Journal of Health Politics, Policy and Law

T0313418

Editor Eric M. Patashnik, Brown University

Associate Editors Nicholas Bagley, University of Michigan; Helen Levy, University of Michigan; Elizabeth Rigby, George Washington University

Book Review Editor Rick Mayes, University of Richmond

Special Section Editors Beneath the Surface: Joseph White, Case Western Reserve University; The Politics and Policy of Health Reform: Heather Howard, Princeton University, and Frank J. Thompson, Rutgers University

Social Media Editor Harold A. Pollack, University of Chicago

Managing Editor Jennifer N. Costanza

Former Editors Ralph A. Straetz, New York University; Theodore R. Marmor, Yale University; Lawrence D. Brown, Columbia University; James A. Morone, Brown University; Mark A. Peterson, University of California, Los Angeles; Mark Schlesinger, Yale University; Michael S. Sparer, Columbia University; Colleen M. Grogan, University of Chicago

Volume 42, Number 2, April 2017
Published by Duke University Press

Contents

Commentaries

Behind the Jargon

Books

Editorial Note/Introduction

Diffusion of ACA Policies across the American States

Editor:
Colleen M. Grogan
University of Chicago

Guest Editors:
David K. Jones
Boston University

Julianna Pacheco
University of Iowa

When the Affordable Care Act (ACA) was passed in 2010, there was a key role for states in its implementation. States were supposed to set up their own health care exchanges, or Marketplaces as they are now called, expand their Medicaid programs, and respond to the many financial incentive-based programs to reform both their local public health systems and health care delivery systems. Despite the rejection of the ACA from conservative-leaning states and the very real possibility that all or significant parts of the ACA will be repealed, implementation questions still loom large for all the states.

By the time this issue goes to press in 2017, states will have had seven years of experience implementing the vast array of ACA policies. This raises many questions: have the states been learning from one another? Do they only take cues from similar ideologically leaning states? Does evidence of effectiveness among first adopters matter for later adopters? Does public opinion affect state adoption and does it influence opinion in non-adopting states? How does framing of policy reforms matter? All these questions and more are addressed in the articles that follow.

These questions are more than mere academic pursuits. And they still matter despite the changing political dynamic that calls into question the stability of ACA-related reforms. The ACA represents the biggest social reform since the passage of Medicare and Medicaid in 1965, and has already dramatically upended how health care is organized in the United States. What states decide to do, or not do, affects whether people have access to insurance (through the Medicaid expansion), what they have

Journal of Health Politics, Policy and Law, Vol. 42, No. 2, April 2017
DOI 10.1215/03616878-3766691   © 2017 by Duke University Press

access to (through decisions about essential health benefits), and how they receive their care (through delivery model reforms). It is difficult to overstate the importance of prior and future state decisions.

This special issue came about largely due to the insight of the late Andrew Hyman. As Heather Howard's tribute makes clear, Andy was particularly devoted to an RWJF-funded project (directed by Heather Howard), which provided technical assistance to ten states implementing insurance expansions under the ACA. Although Andy cared about improving reforms in those ten states, he would often say, "I want to learn about reform in these states to help improve the implementation of reform across all fifty states." And then he would ask, "Do we know anything about how to nudge the diffusion of effective policies across the states?" This special issue is an attempt to answer that question. We are thankful for funding from the Robert Wood Johnson Foundation, under the direction of Andy, to hold a workshop focused on the diffusion of ACA policies and to support the development of this special issue.

While seven years is a long time, many of the ACA's major reforms were not fully implemented until 2014, and so it is still difficult to study how ACA policies have diffused across the states. Because of that, we pursued this issue with two objectives in mind: first, we asked scholars with expertise on policy diffusion to write on a topic they know well and with an eye toward what can be learned for ACA policy diffusion; and second, we asked scholars who are knowledgeable about the ACA to study early trends in policy diffusion with an eye toward lessons for future adoption. The result is a combination of articles in this issue: some focused on the ACA, but other articles focused on policies ranging from sales tax for e-commerce to a sample of eighty-seven policies spanning multiple domains and dating back to 1912.

The approach yields some important lessons both for the field of policy diffusion and for thinking back to Andy's question about nudging states along in a meaningful way.

Two articles focus specifically on the ACA, examining the diffusion of state-level decisions about health insurance exchanges and Medicaid expansion. Callaghan and Jacobs use a multivariate analysis to examine what accounts for the variation across states in enrollment. They point out that this question is particularly interesting given the federal government's incentives and mandates, and the "menacing conditions that generally discourage participation" in many states. They find that the early decisions by states are largely explained by party control, but that enrollment is driven by different political and administrative factors for the exchanges and Medicaid. States with higher unemployment had lower levels of enrollment in their exchanges, while enrollment was positively associated with President Obama's vote share. On the other hand, states with higher levels of unemployment had larger enrollment in Medicaid, as did states with higher levels of administrative capacity.

Grogan, Singer, and Jones examine the rhetoric used by seven Republican-led states to secure 1115 waivers in order to pass legislation expanding Medicaid. These waivers have been integral to convincing conservative legislators in these states that the changes to Medicaid are sufficiently different from the traditional program and from the ACA. Grogan, Singer, and Jones use a content analysis of media coverage and press releases to argue that the policies proposed in each subsequent waiver were further to the right of their predecessors though the associated rhetoric remained consistent. Proposals for introducing premiums, cost sharing, and work requirements into Medicaid were discussed as returning the program to its original intent of caring only for the "truly needy."

Two articles add to the growing political science literature about how policies spread across governmental units, with an eye toward lessons for the ACA. Boehmke et al. take an applied approach by performing simulations to understand which states have the largest impact on speeding up the diffusion process. They select a variety of different "seed" states and find that policies spread much faster and more extensively when policies are adopted first in leader states. This is important for policy advocates who have limited resources, but who want to have the largest impact across the American states. If we want to "nudge" policy along, Boehmke et al. suggest concentrating efforts in states that are policy leaders.

Pacheco and Maltby explore the role that public opinion plays in the diffusion of ACA policies. They find that both gubernatorial ACA announcements and grant activity increased support for the ACA in nearby states. However, only gubernatorial announcements respond to shifts in ACA support, presumably because it is a more salient policy than grant activity. They also look at whether shifts in public opinion in other states provide a signal to elected officials about the viability of decisions in their own state. They find states are more likely to emulate other states with similar ACA policy preferences when deciding about when to announce their decisions. Public opinion may be a potential lever that advocates use to accelerate the diffusion process—either by actively framing the policy debate in ways that are favorable toward their policy or by advising state legislators about public support in similar states.

Karch and Rosenthal look to the debate over applying a sales tax to electronic commerce to draw lessons for the ACA. They argue that this episode, along with the scholarly literature on framing effects, should cause us to question whether supporters of the law will be able to improve public opinion about the ACA by shifting attention to its more popular components. Instead, engagement would be a more effective rhetorical strategy. Advocates should address the same policy dimensions as their opponents and try to convince conservatives that the reform can accomplish what they care about, such as reducing taxes or expanding the role of the private sector in government programs.

We also have two commentaries: one from Craig Volden and a coauthored piece from Rena Conti and David K. Jones. Volden considers how the articles in this special issue contribute toward what we know about the diffusion of policy choices across the American states, and how that knowledge may help us understand the past, present, and future of the ACA. He argues and illustrates how both the ACA and policy diffusion more generally have been significantly affected by the polarized times in which we live. Conti and Jones focus on what policy diffusion research might gain from literatures that focus on the role of private actors. They highlight two important insights for future research: first, after detailing how multiple ACA policies are simultaneously under consideration for adoption in each state, they argue for shifting the focus on the diffusion of specific policies to a diffusion of "policy packages"; second, they discuss why it is important to consider how federal policies impact private actors, especially because a changed private health care marketplace will impact how states approach the adoption and design of specific ACA policies.

Taken together, these articles paint a comprehensive picture of the complex nature of the diffusion of policies stemming from the ACA. We learn that there are some predictable patterns at work, but that policies do not necessarily spread because they are the "best." Diffusion does not necessarily happen because policy makers are learning, and when there is learning it can be about the political effects as well as the policy outcomes. Thus, to return to Andy's question, there are levers for change that state policy makers and other political actors can pursue, but these levers do not distinguish between "good" and "bad" policies. Obviously, these terms are subjective. We want to create a nudge for diffusion of effective policies, but who decides which policies are most effective? We want states to learn from one another, but not at the expense of a democratic process. Sometimes bad policies diffuse. What then? And, what happens if we want to stop a policy? Perhaps this is the story of the ACA: those who want the reform are busy implementing and learning from similarly reform-minded states, and those who are against reform are busy fighting to stop it and learning from similarly resistant states.

This is the essence of democracy under a federal system, for better and for worse. There is enduring debate about whether or not just policies are most likely to emerge from democratic systems. We know that some of our worst, most inhumane policies have emerged out of democratic systems. Yet, we also know that many of our state political processes fall far short of the democratic ideal and many voices are systematically excluded. So, if we strive for any lever to nudge change in the right direction, perhaps it should be that which brings about the most fair and open democratic process in each state, with no guarantees but hope that just policies will prevail.

Finally, we have one last *Behind the Jargon* in this issue. I want to thank David Frankford for acting as editor of this special section for six years. He has brought forth numerous gems for helping us think more deeply about the assumptions underlying some of the most popular jargon used in our health policy lexicon. These essays force us to confront what's at stake when jargon, such as "crowd-out" and "moral hazard" (just two examples of many essays), are used unquestioningly. Jargon assumes agreement on defining a health policy problem, and equally important, it often points in one direction for policy solutions at the expense of considering alternative paths. We use jargon unquestioningly, often to our peril, and David has helped us see that.

Tribute to Andy Hyman

Heather Howard
Princeton University

We miss our friend and colleague Andy Hyman enormously. He leaves an enduring legacy as a leader in the fight for comprehensive, affordable health insurance coverage, and we welcome this opportunity today to honor his achievements and recommit to this work.

Andy had a tremendous passion for expanding access to health insurance coverage—certainly not the safest area of health policy—from a political and funder perspective. But Andy was committed to the idea that if we all just worked a little bit harder, we could make so many more people healthier and life a bit fairer. In fact, Andy embraced the risk inherent in the work—we talked often about how, if it were easy, it would have already been done, or everyone in this space would be doing it.

Quite simply, he wasn't afraid to fail. While generations had fought for universal coverage and stumbled, Andy never gave up, relentlessly plotting strategy and rallying the troops when things looked dark. That optimism was infectious, and no one could fill a room with Washington, DC, policy wonks like Andy when he called a meeting.

Of course, Andy also recognized that passage of ACA was just the beginning. He knew the work of getting people covered was going to move outside the beltway, and he wanted to be there in the trenches, working with states on complex implementation challenges, so that the ACA's promise would be achieved. That's why he created the State Health Reform Assistance Network, to provide technical assistance to states implementing the ACA's coverage provisions.

Journal of Health Politics, Policy and Law, Vol. 42, No. 2, April 2017
DOI 10.1215/03616878-3766700   © 2017 by Duke University Press

We struggled with what to call our ultimate goal—entrenchment of the ACA? Institutionalization of its reforms? Eventually, we settled on a more unorthodox term: *permanantizing* the new coverage paradigm.

Andy had a strategic vision of a three-legged stool to support the successful implementation of the ACA: direct operational support for states through the State Network, consumer advocacy through Consumer Voices for Coverage, and rigorous research and monitoring of implementation, including tracking reports, the Health Reform Monitoring Survey, and programs like today's conference.

Each of these efforts reinforced the other. For instance, Andy recognized that states were at the forefront of implementation and, given their budget and capacity constraints, needed technical assistance and help learning from each other. At the same time, he believed in consumer advocacy and strategically decided to fund consumer advocates in those same states where we provided technical assistance, to push those states and to ensure transparency and accountability. Finally, he wanted to document the process to ensure that we could use our states as examples for the rest of the country and to show how implementation can be done—the good, the bad, and the ugly. And ironically, this nuanced approach was developed by a guy who was a fed at heart! He'd worked at HHS on intergovernmental affairs, tussling with states on waivers.

The JHPPL partnership that brings us together today is a terrific example of how Andy sought to bridge the gap between research and policy. He wanted policy makers to help shape the research agenda, and he wanted researchers to see the value in short, timely analysis that would inform and strengthen policy making. He was so proud of the work of many of you in this room, and proud of this effort and others to bring researchers and practitioners together.

Andy made the people he worked with better. Any idea that you had was probed and prodded, not because he didn't trust you or your idea, but because he knew that you could always be just a little better. And Andy could play three-dimensional chess—calculating several moves ahead, taking into account not just policy nuance but political challenges and operational realities.

Today, he would be proud that we have achieved the biggest expansion in health coverage since the 1960s. But he would want us to continue to push and probe, to ask tough and even uncomfortable questions, in order to strengthen the work we are doing and to ensure it is as relevant as possible to the coming debates and challenges.

▪ ▪ ▪

Heather Howard is a lecturer at Princeton University's Woodrow Wilson School of Public and International Affairs and director of two Robert Wood Johnson Foundation-funded programs that help states implement health reforms. She served as New Jersey's Commissioner of Health and Senior Services from 2008 to 2010. She also has significant federal experience, having worked as Senator Jon Corzine's Chief of Staff, as Associate Director of the White House Domestic Policy Council and Senior Policy Advisor for First Lady Hillary Clinton, as an Honors Attorney in the US Department of Justice's Antitrust Division Health Care Task Force, and for the House of Representatives. She received her B.A. from Duke University and her J.D. from NYU School of Law.

Howard, Heather. "Tribute to Andy Hyman." Speech presented at JHPPL Policy Diffusion Workshop, University of Chicago, June 2, 2015, conference.

The Future of Health Care Reform: What Is Driving Enrollment?

Timothy H. Callaghan
Texas A&M University

Lawrence R. Jacobs
University of Minnesota

Abstract Against a backdrop of ongoing operational challenges, insurance market turbulence, and the ever present pull of partisanship, enrollment in the ACA's programs has soared and significant variations have developed across states in terms of their pace of coverage expansion. Our article explores why ACA enrollment has varied so dramatically across states. We explore the potential influence of party control, presidential cueing, administrative capacity, the reverberating effects of ACA policy decisions, affluence, and unemployment on enrollment. Our multivariate analysis finds that party control dominated early state decision making, but that relative enrollment in insurance exchanges and the Medicaid expansion are driven by a changing mix of political and administrative factors. Health politics is entering a new era as Republicans replace the ACA and devolve significant discretion to states to administer Medicaid and other programs. Our findings offer insights into future directions in health reform and in learning and diffusion.

Keywords health reform, diffusion, ACA enrollment

Introduction

Since the enactment of the Affordable Care Act (ACA) in 2010, its implementation has faced a series of policy and political hurdles. One obstacle is partisanship—the "workhorse" of American politics (Bafumi and Shapiro 2009). Congressional Republicans continue to uniformly oppose the ACA and most Republicans nationwide share that antipathy. This intense, sustained partisan hostility has been particularly threatening to health reform because Republicans control Congress as well as all

Journal of Health Politics, Policy and Law, Vol. 42, No. 2, April 2017
DOI 10.1215/03616878-3766710   © 2017 by Duke University Press

branches of government or at least one of the levers of power in forty-three of fifty states (86 percent).

The fiery partisan resistance is compounded by persistent—if shrinking—website snafus and administrative problems combined with nearly unrelenting press scrutiny that spotlights the failings of the program. Political opponents as well as independent experts predicted that the balky implementation would discourage enrollment; some Republican leaders went as far as to call "the rollout of the Affordable Care Act . . . an unmitigated disaster," and insisted that the law would not work (Fox News 2014).

The double whammy of implementation snags and partisan roadblocks reinforce other well-known limits on individual engagement that worked to obstruct the diffusion of health reform across states. Gathering the kind of information that would be necessary to sort through coverage options and then sign up imposes substantial costs; prior research demonstrate that these costs often deter other forms of political and policy participation. In addition, accurate learning about policy is often skewed away from those most benefiting from new policies such as the ACA and toward the higher income strata that have less need for coverage. Moreover, negative framing (as illustrated by the attacks on the ACA) activates perceptions of risk, which have been connected in prior research to distrust and disengagement (Kahneman and Tversky 1984; Fiorina 1990; Popkin 1991; Cappella and Jamieson 1997; Kuklinski and Quirk 2000; Druckman 2004). These cognitive and communicative difficulties are intensified by the actual costs that loom over individuals who fail to enroll in insurance and face the threat of penalty.

Expectations about enrollment in the ACA should be humbled by the substantial impact that comparatively mild hurdles (such as registering to vote) exert in discouraging participation (Downs 1957). Put simply, the multiple hurdles—intense partisan polarization, implementation stumbles, and limits on individual cognition and behavior—should lead us to expect low enrollment in the ACA.

The ACA raises a general puzzle: its drive to engage individuals in enrolling for coverage should, according to prior research, be severely hampered by these hurdles and yet, large and sharply rising numbers of people are taking on taxing barriers and enrolling. During the first enrollment period that started in October 2013, 7.3 million people decided to sign up and pay their premiums on insurance exchanges. During the next year, exchange sign-ups rose by 27 percent to 9.3 million and by year 3, sign-ups for the exchanges rose to 12.7 million (actual enrollment may decline to approximately 10 million because individuals fail to pay their premiums or other issues) (US Department of Health and Human Services 2014 and 2015; Galewitz 2016). Over the same period, the state-based expansion of Medicaid experienced a dramatic growth of coverage for low-income Americans, with 14.5 million individuals gaining Medicaid coverage from 2013 to 2015 (CMS 2016).

Why is enrollment in the ACA as high as it is despite menacing conditions that generally discourage participation? Moreover, what accounts for the variation across states in enrollment given the federal government's incentives and mandates? With enrollment exceeding expectations, we need to explain why ACA participation is more extensive in Vermont and Massachusetts than in Alaska and Oklahoma even though the latter states exhibit a far larger pool of uninsured to tap.

The differential impact of federal government incentives on states to implement the ACA poses important puzzles for students of health policy and analysts of diffusion. On the one hand, the ACA fits within past research on vertical diffusion—the federal government's use of financial incentives and mandates to coax states into implementing its new policies (Allen, Pettus, and Haider-Markel 2004; Karch 2006; Shipan and Volden 2006; Shipan and Volden 2008).[1] On the other hand, however, the implementation of the ACA has occurred against a backdrop of formidable obstacles that may disrupt common patterns in policy diffusion and produce striking variations across states in the successful implementation of the ACA's programs.

In the discussion below, we explore general explanations for political and policy development and their feedback effects. We then use these bodies of research to structure our analysis of state ACA enrollment in Medicaid and the exchange. Our analysis confirms earlier findings that party control of state government drives early state decisions about the type of exchange to establish and whether or not to pursue Medicaid expansion, but it also reveals that partisanship is less influential in capturing the unique variations in state enrollment in each program. For the exchange, we find that enrollment is lower in states with high unemployment and higher in states that are more supportive of President Obama, after controlling for party control of government. For Medicaid, we find that variations in enrollment are driven by new policy and strengthened administration, Democratic control of the legislature, and high unemployment. Although

---

1. There is also growing evidence of horizontal diffusion in the implementation of the ACA. While not a focus of our analysis here, we conclude by speculating about horizontal diffusion as part of the new politics of health reform.

our research was conducted before the Republicans gained unified control in Washington and pursued their plans to repeal and replace the ACA, our findings about the variations in ACA enrollment offer important insights into the future of health reforms that are devolved to the states.

Explanations for Strenuous Participation

It may appear to be simple common sense for America's low- and middle-income people to sign up for new health benefits: better coverage of needed medical care and, for most people, lower costs—Medicaid is free for those under 138% of the federal poverty line, and 86% signing up on exchanges in 2015 received subsidies to purchase insurance (KFF 2014; Pear 2015).

Extensive research points to a number of reasons, however, that individuals and groups fail to invest in gaining the necessary information and refrain from taking action despite intuitive payoffs. One barrier is a lack of adequate interest and information to act—even if participation is a "good deal." Awareness of potential payoffs from participation often elude those who would most benefit, and the information that is available is routinely incomplete, imperfect, and clouded by uncertainty about its veracity (Converse 1964; Delli Carpini and Keeter 1996).

Opponents of change work hard to fend off threats to the status quo that serves them. Depending on the repertoire of available tools, they may use intimidation through negative sanctions and physical retribution, and sow doubt through misinformation in hopes of raising the costs of change and creating a distraction from the payoffs (Tilly 1978; Gaventa 1982). Opponents of reform in America can tap a deep well of distrust in government that they can activate by spotlighting costs and risks against incumbent officeholders and new programs (Cappella and Jamieson 1997; Hetherington 1999; Hetherington and Globetti 2002). There is also a repertoire of administrative tools to dampen participation in American social policy. Poor relief as far back as sixteenth-century England literally branded those who sought assistance. In America, the process of receiving welfare is notoriously convoluted, demeaning, and punitive in order to dampen requests for aid from eligible people (Soss 1999; Soss, Fording, and Schram 2011). Enrollment in Medicaid, which is administered by states, has long exhibited substantial gaps between eligibility and actual enrollment in part because states developed laborious and confusing steps that deterred participation (e.g., Selden, Banthin, and Cohen 1998).

Decisions by Americans to seek coverage in the new ACA programs faced intense and familiar barriers. After two years of enrollment, public knowledge remained limited, especially among the most affected—about half of the uninsured reported not knowing when to sign up for insurance or about the payoff of the new benefits for them (KFF 2015, fig. 16). What awareness and knowledge that did exist was compromised by aggressive efforts by reform opponents to highlight website problems (even if resolved) and to prime political distrust of Washington; this has contributed to disapproval of the ACA by a consistent three-quarters of Republicans and nearly half of independents (KFF 2015, fig. 2). Moreover, the ACA funded states to designate "navigators" who would work with target populations to sign them up for new programs, but some southern states that harbored the largest uninsured populations obstructed the efforts of navigators (Seitz-Wald 2013; Emanuel 2014). All of these hurdles to seeking the payoff of health coverage are higher for vulnerable populations where awareness and knowledge are low and distrust of the government is particularly high (Doty, Rasmussen, and Collins 2014).

Despite the imposing impediments, large numbers of Americans decided to invest the time and effort to sign up for insurance on exchanges and to register for the expanded Medicaid program. This rising coverage did not occur equally across the country; it rose more sharply in some states and less in others. What accounts for the higher participation in ACA coverage and the variations across states?

Four accounts may explain both the increasing number of Americans who enrolled in ACA programs despite impediments as well as the variations across states.

Partisanship

Partisanship is the "workhorse" of American national and state politics (Bafumi and Shapiro 2009), sorting lawmakers and voters into consistent blocks. The rising partisan polarization in Washington has now spread to states; the partisan conflict over salient policies in states can over-ride or significantly offset financial and other attractions of new federal programs (Deering and Shelly 2009; Layman et al. 2010; Shor and McCarty 2011; Doan and McFarlane 2012). Party exerts a strong and sustained hold on government officials who face elections because of party activists: they insist on fidelity to single issues and reward or punish lawmakers who compromise these core policy goals by withholding campaign contributions, volunteer help, and support during the nomination process. Constituency may modify, however, the pull of partisanship: legislators are beholden to narrow districts that might be particularly ideological while governors are elected by broader state constituencies.

The ACA poses a stark test of partisanship given the law's generous financial terms. On the one hand, the federal government offered large grants to plan and set up state insurance exchanges as well as new Medicaid funding to cover all of the costs for extending coverage for the first three years and, afterward, 90 percent of expenses. In addition, the federal government's new funding of coverage reduces enormous and rising pressure on state budgets to pick up the cost of "uncompensated care" for the uninsured; states that refused to adopt the new funding from the expanded Medicaid program are experiencing rising rates of hospital closures (Angeles 2010; Conlan and Posner 2011; Reiter, Noles, and Pink 2015). This kind of exceptionally generous financing typically energizes the pressure groups at state capitols that stand to gain and convinces lawmakers to accept the new federal support (Thomas and Hrebenar 1999; Singhal 2008).

On the other hand, the sharp partisan divide that enveloped the ACA since congressional debates in 2009 and 2010 when no Republicans voted for its passage has persisted at the national level in Congress and in states (Oberlander 2011; Jacobs and Callaghan 2013; Rigby and Haselswerdt 2013; Frean, Gruber, and Sommers 2016; Jacobs and Skocpol 2016). Although Republican governors in Ohio, Arizona, and a few other states pressed for the adoption of Medicaid's expansion to secure federal financing and respond to pressure from medical providers, the political influence of party propelled many Republican governors and nearly all GOP-controlled legislatures to resist health reform. With Republicans enjoying one-party control in twenty-four states, and wielding a veto through their control over at least one branch of government in nineteen more states, elite partisanship generally obstructed the ACA's implementation. States controlled by Democrats—such as Connecticut and Rhode Island—adopted the expansion of Medicaid, and most established state exchanges; among states where Republicans leaders controlled all levers of power, most have rejected state exchanges (with the exception of Nevada, Michigan, Idaho, and Arkansas) and two-thirds (17 of 24) refused to approve the new Medicaid benefits.

Party control of government conditioned ACA enrollment. Republican control ruled out the option of state insurance exchanges and often precluded the opportunity to seek expanded Medicaid coverage, while individuals in states run by Democrats enjoyed more opportunities to seek new health benefits. In addition, some Republican-controlled states actively discouraged their residents from registering on federal insurance exchanges (Seitz-Wald 2013).

There are some indications, however, that there has been divergence in the motivation of Republican policy makers. Governors who represent the entire state and a wide range of interests (including businesses, medical care providers, and uninsured who seek medical care funded by the state) may diverge from Republican legislators who represent a narrow district and may be especially attuned to the Tea Party and other conservative activists (Skocpol and Williamson 2012). For instance, Republican governors in Ohio and Arizona pushed their states to adopt Medicaid expansion even though the GOP-controlled legislatures and conservative activists opposed the reforms. While Republicans from both branches of government are prone to be less supportive of health reform than their Democratic counterparts, GOP governors appear more willing to accept the federal government's generous financial terms and implement reform than their legislative counterparts.

Presidential Cueing

Presidents enjoy unrivaled public attention and can influence, if they are popular, how Americans evaluate government policy as well as members of Congress and other politicians. A long line of research finds that presidents with strong support in elections or favorable approval ratings affect public support of members of Congress from the president's party; conversely, antipathy to the president prompts Americans to vent their anger against them by, for instance, voting against the president's partisans in Congress (Fiorina 1983; Abramowitz 1985; Cover 1986; Gronke, Koch, and Wilson 2003).

Presidents exert an independent effect that "cues" the public, beyond the influence of party affiliation. As one study explains, "Citizens look to the President for a cue as to how the country is doing, how things are going in Washington, and how well Congress is doing its job" (Gronke, Koch, and Wilson 2003: 805). The effect can be significant: the president can cue Americans as they assess new policy initiatives and competing candidates. Cueing on presidential support is a cognitive shortcut for Americans with low levels of information; it gives them some basis to assess complicated government programs (Popkin 1991).

Public support for President Obama may have had particular relevance to the public's evaluations of the ACA and commitment to enroll in its programs. Rarely has a new program been as closely associated with a president as the ACA, which is widely referenced as "Obamacare."

The cueing account anticipates that states with higher levels of support for Obama will experience higher enrollment. Given the barriers to enrolling in the exchanges and Medicaid, Democrats or independents who harbor reservations about the ACA but support Obama may be more willing to take on the taxing barriers to enroll in the ACA's programs. This dynamic may even apply to a relatively small number of Republicans who are "weak partisans" but respect the president. In these cases, Americans are following the cue of President Obama despite their partisanship or, in the case of Democrats, their reservations about health reform.

Feedback Effects and Institutions

A growing body of research reveals that established government programs are not just a product of politics but also influence politics. The "feedback effects" of established programs generate resources and motivation for potential program beneficiaries to become aware of new programs and invest the time in enrolling in them and then supporting them. The passage of Social Security in 1935, for instance, influenced the decisions of senior citizens to learn about the program and join it as well as to increase their political engagement, which produced the higher levels of voting that are evident today (Campbell 2003; see also Mettler and Soss 2004).

In addition, historical institutionalists find that existing administrative capacity fosters "path dependence" that predisposes policy developments along established paths (Skocpol and Ikenberry 1983; Skocpol 1992; Pierson 2000). In particular, hierarchical structures that facilitate coherent direction, as well as well-trained and rule-guided civil servants, enhance the confidence and capability of lawmakers and citizens in pursuing new programs. For instance, the Medicare program of hospital insurance for seniors was constructed in the mid-1960s on the existing and widely respected Social Security system for administering the financing and delivery of benefits (Jacobs 1993). Research on state health policy reveals that competent administrative capacity generates support among policy makers for creating effective eligibility determination, enrollment processing, provider reimbursement, and quality assessments (Gold, Sparer, and Chu 1996; Holahan et al. 1998; Miller 2005).

States with a history of competent administration and adopting generous health policy created a trajectory of policy change that facilitated the adoption of the expanded Medicaid program and the establishment of state-based exchanges. Research on path dependence suggests that states with a history of effectiveness and health reform both boost the confidence of lawmakers in the feasibility of policy change and distribute tangible benefits in a way that activates organized groups and voters to press for further reform. In addition, states with well-formed health reform trajectories motivate lawmakers and civil servants to invest in competent and coherent administration. In the case of the ACA, prior research suggests that these states will use available federal funding to strengthen their administrative capacity to subsidize the cost of enrolling by distributing information, paying "navigators" to provide assistance, and staffing call centers. As a result, states with higher capacity are expected to handle enrollment in a smooth and consistent manner that enables more individuals to sign up for ACA coverage; states with weak administration obstruct enrollment by leaving individuals to absorb the costs of signing up.

State Economic Circumstances

The economic prosperity of states conditions the generosity and scope of policy making, according to a number of studies. Research finds that states that are affluent with robust employment are, in general, more innovative and receptive to developing new federal initiatives, while less well-off states are less inclined to adopt new fiscal commitments—even if they are heavily subsidized by the federal government (Welch and Thompson 1980; Davies and Derthick 1997: 229–31; Rigby and Haselswerdt 2013). In the health policy arena, a notable body of research similarly reports that prosperous states are more likely to innovate, adopt Medicaid programs, and implement managed care models (Grogan 1993; Satterthwaite 2002; Miller 2005).

The economic circumstances within a state might also condition ACA enrollment across states. Specifically, a state's affluence as well as its unemployment rate might influence the generosity and scope of state policy makers, and thereby factor into their willingness to adopt Medicaid reform and back the operations of insurance exchanges.

The implication, then, is that weaker state economies—as evident in higher unemployment rates or lower personal income—will tilt against ACA implementation because policy makers and other elites conclude that they are unable to afford even modest investments, while better-off states will be more confident and able to invest in adopting health reform. This drag on coverage may be particularly apparent in the insurance exchanges; even with government subsidies, the costs on economically strapped individuals to enroll may prove too high.

There is, however, some uncertainty about the application of past research to the ACA. The reformers who designed the ACA and worked to implement it challenged the finding of prior research that reported a positive relationship between economic well-being and the adoption of new policy. They created unusually generous financial terms precisely to entice states that were struggling to generate employment and lift personal income to expand Medicaid (Jacobs and Skocpol 2016).

Theoretical Expectations

What explains the number of individuals in each state that decided to enroll in the new insurance exchanges and expanded Medicaid program despite intimidating obstacles? We investigate four sets of hypotheses to explain variation in enrollment across states.

Partisanship

H1A   Individuals in states with Democratic governors will enroll in Medicaid and the exchange at higher rates than those in states with Republican governors.
H1B   Individuals in states with more extensive Democratic control of the state legislature will enroll in Medicaid and the exchange at higher rates than those in states with more Republican control.

Presidential Cueing

H2   Individuals in states with higher levels of public support for President Obama will enroll in Medicaid and the exchange at higher rates than those in states with lower levels of support for Obama.

Institutional Effects

H3A   Individuals in states with histories of strong administrative capacity will enroll in Medicaid and the exchange at higher levels than those in states with weaker administrative capacity.
H3B   States with greater control over their insurance exchanges will have higher levels of enrollment in the exchange.
H3C   States with greater progress implementing Medicaid reform as stipulated by the ACA will have higher enrollment in Medicaid.

State Economic Circumstances

H4A   Individuals in states with higher personal income will enroll in Medicaid and the exchange at higher rates than those in less affluent states. H4B   Individuals in states with higher levels of unemployment will be less likely to enroll in insurance exchanges but more likely to enroll in Medicaid.

Studying ACA Enrollment

The absolute number of Americans who enrolled in the ACA conveys the sheer magnitude of participation across the country—even in conservative states such as Texas where the third largest sign-up in the insurance exchange was registered.

The use of absolute numbers, however, conveys an incomplete picture and omits the context of participation. Texas had a large number of individuals enroll in the exchange, but it was also was home to one of the largest populations of uninsured people (5.8 million in 2013). We need measures of state progress in implementing health reform that can control for the context of insurance availability. This will allow us to assess each state's relative exertion and opportunity to sign up the uninsured.

Explaining Relative Enrollment

Variations across states in ACA enrollment are revealed by studying the decisions of individuals to sign up for coverage. We track state variation using relative measures of enrollment in the ACA's two primary programs to expand coverage: the insurance exchange and the expansion of Medicaid. We created a relative measure of exchange enrollment based on the number of individuals who signed up with a qualified health plan (QHP) in each state through the end of the 2015 open enrollment period as a proportion of the total number of uninsured in each state in 2013.[2] Similarly, we calculated the change in Medicaid enrollment from the pre-ACA monthly average Medicaid and CHIP enrollment for July–September 2013 and the end of the 2015 open enrollment period, and then divided this amount by the total number of uninsured in each state. Our measures reflect developments as of February 22, 2015—the end of the 2015 open

2. Our measure of the number of uninsured is incomplete but provides the most current available data. The Small Area Health Insurance Estimates (SAHIE) offers more accurate measures of the number of uninsured, but it will not be available for analysis until later in 2016.

enrollment period.[3] (See appendix for detailed information on the construction of our enrollment measures as well as our independent variables.)

Our measures of relative enrollment, which are presented in figures 1 and 2, show that Texas and other Republican-controlled states which boast large absolute numbers of exchange enrollment trail Vermont, Massachusetts, and other states in covering their population of uninsured. For the exchange, well over half the uninsured in Vermont and Massachusetts enrolled while less than a quarter signed up in Oklahoma, Texas, and Alaska. In terms of increased Medicaid coverage since the ACA's passage, three-quarters of the uninsured enrolled in Massachusetts, Kentucky, and Oregon while only a half or less enrolled in Texas, Oklahoma, and Alaska.[4] These are startling differences in the relative progress of states in reaching their uninsured that require rigorous and comprehensive explanation.

Our measures of relative enrollment point to the influence of partisanship. The highest scores in figure 1 are among states with strong Democratic Party control (Vermont and Massachusetts), and the lowest are among states with unified Republican Party control (Nevada). Similarly, in figure 2, the highest scores are in Democratic strongholds such as Oregon and Massachusetts, and the lowest scores are found in Republican-controlled states such as Nebraska and Utah.

There are also signs, however, that partisan control of state government may not fully account for the wide variation in relative enrollment across states. Republican states such as Florida and Wisconsin score quite well on the exchange measure, for example, and a few states with Democratic control—such as Hawaii—do comparatively less well, finishing outside the top 15 on both measures.

Explanatory Variables

What explains the variation in individual decisions across states as reflected in relative enrollment? We examine four explanations, creating distinct independent variables for each.

---

3. The ACA explicitly bars the undocumented from enrolling in the insurance exchanges. Our study makes no effort to confirm this legal requirement. In terms of our measures of Medicaid enrollment and the number of uninsured, there are no reliable and readily available data that differentiate the undocumented from citizens.

4. It is important to note that our estimates are rough gauges for relative enrollment. Although Massachusetts appears to cover 100 percent of its population in figure 2, this does not presume that there are no uninsured in the state. Instead, it reflects the timing and imperfections of data collection.

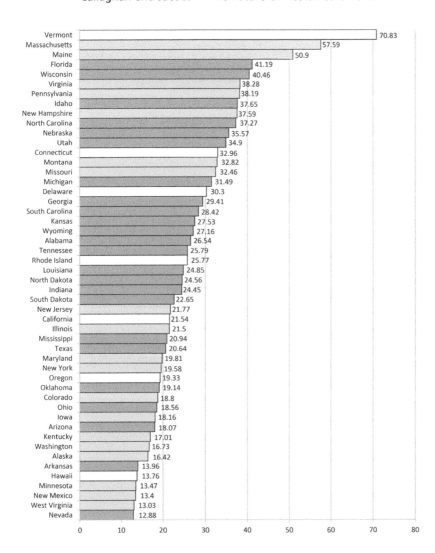

Figure 1   Relative Exchange Enrollment in the ACA
(results for 11/15/14–2/22/15)

Notes: White - full Democratic control of state government, Light gray - partial Republican control, Dark gray - full Republican control—as of 12/1/15.

The first explanation is focused on partisanship and is measured with two key variables. One is a dummy variable for whether or not the state has a Democratic governor; the other is a three-point variable capturing full, partial, or no Democratic control of the state legislature. Our distinct measures for each lawmaking branch allow us to account for differential

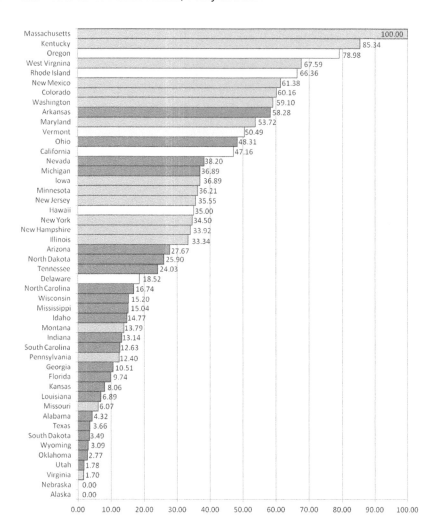

Figure 2 Relative Medicaid Enrollment in the ACA
(results for 11/15/14–2/22/15)

Notes: White - full Democratic control of state government, Light gray - partial Republican control, Dark gray - full Republican control—as of 12/1/15.

institutional interests regarding health reform. Governors—including some Republicans—may have focused on the state's broad interests in securing the generous federal government financial support to reduce budgets and in supporting medical providers who pressed for widening coverage. Alternatively, legislators focused on narrower regional and political interests, with Republicans opposing reform in response to intense pressure by conservative constituents (including well-organized and vocal Tea Party groups from their districts). Prior research has also used split-party measures to track the differential political incentives of state lawmakers (Ferguson 2003; Miller and Blanding 2012; Rigby and Haselswerdt 2013).

The second explanation is presidential cueing and measures the support for Obama through his vote share in each state during the 2012 presidential election. Presidential vote share has been used previously to account for public support of presidents and is a useful measure here given the close ties between President Obama and the ACA (Cover 1986; Abramowitz 2008; Shelly 2012; Barrilleaux and Rainey 2014).

The next explanation is institutional and focuses on two potential effects. Administrative capacity differentially equips states to implement health reform and help individuals enroll but, unfortunately, past research has not produced an appropriate measure of administrative capacity for us to borrow. In this context, we rely on a rough gauge of state capacity to handle insurance oversight, which is a component of exchange operation, and to aid the poor and vulnerable developed in prior work (see Jacobs and Callaghan 2013; Callaghan and Jacobs 2016). The variation in our measure has a strong degree of face validity as it corresponds with expected differences across states—from the weak resources of Alabama to the greater capabilities in Maryland, Massachusetts, and Connecticut (Gold, Sparer, and Chu 1996).

Another potential institutional effect relates to policy feedbacks and, specifically, the impact of states adopting insurance exchanges and the expanded Medicaid program on enrollment. Our measure of insurance exchanges used a three-point scale to score greater state involvement: No points were assigned where states played little or no significant role and defaulted to the federal exchange; one point was granted to states that formed a "partnership" with the federal exchange to share responsibility; and two points were awarded for states that established their own exchange.[5] In addition, we designed a six-point scale to measure greater state progress toward implementing steps to adopt Medicaid expansion: zero points were awarded for no progress; one point was granted to states that obtained planning grants; two were assigned when the governor made a public announcement of support; three points were given for the formal submission of a waiver proposing a Medicaid reform alternative; four

5. Nevada, New Mexico, and Oregon received scores of "1": they approved state exchanges and assumed significant responsibilities while also deferring to the federal exchange's website to handle much of the process of eligibility determination and enrollment.

points were awarded if the state implemented the alternative and it was considered compliant with federal law; and five points were awarded to states that implemented the program stipulated by the ACA. Higher scores on our measures for exchange and Medicaid reform indicated that states supplied more resources to individuals who might consider ACA enrollment.

The fourth explanation focuses on economic circumstances and is measured in two ways. The first is with state affluence which is measured by real, price-adjusted estimates of per capita personal income for states. These data were obtained from the Bureau of Economic Analysis and are updated to the most recent year available, 2014.[6] The second measure is the unemployment rate in each state. This measure is a twelve-month average of the unemployment rate in each state in 2014 and is taken from the National Conference of State Legislatures.

We also tested for a fifth explanation related to groups external to the state that aggressively targeted ACA enrollment through a dummy variable for whether or not a state was an Enroll America state. This variable was excluded from final analysis because it failed to exert a statistically significant effect on enrollment.[7]

Method of Analysis

We study the impact on relative exchange enrollment and relative Medicaid enrollment by the sets of variables we outlined: party control of state government, Obama vote share, the institutional effects of administrative capacity and establishing new ACA programs (insurance exchanges and new Medicaid benefits), economic affluence and unemployment. Specifically, party control, Obama vote share, administrative capacity, state affluence, and unemployment are theorized to exert direct effects on enrollment as well as to work through the intervening variables of established exchanges and expanded Medicaid programs.

Our study relies on path analysis with standardized coefficients to investigate the effect of our explanatory variables on exchange and Medicaid

6. We also tested state revenue per capita in place of economic affluence but ultimately excluded it because it performed similarly. Revenue per capita never reaches statistical significance in the exchange path analysis and in the Medicaid path analysis; it is an insignificant predictor of Medicaid enrollment and has an insignificant total effect, although it does have a marginally significant influence on Medicaid status.

7. Tests determined that the Enroll America variable had no statistically significant direct or total effect on relative exchange enrollment or relative Medicaid enrollment. It was, however, a negative and significant predictor of exchange type.

enrollment. We use path analysis and structural equations to estimate the links (or paths) among variables in order to examine the underlying causal connection between our measures (Asher 1983: 30; Bohrnstedt and Knoke 1994). This approach is particularly helpful because we are interested in studying the paths that run from our four sets of independent variables to our dependent variables (exchange and Medicaid enrollment), either directly or indirectly through the intervening (or endogenous) variables — state decisions regarding the type of exchange to establish and whether to adopt Medicaid expansion (Asher 1983; Bohrnstedt and Knoke 1994; Cook, Jacobs, and Kim 2010).

In short, relative exchange enrollment is modeled as a function of exogenous variables (party control, Obama vote share, administrative capacity, state affluence, and unemployment), and an endogenous variable (exchange type). Similarly, relative Medicaid enrollment is modeled as a function of the same exogenous variables but replaces exchange type with Medicaid status as the endogenous variable.

Understanding State Variation

Our analyses partly confirm earlier findings that pointed to the impact of partisanship. What is striking, however, is that partisanship is neither a consistent nor a dominant influence on exchange and Medicaid enrollment across states. Other political and economic factors are crucial to understanding ACA implementation.

Only two factors account for the variations in exchange enrollment across states, as shown in figure 3. First, unemployment exerts a negative and significant influence on relative exchange enrollment. Figure 3 shows that a one-unit increase in unemployment decreases exchange enrollment by .30 standard deviations. While this finding is consistent with our hypothesis and prior research, we found little support for our other measure of economic circumstances — affluence. Affluence appears to be unrelated with either exchange type or enrollment.

The second and strongest influence on state exchange enrollment is presidential cueing. As anticipated by prior research, Obama vote share has a positive and significant effect. Specifically, a 1 percent increase in Obama vote share increases relative exchange enrollment by .43 standard deviations (see fig. 3). This effect remains after controlling for the partisanship of the governor and legislature, neither of which reach statistical significance. This suggests that presidential cueing has an independent effect beyond the partisan control of the lawmaking branches.

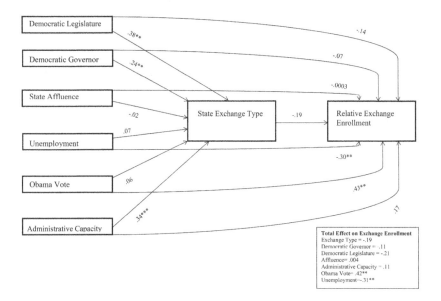

Figure 3 Relative Exchange Enrollment by States

Notes: * $p<0.10$, ** $p<0.05$, *** $p<0.01$; R^2 for full model is .66. Results obtained using structural equation modeling with standardized coefficients.

Finally, our institutional variables exert little impact on exchange enrollment. Administrative capacity is a positive and significant predictor of exchange type, but both exchange type and administrative capacity are insignificant predictors of exchange enrollment.

What happens when we focus on Medicaid enrollment in figure 4? Medicaid enrollment is driven by a different dynamic. Democratic legislatures exert a positive and significant influence. As expected, Democratic bodies expand enrollment but only when analyzing Medicaid enrollment.

Second, in exploring economic circumstances, we once again find that unemployment is a significant predictor and that state affluence is an insignificant predictor of relative enrollment. Critically, however, the sign on unemployment flips and the measure is a positive and significant predictor of Medicaid enrollment as was expected in our hypotheses. Where unemployment deterred Americans from paying for insurance on exchanges, it encouraged them to seek Medicaid coverage, which does not charge a premium.

Finally, we find considerable support for the institutional account when studying relative Medicaid enrollment. State decisions to adopt the Medicaid expansion are a positive and significant predictor of relative Medicaid

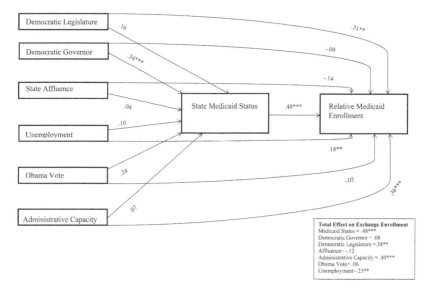

Figure 4   Relative Medicaid Enrollment by States

Notes: * *p*<0.10, ** *p*<0.05, *** *p*<0.01; R² for full model is .70. Results obtained using structural equation modeling with standardized coefficients.

enrollment: states that take a one-point increase (on a six-point scale) toward further implementing Medicaid produce a .48 standard deviation increase in Medicaid enrollment. This finding should be intuitive: states that implement Medicaid expansion are able to enroll more people. More intriguing, however, is the positive and significant effect for administrative capacity. While administrative capacity plays no role in determining exchange enrollment, states with stronger administrative capacity do have higher levels of Medicaid enrollment, perhaps reflecting the fact that they are better equipped to use their capacity to locate and enroll newly eligible individuals.

Partisanship, administrative capacity, and unemployment swamp presidential cueing. Obama vote share fails to exert a significant effect.

The New Politics of Health Reform

For six years, the ACA's journey through Congress to President Obama's desk and then the pitted political and judicial fight over implementing the law has appropriately dominated the study of health politics. A new politics of health reform is, however, dawning that pits the normalization of the

ACA against Republican efforts to change the law. On the one hand, the ACA has started its normalization into American health care—it has provided health coverage to millions of Americans and millions more have been impacted by its insurance regulations, prescription drug coverage, and other provisions (Congressional Budget Office 2016). On the other hand, this growing normalization will be interrupted by the efforts by the Trump administration and Republican majorities in Congress to replace the ACA.

Our research was conducted before the Republican replacement was pursued and its parameters introduced. Our research does point to three themes that may color the debates over replacing the ACA and the new directions of health reform. First, the ACA's new benefits have created new expectations among Americans and new business for stakeholders, which will create pressure for risk aversion among politicians. Enrollment in insurance exchanges and Medicaid has, as we demonstrated, increased throughout the country—even in regions where opposition was strongest. There is no case in US social policy of entirely terminating a comparatively inclusive program impacting massive numbers of Americans.[8] The political backlash for doing so would be intense.

Indeed, there are telltale signs of the active or tacit acceptance of parts of the ACA. Political attacks and much of the critical press coverage focus on a relatively small part of the ACA's policy interventions—the 9 percent of the country in the individual insurance market (as of 2007) who were the original targets of the insurance exchanges (US Census Bureau 2008). Few politicians and press reports are making it a priority to take away the new prescription drug coverage for seniors, the new protections for all Americans against insurance companies excluding the ill or charging them exorbitant rates, the new safeguard against elder abuse, and other provisions. Another tacit sign of the law's normalization: the arrival of the familiar dynamics of interest group politics (Lowi 1979). Pressure groups representing insurers, medical device manufacturers, and others have shifted their fire from seeking repeal to seeking a better deal (Ario and Jacobs 2012). The eventual Republican plan to replace the ACA will be a function, in part, of the new political reality created after 2010 and the implementation of health reform.

The second feature of the new politics of health reform is the emerging effects of new policies across states (Mettler and Soss 2004; Jacobs and Mettler 2011). Our evidence is clearest with regard to Medicaid enrollment where stronger administrative capacity and progress toward adopting

---

8. Pensions for Civil War veterans and their dependents reached millions of Americans but its scope was limited to those with a connection to the Civil War. The program died off with them (Skocpol 1992).

Medicaid expansion contribute to higher enrollment. This particular dynamic is not, so far, evident with regard to insurance exchanges; the decision of most states to default to Washington may account for this difference. Our quantitative research does indicate, however, that Republican control of state government does not deter exchange enrollment, despite media speculation that it does. The broader point is that the ACA's concrete programs gained traction to the point that partisanship did not— prior to 2017—suffocate state implementation and enrollment.

The dynamics of policy evolution before the Republican replacement of the ACA are likely to be imprinted on their plans. For instance, Republican decisions to grant states greater discretion and control over budget and benefit structure will produce national variations. Based on our findings, we expect administrative capacity and relative progress implementing the ACA may continue to characterize state decisions about whether and how to use their new flexibility.

Finally, state innovations—from liberal approaches in Massachusetts and elsewhere to the "private option" in Arkansas and the "consumer-driven" model in Indiana—are likely to contribute to state-to-state learning and diffusion after 2017. Even with the repeal and replacement of the ACA, the performance and budgetary gains of states implementing the ACA introduced a new chapter to America's history of state experimentation and diffusion of effective programs across the US, or what is known as "horiztonal diffusion" (Volden 2006; Gilardi, Füglister, and Luyet 2009; Shipan and Volden 2012). In particular, the ACA's early outcomes suggest that developing administrative capacity and choosing to implement the Medicaid expansion facilititate wider coverage of the uninsured. Research on "horizontal diffusion" suggests that states with relatively low enrollment of the uninsured may look to the successes of other states to try to secure the budgetary benefits and, possibly, the political rewards of improved coverage. In short, increased state discretion in health care under President Trump could accelarate this learning and diffusion, with states building on what has worked under the ACA to effectively and affordably cover their residents.

Much remains for future research. Whether and to what extent the ACA's particular provisions lock in or are watered down or terminated are uncertain on the eve of Donald Trump's inauguration. While the ACA will experience significant change, policy continuity is also likely. Attention to policy feedback—how the ACA's implementation impacted the expectations and preferences of Americans and stakeholders—offers an analytic framework for studying the mix of change and continuity (Jacobs and Mettler 2011).

Major social policy reform in the United States—whether Social Security in 1935 or Medicare and Medicaid in 1965—often triggers a cycle of intense struggles to establish new programs. Take Social Security: its formulation and enactment enjoyed some bipartisan support, but its passage ignited decades of pitched ideological battles that included efforts to repeal it outright or to undercut it by converting it into a voluntary program (as Ronald Reagan proposed for decades). What is significant is that the contention at the birth of Social Security and Medicare was followed by a normalization of politics: partisan acceptance, quiet interest group negotiation, the diffusion of successful innovations, and the formation of supportive voting blocs and organizations (Jacobs 1993; Brown and Jacobs 2008).

Direct comparisons with the ACA will be incomplete and inaccurate after the Republicans repeal and replace the ACA. But these comparisons were always imperfect because the ACA's benefits are more diffuse and not limited to a single program.

Nonetheless, it appears that aspects of normalization have begun in the form of interest group acceptance, state borrowing of innovations, and the activation of advocates for specific programs. The pressure of nomalization is evident in the Republican rejection of the outright termination favored by its most conservative supporters and its pursuit of a replacement plan that acknowledges the new reality of public and stakeholder expectations. Perhaps the most salient lesson of American political development and the history of social policy reform is that the new path of health reform inaugruated in 2010 and recast in 2017 set the conditions for future debate. Over time, the 2017 replacement may well stand out for significant reversals of the ACA as well as the Republican Party's acceptance of health reforms that it had firmly rejected. Future debates over health reform will respond to the new policies and incorporate Republican ideological concessions to government's expanded role in health policy.

■ ■ ■

Timothy H. Callaghan is an assistant professor in the Department of Health Policy and Management at Texas A&M University. He received his PhD in political science from the University of Minnesota in 2016. His research focuses on the linkages between policy, politics, and public attitudes with an emphasis on the US health care system and the Affordable Care Act. His work has appeared in journals such as the *American Journal of Public Health*, *Political Communication*, *Publius*, and the *International Journal of Public Opinion Research*.

Lawrence R. Jacobs is the Mondale chair and director of the Center for the Study of Politics and Governance in the Hubert H. Humphrey School and Department of Political Science at the University of Minnesota. He has written or edited sixteen books as well as authoring numerous articles on health policy, public opinion and elections, the US presidency, and American political development. His book with Theda Skocpol, *Health Reform and American Politics*, is in its third edition with Oxford University Press. His latest books are: *Who Governs? Presidents, Public Opinion, and Manipulation* with James Druckman (University of Chicago Press, 2015); and *Fed Power: How Finance Wins* with Desmond King (Oxford University Press, 2016).

References

Abramowitz, Alan I. 1985. "Economic Conditions, Presidential Popularity, and Voting Behavior in Midterm Congressional Elections." *Journal of Politics* 47, no. 1: 31–42.

Abramowitz, Alan I. 2008. "Forecasting the 2008 Presidential Election with the Time-for-Change Model." *PS: Political Science and Politics* 41, no. 4: 691–95.

Allen, Mahalley D., Carrie Pettus, and Donald P. Haider-Markel. 2004. "Making the National Local: Specifying the Conditions for National Government Influence on State Policymaking." *State Politics and Policy Quarterly* 4, no. 3: 318–44.

Angeles, January. 2010. "Health Reform Is a Good Deal for States." Center on Budget and Policy Priorities. Washington, D.C. www.cbpp.org/cms/index.cfm?fa=view &id =3171.

Ario, Joel, and Lawrence Jacobs. 2012. "In the Wake of the Supreme Court Decision over the Affordable Care Act, Many Stakeholders Still Support Health Reform." *Health Affairs*. Web version, July 11, 2012. Print version, August 2012.

Asher, Herbert. 1983. *Causal Modeling*. Newbury Park, CA: Sage.

Bafumi, Joseph, and Robert Y. Shapiro. 2009. "A New Partisan Voter." *Journal of Politics* 71, no. 1: 1–24.

Barrilleaux, Charles, and Carlisle Rainey. 2014. "The Politics of Need: Examining Governors' Decisions to Oppose the 'Obamacare' Medicaid Expansion." *State Politics and Policy Quarterly* 14, no. 4: 437–60.

Bohrnstedt, George, and David Knoke. 1994. *Statistics for Social Data Analysis*. 3rd ed. Itasca, IL: F. E. Peacock.

Brown, Lawrence, and Lawrence R. Jacobs. 2008. *The Private Abuse of the Public Interest*. Chicago: University of Chicago Press.

Callaghan, Timothy, and Lawrence R. Jacobs. 2016. "Interest Group Conflict over Medicaid Expansion: The Surprising Impact of Public Advocates." *American Journal of Public Health* 106, no. 2: 308–13.

Campbell, Andrea. 2003. *How Policies Make Citizens: Senior Political Activism and the American Welfare State*. Princeton, NJ: Princeton University Press.

Cappella, Joseph, and Kathleen Hall Jamieson. 1997. *Spiral of Cynicism: The Press and the Public Good*. New York: Oxford University Press.

CBO (Congressional Budget Office). 2016. "Federal Subsidies for Health Insurance Coverage for People under Age 65: 2016–2026." www.cbo.gov/sites/default/files /114th-congress-2015-2016/reports/51385-HealthInsuranceBaseline.pdf.

CMS (Centers for Medicare and Medicaid Services). 2016. "Medicaid and CHIP: December 2015 Monthly Applications, Eligibility Determinations and Enrollment Report." February 29. Baltimore: CMS.

Conlan, Timothy J., and Paul L. Posner. 2011. "Inflection Point? Federalism and the Obama Administration." *Publius: The Journal of Federalism* 41, no. 3: 421–46.

Converse, Philip. 1964. "The Nature of Belief Systems in Mass Publics." In *Ideology and Discontent*, edited by David Apter, 206–61. New York: Free Press.

Cook, Fay Lomax, Lawrence R. Jacobs, and Dukhong Kim. 2010. "Trusting What You Know: Information, Knowledge, and Confidence in Social Security." *Journal of Politics* 72, no. 2: 397–412.

Cover, Albert D. 1986. "Presidential Evaluations and Voting for Congress." *American Journal of Political Science* 30, no. 4: 786–801.

Davies, Gareth, and Martha Derthick. 1997. "Race and Social Welfare Policy: The Social Security Act of 1935." *Political Science Quarterly* 112, no. 2: 217–35.

Deering, Christopher J., and Shelly, Bryan. 2009. "State Resistance to Federal Mandates: A Cross-Case Analysis." Paper Presented at the 2009 American Political Science Association Annual Meeting, Toronto, CA, September 3–6.

Delli Carpini, Michael X., and Scott Keeter. 1996. *What Americans Know about Politics and Why It Matters*. New Haven, CT: Yale University Press.

Doan, Alesha E., and Deborah R. McFarlane. 2012. "Saying No to Abstinence-Only Education: An Analysis of State Decision-Making. *Publius: The Journal of Federalism* 42, no. 4: 613–35.

Doty, Michelle, Petra W. Rasmussen, and Sara R. Collins. 2014. "Catching Up: Latino Health Coverage Gains and Challenges under the Affordable Care Act." Commonwealth Fund. ow.ly/L6rTb.

Downs, Anthony. 1957. *An Economic Theory of Democracy*. New York: Harper.

Druckman, James N. 2004. "Political Preference Formation: Competition, Deliberation, and the (Ir)relevance of Framing Effects." *American Political Science Review* 98, no. 4: 671–86.

DSS (US Department of Health and Human Services). 2014. "Enrollment in the Health Insurance Marketplace Totals over 8 Million People." May 1, 2014. www.hhs.gov /news/press/2014pres/05/20140501a.html.

DSS (US Department of Health and Human Services). 2015. "Health Insurance Marketplaces." March 10, 2015. aspe.hhs.gov/health/reports/2015/MarketPlace Enrollment/Mar2015/ib_2015mar_enrollment.pdf.

Emanuel, Ezekiel. 2014. *Reinventing American Health Care*. New York: Public Affairs.

Ferguson, Margaret R. 2003. "Chief Executive Success in the Legislative Arena." *State Politics and Policy Quarterly* 3, no. 2: 158–82.

Fiorina, Morris. 1983. "Who Is Held Responsible? Further Evidence on the Hibbing-Alford Thesis." *American Journal of Political Science* 27: 158–64.

Fiorina, Morris. 1990. "Information and Rationality in Elections." In *Information and Democratic Processes*, edited by John A. Ferejohn and James Kuklinski, 329–42. Urbana: University of Illinois Press.

Fox News. 2014. "Failures in Management Led to ObamaCare Website Woes, Investigation Finds." *FoxNews.com.* July 31, 2014. www.foxnews.com/politics /2014/07/30/failures-in-management-led-to-obamacare-website-woes-investigation -finds.html.

Frean, Molly, Jonathan Gruber, and Benjamin D. Sommers. 2016. "Premium Subsidies, the Mandate, and Medicaid Expansion: Coverage Effects of the Affordable Care Act." NBER Working Paper No. 22213. Cambridge, MA: National Bureau of Economic Research.

Galewitz, Phil. 2016. "2016 Obamacare Enrollment Tops Expectations at 12.7 Million." *Kaiser Health News.* February 4, 2016. khn.org/news/2016-obamacare -enrollment-tops-expectations-at-12-7-million/.

Gaventa, John. 1982. *Power and Powerlessness: Quiescence and Rebellion in an Appalachian Valley*. Urbana: University of Illinois Press.

Gilardi, Fabrizio, Katharina Füglister, and Stéphane Luyet. 2009. "Learning from Others: The Diffusion of Hospital Financing Reforms in OECD Countries." *Comparative Political Studies* 42, no. 4: 549–73.

Gold, Marsha, Michael Sparer, and Karyen Chu. 1996. "Medicaid Managed Care: Lessons from Five States." *Health Affairs* 15, no. 3: 153–66.

Grogan, Colleen M. 1993. "Federalism and Health Care Reform." *American Behavioral Scientist* 36, no. 6: 741–59.

Gronke, Paul, Jeffrey Koch, and J. Matthew Wilson. 2003. "Follow the Leader? Presidential Approval, Presidential Support, and Representatives' Electoral Fortunes." *Journal of Politics* 65 (August): 785–808.

Hetherington, Marc. 1999. "The Effect of Political Trust on the Presidential Vote, 1968–96." *American Political Science Review* 93: 311–26.

Hetherington, Marc, and Suzanne Globetti. 2002. "Political Trust and Racial Policy Preferences." *American Journal of Political Science* 46 (April): 253–75.

Holahan, John, Stephen Zuckerman, Alison Evans, and Suresh Rangarajan. 1998. Medicaid Managed Care in Thirteen States. *Health Affairs* 17, no. 3: 43–63.

Jacobs, Lawrence R. 1993. *The Health of Nations: Public Opinion and the Making of American and British Health Policy*. Ithaca, NY: Cornell University Press.

Jacobs, Lawrence R., and Timothy Callaghan. 2013. "Why States Expand Medicaid: Party, Resources, and History." *Journal of Health Politics, Policy and Law* 38, no. 5: 1023–50.

Jacobs, Lawrence and Suzanne Mettler. 2011. "Why Public Opinion Changes: The Implications for Health and Health Policy." *Journal of Health Politics, Policy and Law* 36, no. 6: 917–33.

Jacobs, Lawrence, and Theda Skocpol. 2016. *Health Care Reform and American Politics: What Everyone Needs to Know*. 3rd ed. New York: Oxford University Press.

Kahneman, Daniel, and Amos Tversky. 1984. "Choices, Values, and Frames." *American Psychologist* 39 (April): 341–50.

Karch, Andrew. 2006. "National Intervention and the Diffusion of Policy Innovations." *American Politics Research* 34, no. 4: 403–26.

KFF (Kaiser Family Foundation). 2015. "Kaiser Health Tracking Poll: March 2015." March 19. ow.ly/L6n0B.

KFF (Kaiser Family Foundation). 2014. "Explaining Health Care Reform." October 24. kff.org/health-reform/issue-brief/explaining-health-care-reform-questions-about -health/.

Kuklinski, James, and Paul Quirk. 2000. "Reconsidering the Rational Public: Cognition, Heuristics, and Mass Opinion." In *Elements of Reason: Cognition, Choice, and the Bounds of Rationality*, edited by A. Lupia, M. D. McCubbins, and S. L. Popkin, 153–82. New York: Cambridge University Press.

Layman, Geoffrey C., Thomas M. Carsey, John C. Green, Richard Herrera, and Rosalyn Cooperman. 2010. "Activists and Conflict Extension in American Party Politics." *American Political Science Review* 104, no. 2: 324–46.

Lowi, Theodore. 1979. *The End of Liberalism: The Second Republic of the United States*. New York: W. W. Norton.

Mettler, Suzanne, and Joe Soss. 2004. "The Consequences of Public Policy for Democratic Citizenship: Bridging Policy Studies and Mass Politics." *Perspectives on Politics* 2, no. 1: 55–73.

Miller, E. A. 2005. "State Health Policy Making Determinants, Theory, and Methods: A Synthesis." *Social Science and Medicine* 61, no. 12: 2639–57.

Miller, E. A., and David Blanding. 2012. "Pressure Cooker Politics: Partisanship and Symbolism in State Certification of Federal Stimulus Funds." *State Politics and Policy Quarterly* 12, no. 1: 58–74.

Oberlander, Jonathan. 2011. "Under Siege—The Individual Mandate for Health Insurance and Its Alternatives." *New England Journal of Medicine* 364 (March 11): 1085–87.

Pear, Robert. 2015. "Eighty-six Percent of Health Law Enrollees Receive Subsidies." *New York Times*, March 10. ow.ly/L6a1M.

Pierson, Paul. 2000. "Increasing Returns, Path Dependence, and the Study of Politics." *American Political Science Review* 94 (June): 251–67.

Popkin, Samuel. 1991. *The Reasoning Voter*. Chicago: University of Chicago Press.

Reiter, Kristin, Marissa Noles, and George Pink. 2015. "Uncompensated Care Burden May Mean Financial Vulnerability for Rural Hospitals in States That Did Not Expand Medicaid." *Health Affairs* 34, no. 10: 1721–29.

Rigby, Elizabeth, and Jake Haselswerdt. 2013. "Hybrid Federalism, Partisan Politics, and Early Implementation of State Health Insurance Exchanges." *Publius: The Journal of Federalism* 43, no. 3: 368–91.

Satterthwaite, Shad B. 2002. "Innovation and Diffusion of Managed Care in Medicaid Programs." *State and Local Government Review* 34, no. 2: 116–26.

Seitz-Wald, Alex. 2013. "The Fight of Obamacare's 'Navigators' against Republican Hurdles." *National Journal*, October 30, 2013. ow.ly/L6r9C.

Selden, Tom, Jessica Banthin, and Joseph Cohen. 1998. "Medicaids Problem Children: Eligible but Not Enrolled." *Health Affairs* 17, no. 3: 192–200.

Shelly, Bryan. 2012. "Flexible Response: Executive Federalism and the No Child Left Behind Act of 2001." *Educational Policy* 26, no. 1: 117–35.

Shipan, Charles R., and Craig Volden. 2006. "Bottom-Up Federalism: The Diffusion of Antismoking Policies from U.S. Cities to States." *American Journal of Political Science* 50, no. 4: 825–43.

Shipan, Charles R., and Craig Volden. 2008. "The Mechanisms of Policy Diffusion." *American Journal of Political Science* 52, no. 4: 840–57.

Shipan, Charles R., and Craig Volden. 2012. "Policy Diffusion: Seven Lessons for Scholars and Practitioners." *Public Administration Review* 72, no. 6 (2012): 788–96.

Shor, Boris, and Nolan McCarty. 2011. "The Ideological Mapping of American Legislatures." *American Political Science Review* 105, no. 3: 530–51.

Singhal, Monica. 2008. "Special Interest Groups and the Allocation of Public Funds." *Journal of Public Economics* 92, no. 3: 548–64.

Skocpol, Theda. 1992. *Protecting Soldiers and Mothers: The Politics of Social Provision in the United States, 1870s–1920s.* Cambridge, MA: Harvard University.

Skocpol, Theda, and John Ikenberry. 1983. "The Political Formation of the American Welfare State in Historical and Comparative Context." *Comparative Social Research* 6: 87–148.

Skocpol, Theda, and Vanessa Williamson. 2012. *The Tea Party and the Remaking of Republican Conservatism.* New York: Oxford University Press.

Soss, Joe. 1999. "Lessons of Welfare: Policy Design, Political Learning, and Political Action." *American Political Science Review* 93: 363–80.

Soss, Joe, Richard C. Fording, and Sanford F. Schram. 2011. *Disciplining the Poor: Neoliberal Paternalism and the Persistent Power of Race.* Chicago: University of Chicago Press.

Thomas, Clive S., and Ronald J. Hrebenar. 1999. "Interest Groups in the States." In *Politics in the American States: A Comparative Analysis*, 7th ed., edited by Virginia Gray, Russell L. Hanson, and Herbert Jacobson, 113–43. Washington, DC: Congressional Quarterly.

Tilly, Charles. 1978. *From Mobilization to Revolution.* Reading, MA: Addison-Wesley.

US Census Bureau. 2008. "Income, Poverty, and Health Insurance Coverage in the United States: 2007." www.census.gov/prod/2008pubs/p60-235.pdf.

Volden, Craig. 2006. "States as Policy Laboratories: Emulating Success in the Children's Health Insurance Program." *American Journal of Political Science* 50, no. 2: 294–312.

Welch, Susan, and Kay Thompson. 1980. "The Impact of Federal Incentives on State Policy Innovation." *American Journal of Political Science* 24, no. 4: 715–29.

Williams, Misty. 2015. "The Red State Solution: Arkansas' 'Private Option' on Medicaid." *Atlanta Journal-Constitution*, March 21, 2015. www.myajc.com/news /news/state-regional-govt-politics/the-red-state-solution-arkansas-private-option -on-/nkYkM/?icmp=AJC_internallink_032315_AJCtoMyAJC_ArkansasMedicaid.

Appendix: Variable Measurement

Relative Exchange Enrollment DV

Our exchange enrollment measure is captured using the equation (QHP/ Uninsured pre-ACA). The numerator of the equation reflects the number of individuals determined eligible to enroll in a plan through the exchange marketplace who have selected a plan from 11/15/14 to 2/22/15. The number uninsured in each state is based on American Community Survey Estimates for 2013 and population data originally from the census bureau's March 2014 Current Population Survey as reported by Kaiser.

>   aspe.hhs.gov/health/reports/2015/MarketPlaceEnrollment/Mar2015
>   /ib_2015mar_enrollment.pdf
>   kff.org/uninsured/state-indicator/total-population-2/
>   kff.org/other/state-indicator/total-residents/

Relative Medicaid Enrollment DV

Our Medicaid enrollment measure is captured using the equation (Medicaid Change/Uninsured pre-ACA). Our Medicaid data is state reported and recorded by Kaiser and represents the difference between total enrollment in March 2015 and Pre-ACA monthly average Medicaid and CHIP enrollment for July–September 2013. Please note that not all changes in enrollment in Medicaid may be related to the ACA. The number uninsured in each state is based on American Community Survey Estimates for 2013 and population data originally from the census bureau's March 2014 Current Population Survey as reported by Kaiser.

>   kff.org/health-reform/state-indicator/total-monthly-medicaid-and
>   -chip-enrollment/#
>   kff.org/uninsured/state-indicator/total-population-2/
>   kff.org/other/state-indicator/total-residents/

Democratic Governor

This variable is a dummy variable which is scored as a "1" if the governor is a Democrat and "0" if the governor is not a Democrat. It is updated to 2015.

>   www.ncsl.org/legislatures-elections/elections/statevote-charts.aspx
>   www.ncsl.org/legislatures-elections/elections/statevote-election-night
>   -governor-map.aspx

Democratic Legislature

1 point = full Democratic control of both houses of the state legislature.
.5 points = Democratic control of only one house of the state
  legislature . . . includes splits.
0 points = full Republican control of the state legislature
Results updated to 2015.

  http://www.ncsl.org/legislatures-elections/elections/statevote-charts
    .aspx
  http://www.ncsl.org/legislatures-elections/elections/statevote-election
    -night-governor-map.aspx

Obama Vote 2012

This variable is taken from data made available by the Federal Election
Commission and reflects the percentage of the popular vote won by President Obama in the 2012 presidential election against Mitt Romney.

  http://www.fec.gov/pubrec/fe2012/federalelections2012.pdf

State Affluence

State affluence is a measure of state per capita personal income dollars for
the most recent year available, 2014. This information is available through
the Beaureau of Economic Analysis.

  http://www.bea.gov/newsreleases/regional/spi/2015/spi0315.htm

State Unemployment

State unemployment is a measure of the average unemployment in each
state that was created by averaging state unemployment in each month of
2014. This data is available through the National Conference of State
Legislatures.

  http://www.ncsl.org/documents/employ/STATE-UI-RATES-2014.pdf

Exchange Type

This variable scores states along 3 points with higher scores reflecting
increased state control over the exchange. Zero points were awarded for a

federal exchange, 1 point was awarded for a partnership exchange, and 2 points were awarded for a state exchange. Nevada, New Mexico, and Oregon, which operate federally supported state-based marketplaces, are coded as 1's.

> http://kff.org/health-reform/state-indicator/state-health-insurance -marketplace-types/

Medicaid Status

Stage 1: Level 1 Grant Application
1 = States who applied for a level one grant from the federal government to implement ACA reform
0 = No level one grant application by state
Source: http://www.healthcare.gov/news/factsheets/2011/05 /exchanges05232011a.html
Stage 2: Public Statement in Support of Reform from Governor
1 = Clear statement from governor in support of reform
0 = No indication of gubernatorial support for ACA related Medicaid reform including outright opposition to reform
Sources: http://kff.org/medicaid/state-indicator/state-activity-around -expanding-medicaid-under-the-affordable-care-act/
http://www.advisory.com/Daily-Briefing/2012/11/09/Medicaid Map#lightbox/1/.
Stage 3: Medicaid Alternative Approval Sought/Non-ACA Alternative Implemented
1 = State pursuit of federal approval for an ACA alternative or outright implementation of Medicaid expansion not categorized as ACA compliant
0 = No alternative sought or implemented
Sources: http://kff.org/medicaid/state-indicator/state-activity-around -expanding-medicaid-under-the-affordable-care-act/
Stage 4: Federally Approved ACA Medicaid Alternative Implemented
1 = State implementation of a federally approved ACA alternative
0 = No alternative implemented
Sources: http://kff.org/medicaid/state-indicator/state-activity-around -expanding-medicaid-under-the-affordable-care-act/
Stage 5: Implementation of Federally Stipulated Medicaid Reform
1 = State implementation of Medicaid reform as stipulated under federal law
0 = No state implementation of ACA compliant Medicaid reform

Sources: http://kff.org/medicaid/state-indicator/state-activity-around
-expanding-medicaid-under-the-affordable-care-act/

This variable is scored 0–5 with states awarded points based on the highest stage they have achieved towards reform. The stages do not represent a temporal sequence as states may vary in the order of action; instead, they measure state progress in completing increasingly important steps. Thus a state with no level-1 grant but which has implemented Medicaid reform would get a score of 5 despite skipping stage 1. A state that has completed none of the stages is coded as a 0.

Administrative Capacity

Administrative capacity is a cumulative measure based on the following: 1 point in the small group market if states guarantee and issue all products, have special rules for groups of one, have state-imposed limits on rating, have health insurance subsidies and up to 1 point for state authority to review rates. The same number of points was available for the same subjects in the individual market and 1 point was also added for guarantee issuing some products. One point was also awarded for the presence of a high-risk pool program, the high-risk pool being open to Health Insurance Portability and Accountability Act–eligible individuals, the high-risk pool being open to medically needy individuals, and the high-risk pool being open to health coverage tax credit–eligible individuals. One point was also awarded for state-mandated coverage of infertility treatment and eating-disorder coverage in the individual and small group markets. Three points were awarded for a state having an all-payer claims database, up to 1 point was given (based on Kaiser-established categories) for federal hazard preparedness funding, and 1 point each were given for state conversion coverage in small firms, state restrictions against balance billing in preferred provider organizations, and out-of-network providers in health maintenance organizations.

> www.statehealthfacts.org/comparetable.jsp?ind=350&cat=7
> www.statehealthfacts.org/comparetable.jsp?ind=351&cat=7
> www.statehealthfacts.org/comparereport.jsp?rep=4&cat=7#
> www.statehealthfacts.org/comparetable.jsp?ind=888&cat=7
> www.statehealthfacts.org/comparetable.jsp?ind=353&cat=7
> www.statehealthfacts.org/comparetable.jsp?ind=354&cat=7
> www.statehealthfacts.org/comparereport.jsp?rep=3&cat=7

www.statehealthfacts.org/comparetable.jsp?ind=887&cat=7
kff.org/womens-health-policy/state-indicator/infertility-coverage/
www.statehealthfacts.org/comparereport.jsp?rep=65&cat=7
apcdcouncil.org/state/map
kff.org/state-category/health-costs-budgets/
statehealthfacts.org/comparetable.jsp?ind=358&cat=7
kff.org/private-insurance/state-indicator/state-restriction-against
    -providers-balance-billing-managed-care-enrollees/
statehealthfacts.org/comparereport.jsp?rep=66&cat=7
www.statehealthfacts.org/comparetable.jsp?ind=602&cat=7
www.statehealthfacts.org/comparetable.jsp?ind=604&cat=7

Rhetoric and Reform in Waiver States

Colleen M. Grogan
University of Chicago

Phillip M. Singer
University of Michigan

David K. Jones
Boston University

Abstract   Seven states have used Section 1115 waivers to expand Medicaid as part of the Affordable Care Act (ACA). While each state pursued a unique plan, there are similarities in the types of changes each state desired to make. Equally important to how a state modified their Medicaid programs is how a state talked about Medicaid and reform. We investigate whether the rhetoric that emerged in waiver states is unique, analyze whether the rhetoric is associated with particular waiver reforms, and consider the implications of our findings for the future of Medicaid policy making. We find that proponents in waiver states have convinced a conservative legislature that their reform is sufficiently innovative that they are not doing a Medicaid expansion, and not building on the traditional Medicaid program. Particularly striking is that none of these reforms are entirely new to the Medicaid program. While not new, the way in which waiver states have been allowed to implement many of the reforms is new and has become stricter. We find an emerging consensus utilized by conservative policy makers in framing the Medicaid expansion. Expansion efforts by conservative policy makers in other states have subsequently pushed this framing far to the right.

Keywords   Medicaid expansion, Affordable Care Act, waivers

Introduction

Three major principles were embedded in the Affordable Care Act (ACA) when it passed in 2010: (1) federalism and encouraging state-level innovation; (2) universal coverage; and (3) incentives to bend the cost curve through delivery model innovations. When the Supreme Court ruled on the constitutionality of the ACA in 2012, upholding the individual mandate but allowing states the option to expand Medicaid, the Court consequentially

Journal of Health Politics, Policy and Law, Vol. 42, No. 2, April 2017
DOI 10.1215/03616878-3766719   © 2017 by Duke University Press

privileged the first principle over the second (with no comment or action on the third). Allowing states the option to expand coverage necessarily means universal coverage is no guarantee.[1] By the end of 2015, nearly 33 million people remained uninsured, primarily those residing in the nineteen non-expansion states (KFF 2016b). Although the decision to expand is largely driven by party control in the states, some Republican governors in conservative states have been able to pass their own version of a Medicaid expansion through the use of waivers. Indeed, Republican governors and legislators have used the first principle—federalism and states' rights—to claim that they have expanded coverage to low-income families, thereby allowing them to pull down substantial federal funds, but have taken a path uniquely suited to their state's conservative values.

Seven states have used Section 1115 waivers as a key element of their expansion of Medicaid as part of the Affordable Care Act (ACA): Arkansas, Indiana, Iowa, Michigan, Montana, New Hampshire, and Pennsylvania.[2] This is in addition to the other twenty-four states (including Washington, DC) that have expanded Medicaid. These waivers were negotiated between the Centers for Medicare and Medicaid Services (CMS) and state administrations to make substantial changes to the Medicaid program in these states. Essentially, proponents in these seven states have convinced a conservative legislature that their reform is sufficiently innovative and different that they are *not* doing a Medicaid expansion as called for in the ACA, and *not* building on the traditional Medicaid program, which conservatives view as faulty and dysfunctional. These leaders need to convince CMS that their reform is a legitimate version of a Medicaid expansion and they need to convince their own state legislature that this is not Medicaid at all. While certain reform elements appear crucial to gain conservative support—charging premiums, imposing forms of cost sharing, incentives to modify lifestyle behaviors—equally important (if not more so) is the use of rhetorical devices to sell these reforms to a conservative constituency.

In an effort to distinguish between the diffusion of policy elements versus political rhetoric, we document not only how the elements of waiver reforms have developed in these first adopter waiver states, but also how the reforms have been framed, and whether there is an interaction between reform elements and political discourse. For example, when cost-sharing

1. Of course, even in its original form the ACA excluded undocumented immigrants and legal immigrants in residence for less than five years, which compromised the universality claim.
2. Pennsylvania subsequently rescinded its grant application when a new governor was elected and decided to implement a straight expansion consistent with the ACA.

and premium components are discussed as important waiver components, what arguments (or political frames) appear in political discourse most frequently: Cost containment? Individual responsibility? Similarly, when the private option or Medicaid managed care designs are discussed, what arguments in political discourse appear most frequently: Individual responsibility in a marketplace? Efficiency of private insurance? Cost containment?

Very few scholars studying policy diffusion have looked at the influence of political discourse (Boushey 2016). This study will help illuminate the extent to which political discourse is an important mechanism to nudge policy adoption, and subsequent research can ascertain its import on policy diffusion of waivers in conservative states. Moreover, by looking at both policy reforms and rhetoric, we can examine whether framing becomes more important than the reform itself. In other words, are cost-sharing elements crucial for passage in a conservative legislature or is it the framing of personal responsibility that matters most?

We argue that these waiver states are important because they may act as a harbinger for how far Medicaid may be allowed to move to meet a conservative ideology, and, as such, has the potential to put Medicaid on a distinctive path in these states. Before detailing this argument, we provide a brief history of how Medicaid's past reforms have been framed to set the context to understand how these conservative ACA waiver reforms are similar and different from past reform efforts. Next, we provide a brief review of the policy diffusion literature to locate our contribution. After detailing our methodological approach, we then present our findings. We find a chronological pattern developing where each grouping of conservative states pushed for reforms further to the right of their predecessors and its associated rhetoric remained in sync—questioning the deservingness of the newly eligible, and seeking to return Medicaid to its original intent of only serving the truly needy.

Background: The Framing of Medicaid's Past Reforms

Since 1962, Section 1115 waivers have allowed states to modify, or waive certain requirements associated with entitlement programs, including Medicaid when it was originally passed in 1965. Before 1993, the federal government observed strict budget neutrality requirements and demanded fully developed research designs, which limited the use of states applying for 1115 waivers (Thompson 2012). However, since then, the federal government has loosened requirements and states have used 1115 waivers to expand coverage, reform delivery systems, adjust payment models, and revise benefits and cost-sharing requirements (KFF 2011). As of November 2015, thirty-nine states had a currently approved or pending waiver with the federal government, and all but five states (Alaska, Nebraska, North Dakota, South Carolina, and South Dakota) had applied for a Section 1115 waiver (Medicaid.gov 2016a).

These changes come at a time when Medicaid is already undergoing its most substantial shift in its fifty-year history. States expanding Medicaid as part of the ACA will cover all individuals below 138 percent of the federal poverty level (FPL). Prior to the ACA, Medicaid would only cover individuals who met specific categorical eligibility rules—for example, the elderly and disabled, and children and pregnant women—and were below federally established income thresholds. States were allowed flexibility in expanding the categories of eligibility and for modifying the income threshold to cover more people. However, the ACA Medicaid expansion is the first time the federal government has allowed states to only consider income and completely disregard categorical eligibility (with the important exception of federal policy regarding immigrants). Since children, pregnant women, and parents were already allowed Medicaid coverage, what this reform essentially allows is Medicaid coverage for healthy, single adults.

Questions about whether healthy, single adults are deserving of subsidized public health insurance is an old and long-standing debate in America. When Medicaid and Medicare were passed in 1965, the question of deservingness was central to the ideological wedge between conservatives and liberals. Most liberals at the time were in favor of universal health care coverage and viewed Medicare as the stepping-stone to achieve such coverage. In contrast, most conservatives viewed the dual passage of Medicare and Medicaid as having solved the problem of the uninsured. In particular, they argued that Medicare was now available for the elderly, Medicaid was available for the "truly deserving"—poor mothers and children, and poor aged and disabled persons—and affordable private insurance was available for the remainder of Americans, including able-bodied working men (Grogan 2008; Grogan and Smith 2008).

However, even by the mid-1980s, as health care costs continued to increase, and it became increasingly difficult to argue that private insurance was affordable for lower- and even middle-class Americans, the contours of this debate changed. More and more conservatives were comfortable with expanding the notion of deservingness—acknowledging that, for many working Americans, private insurance was unaffordable. A number of voluntary expansions occurred during the 1980s, and by 1990 Medicaid was required to cover additional groups: children and pregnant women and the low-income elderly up to the FPL (Tanenbaum 1995; Grogan 2008). In response to the inclusion of these sympathetic expansion groups, the program was no longer overlooked, but was rather seen as an essential component of the American safety net.

During this time, both Republicans and Democrats argued that Medicaid was essential, though they differed on the details of how the program should operate. Republican rhetoric after they gained majority control of Congress in 1995 focused on strengthening Medicaid through block-granting the program, rather than retrenchment. At the same time, an analysis of Democratic Party platforms found that Medicaid was now talked about as a broad social entitlement that provided assistance to the middle class (Grogan and Patashnik 2003). In a complete reversal from the views of policy makers at the implementation of Medicaid thirty years earlier, the failure of the Clinton health care plan and unsuccessful state-level health reforms during the early 1990s meant that many policy makers—across political parties—turned willingly to the Medicaid program to expand coverage (Grogan 2008; Thompson 2012).

The State Children's Health Insurance Program (SCHIP) passed in 1997 and expansions to working parents in 2003 were a response of this shift in opinion. Both passed with bipartisan support and allowed states to use Medicaid to expand coverage. However, a backlash against an expanded Medicaid program began to emerge as states took advantage of these options to expand Medicaid and the number of enrollees—as well as Medicaid expenditures—increased dramatically. The backlash started first under the 2008 SCHIP reauthorization debate where conservatives fought strongly against reauthorizing SCHIP, which by that time had expanded coverage to children in working families in some states as high as 300 percent of the FPL. Conservatives argued that states had gone too far in expanding coverage, especially since many of the "truly deserving poor" were still not enrolled (Grogan and Rigby 2009; Grogan and Andrews 2011).

This debate primed the discussion that followed after passage of the ACA. Although most of the disagreement in 2009–10 over the passage of the ACA at the federal level focused on how to design health care reform and not on questions of deservingness,[3] moving the decision to expand

---

3. This is obviously not entirely true given the debates about whether immigrants should have access to the benefits of health reform and the decision to exclude those here lawfully only after a five-year waiting period; however, the older rhetoric related to work and health care benefits was largely absent.

Medicaid to the states allowed the deservingness question to emerge front and center again in conservative states (Grogan 2013). Yet, while the rhetoric of reform is unique in conservative states, many of the policy design elements requested and granted under the waivers are characteristic of broader trends undertaken by many states—conservative and liberal alike. Thus, although proponents of waivers in the conservative states appear to all claim their reforms to be dramatically different from traditional Medicaid, we interrogate the reform elements of waivers separate from their associated rhetoric and framing to determine if it is the policy design, its rhetoric, or aspects of both which makes these waivers unique.

Policy Diffusion

The literature on policy diffusion provides helpful guidance and context on how to examine learning between states. Scholars have studied a variety of mechanisms contributing to the likelihood of a specific policy diffusing across states, including geographic proximity (Case, Rosen, and Hines 1993), shared similar political ideologies (Grossback, Nicholson-Crotty, and Peterson 2004), participation in extra-governmental organizations (Skocpol et al. 1993; Mintrom 1997; Balla 2001), similar institutional factors shared by different states (Boehmke 2005), the success of a policy (Volden 2007), and the expertise and experience of the policy maker within a state (Shipan and Volden 2014). Much of this research has focused on the horizontal spread of policies, for example, among various states within a federated system. However, another strain of research has highlighted the vertical nature of policy diffusion and learning. Vertical diffusion highlights when policy makers at different levels of government—federal, state, and local—learn from and are influenced by the implementation of policies at other levels of government (Shipan and Volden 2006; Karch 2007).

Much of the political science literature on diffusion treats policy as a dichotomous variable. A state has either adopted a policy or not, with the main outcome of interest being the rate of spread from state to state. Our study is better situated in the thread of research focused on reinvention, or the modification of a policy throughout the diffusion process (Rogers 1983). This is an important distinction because, rather than be a laggard slow to act, the fortieth state to adopt a policy might actually be quite innovative in how it adopts a particular policy (Glick and Hays 1991, Hays 1996). Karch and Cravens (2014) point out that policies are often modified after the initial adoption, further emphasizing the importance of paying close attention to the details, rather than the dichotomous rate of adoption. We also build on the recent work of Boushey (2016) who finds that diffusion of state policy is shaped by how the groups affected by a proposal are described in media coverage. Our analysis differs from previous work on policy diffusion in three ways. First, because we are studying the phenomenon of ACA Medicaid waivers very early in the implementation stages, our focus is best described as a study of early adopters. Second, because the design and politics of waivers is complex, we argue that simply studying waiver adoption—as a binary variable—can be misleading. Many waiver reforms are identical to Medicaid reforms adopted in non-waiver states. Despite rhetoric claiming substantial movement away from traditional Medicaid programs, we interrogate this claim to determine which elements of reform are truly unique in these initial waiver states. Third, while most studies of policy diffusion analyze policy adoption as the key unit of analysis, we collect data on policy discourse in addition to reform elements to understand if the framing of reform might be what is novel rather than the reform itself, and to understand better how framing nudges policy adoption.

Methods

We focus on nine states: the six that have used a waiver to expand Medicaid (Arkansas, Indiana, Iowa, Michigan, Montana, and New Hampshire), the one that submitted but subsequently rescinded its waiver application (Pennsylvania), and two in which governors pushed for an expansion waiver but were rebuffed by their legislatures (Tennessee and Utah). These states made for particularly good comparisons given their interesting variation in partisan control. Five of these states (Michigan, Indiana, Iowa, Tennessee, and Utah) were controlled by Republican governors during the entire period of our study (2012–15). Of these, only Iowa did not also have a unified Republican-led legislature. Two states (Montana and New Hampshire) were led by Democratic governors during the entire four-year period. Republicans controlled the legislature in both states except for a two-year period when Democrats controlled the New Hampshire House. Partisan control of the governorship changed in two states, with Arkansas moving from Democrat Mike Beebe to Republican Asa Hutchinson in 2015, and Pennsylvania moving from Republican Tom Corbett to Democrat Tom Wolf in 2015. Both legislatures were controlled entirely by Republicans during this period, except for one year in which Democrats controlled the Arkansas House and Senate (see table 1). This variation in party control,

Table 1 Party Control in Key Positions in Waiver States

States	Governor	House	Senate
Arkansas	2012–2014	2012	2012
	Beebe (D)	(D)	(D)
	2014–Present	2013–2015	2013–2015
	Hutchinson (R)	(R)	(R)
Iowa	2012–Present	2012–2015	2012–2015
	Branstad (R)	(R)	(D)
Michigan	2012–Present	2012–2015	2012–2015
	Snyder (R)	(R)	(R)
Pennsylvania	2012–2015	2012–2015	2012–2015
	Corbett (R)	(R)	(R)
	2015–Present		
	Wolf (D)		
Indiana	2012–2013	2012–2015	2012–2015
	Daniels (R)	(R)	(R)
	2013–Present		
	Holcomb (R)		
New Hampshire	2012–2013	2012	2012–2015
	Lynch (D)	(R)	(R)
	2013–2017	2013–2014	
	Hassan (D)	(D)	
		2015	
		(R)	
Montana	2012–2013	2012–2015	2012–2015
	Schweitzer (D)	(R)	(R)
	2013–Present		
	Bullock (D)		
Tennessee	2012–Present	2012–2015	2012–2015
	Haslam (R)	(R)	(R)
Utah	2012–Present	2012–2015	2012–2015
	Herbert (R)	(R)	(R)

Sources: Statistical Almanac for 2012–2014 Data; National Conference of State Legislatures for 2015 Data.

especially in the governorship because the state executive primarily shapes the framing of the waiver proposal, is methodologically helpful because it allows us to observe whether and how rhetoric changes when party control shifts.

Our methodological approach involved two main data collection efforts. First, we examined each Section 1115 waiver application submitted by the seven states that connected a waiver to the ACA's expansion. We used these applications as primary source material to focus on the structure of the reforms in each of these states. We collected the following seven variables of interest: design of expansion plan, premiums, cost sharing, healthy behaviors, employment regulations, health savings accounts, and employer-sponsored insurance premium supports.

Design of expansion plan includes the main mechanism which the state implemented for their expanded Medicaid program; examples of this variable include premium assistance plans in Arkansas and expansion of Medicaid managed care in Michigan. States vary at the FPL in which they require premiums and cost-sharing from new enrollees. with premiums in Indiana start at 0 percent of the FPL, and the other states require premiums starting at 50 percent and 100 percent of the FPL. Our healthy behaviors variable includes any requirement from the state which demands that enrollees complete health risk assessments, wellness activities, or preventative health activities in return for reduced cost sharing or premiums.

The US Department of Health and Human Services (HHS) has been adamant about not accepting waiver applications which *required* new enrollees to be employed to receive benefits. In an effort to claim success in negotiations with the federal government though, waiver states have pushed for certain employment regulations in a "holistic" approach to poverty reduction, requiring the newly enrolled to be engaged in employment programs or job-seeking efforts as part of their Medicaid benefits. Health savings accounts have an interesting history, introduced into Medicaid programs by Indiana in an earlier 2008 reform effort (Commonwealth Fund 2008). These accounts operate as a repository for enrollee premiums, subsidized by state contributions, and are used by the new enrollees to finance the costs associated with covered Medicaid benefits (i.e., premiums, co-pays and deductibles). The last variable collected, Employer-sponsored insurance premium supports, involve states providing subsidies to newly enrolled Medicaid beneficiaries who have access to employer insurance.

The second main data collection effort involved gathering text from policy and political discourse related to the waiver adoption process. The key sources of data which we collected were speeches and press releases produced by the governor of each of the waiver states; legislator statements, including press releases and floor speeches; and presentations, research briefs, and reports produced by relevant state agencies. We focused on key policy makers in each state, including the governor, state house and senate leadership, chairs of relevant committees, and heads of relevant agencies in each state.

To further support our detailed content analysis of the waiver applications, we also relied on two forms of media data to provide further documentation of the public debate around these waivers. The first was a search of the capital city-based National Public Radio subsidiary in each state. We employed uniform search criteria for each of these news websites of stakeholder first name, stakeholder last name, and Medicaid, with a date range of June 29, 2012, to July 15, 2015. We also completed the same search for the newspaper with the highest circulation in each state in our study: *Arkansas Democrat-Gazette, Indianapolis Star, Des Moines Register, Detroit Free Press, Billings Gazette, New Hampshire Union Leader, Philadelphia Inquirer, Tennessean,* and *Salt Lake Tribune.*[4]

In total, we amassed 1,227 documents as part of our data collection efforts.

Using these data, we conducted detailed content analysis of the frames, rhetoric, and arguments provided by the stakeholders in each of the waiver states. To ensure reliability among the three researchers, we individually coded a subset of press releases, speeches, and newspaper accounts related to Arkansas's Medicaid expansion. Independently, the three researchers identified themes related to the data. The three researchers then cross-checked their results to ensure similar identification of themes as well as developed coding strategies used for the rest of the analysis.

Each coauthor was assigned three states to code: an early adopter state, and two states which successfully expanded Medicaid through a waiver. Two coauthors were assigned states where governors sought a waiver but failed to implement an expansion. We coded several themes for each article included in our content analysis, including who was speaking, the intended audience, the tone of the speech toward the waiver, requested policy design of the waiver, how the deservingness of the expansion population was framed, and the use of evidence by the speaker. The data collected included direct quotations from key policy makers as well as our own notes on the use of frames and phrases changed over time. After finishing each state, the coder wrote a short summary of arguments and framing used to talk about Medicaid expansion within the state.

---

4. Inclusion of National Public Radio in our content analysis was due to subsidiaries located in every state and their emphasis on in-depth state and local news. One challenge we faced was ensuring an ideological balance of media outlet accounts of Medicaid expansion. There is no analogous conservative-leaning media outlet similar in scope to National Public Radio, with a network of state-based subsidiaries. However, the nine newspapers included in our content analysis did exhibit conservative leanings, with five of the newspapers endorsing Mitt Romney for president in 2012, with three supporting Barack Obama, and one abstaining. Additionally, our data collection efforts included press releases and texts of speeches by key stakeholders in each state, ensuring that we also included these primary documents in our content analysis.

Findings: Medicaid Waiver Reforms—Rhetoric and Reality

The most striking pattern about the reform elements passed in the seven waiver states is that the most popular reforms are also those most likely to be passed in non-waiver states. All seven waiver states have implemented some form of cost sharing and Medicaid managed care, five states have included various premium charges, and four states have included incentive policies to encourage healthy behaviors (see table 2). The most novel reform, which also received the most national press coverage, is the creation of the so-called private option which allows the state to draw down federal Medicaid funds for the new Medicaid enrollees to purchase private insurance on the state's ACA health insurance exchange. This is also called premium assistance since the state pays premiums to qualified health plans (QHPs) on the exchange for newly eligible Medicaid recipients. Arkansas was not only the first state to implement an expansion waiver, but also the first state to adopt a private option. Iowa quickly followed with their version of the private option and, a few years later, New Hampshire followed suit.

Much of the rhetoric supporting the uniqueness of the private option reform was that it was reforming Medicaid away from a state-run program since it contracts with private plans. However, as others have pointed out, state Medicaid programs have contracted with private managed care plans since the early 1970s, and today the vast majority of states utilize some form of managed care contracting (Rosenbaum and Sommers 2013). What makes the private option different from Medicaid managed care plans is that under the private option, insurers are not able to distinguish who in their population is a Medicaid beneficiary (Kliff 2013). In contrast, under Medicaid managed care, states contract with private plans who offer a separate Medicaid product, which means that Medicaid enrollees have access to a separate, and often much more limited, network of providers. Nevertheless, while this integration with other non-Medicaid enrollees is new, the reliance on the private sector is not new to the Medicaid program (Rosenbaum and Sommers 2013). When the ACA was signed into law in 2010, nearly 70 percent of the 60 million Medicaid beneficiaries were enrolled in a managed care program (Sparer 2012). This number continues to increase, with 80 percent of Medicaid beneficiaries currently enrolled in managed care plans—most under regular Medicaid expansions, not waivers.

The two other reform elements which were each adopted by three states are health savings accounts (in Indiana, Michigan, and later Arkansas), and

Table 2 Waiver Reform Elements by State

| | Waiver States and Date of Adoption | | | | | | | |
Reform Element	Arkansas September 2013	Iowa December 2013	Michigan December 2013	Pennsylvania* August 2014	Indiana January 2015	New Hampshire March 2015	Montana November 2015	Number of Waiver States Adopting
Cost-sharing	Yes	Yes	Yes	Yes	Yes	Yes	Yes	7
Medicaid managed care	Yes	Yes	Yes	Yes	Yes	Yes	Yes**	7
Premiums	No	Yes	Yes	Yes	Yes	No	Yes	5
Healthy behavior incentives	No	Yes	Yes	Yes	Yes	No	No	4
Premium assistance to purchase QHPs on exchange	Yes	Yes	No	No	No	Yes	No	3
Health savings accounts	Yes***	No	Yes	No	Yes	No	No	3
Voluntary work incentives	No	No	No	Yes	Yes	Yes	No	3
Number of reforms within each state	4	5	5	5	6	4	3	

Source: Adapted from Kaiser Family Foundation.

Notes: *After the election of a new governor, Pennsylvania terminated its waiver and adopted an expansion of traditional Medicaid. Results in Table 1 for Pennsylvania are for the Healthy Pennsylvania Waiver.

**Montana calls this fee for service third-party administrator (FFS TPA), which is a contract with a TPA to manage recipients' care with a designated network of providers. Thus, similar to Medicaid Managed Care reforms, Montana secured a Freedom of Choice waiver to implement FFS TPA.

***Added during reauthorization process in 2015.

voluntary work incentives (adopted by Pennsylvania, Indiana, and New Hampshire). Again, these two reform ideas have been around a long time. Under health savings accounts, individuals are encouraged to save for financial costs associated with out-of-pocket health care expenditures. Many states have utilized the idea of health savings accounts—most notably Indiana, even for its Medicaid program—before the ACA was passed. Job training and counseling have long been offered to recipients of public programs.

So, are these expansion waivers much ado about nothing?[5] First, although most of these reform ideas are not new, the way in which waiver states have been allowed to implement many of the reforms is new and much more aggressive. Second, it is this stronger approach—combined with its associated rhetoric—that arguably helped allow for a Medicaid expansion in these conservative states during this particular time period. While other conservative states passed a "regular" Medicaid expansion, these waiver states are important because they may act as a harbinger for how far Medicaid may be allowed to move to meet a conservative ideology, and, as such, has the potential to put Medicaid on a distinctive path in these states. To detail this argument, we start by discussing the reforms adopted and the framing used in the first three states—Arkansas, Iowa, and Michigan. We then illustrate how Indiana and Pennsylvania adopted additional reforms and pushed the framing further to the right. Third, the more focused reforms adopted under New Hampshire's and Montana's waivers, and Arkansas's reauthorization, suggest an emerging consensus among conservatives that even very poor people must have skin in the private sector game. Finally, local debates surrounding Utah's and Tennessee's failed waiver proposals might suggest an even further push for additional conservative reforms. Conservative states continue to push for a Medicaid work requirement and are looking for ways to impose an expenditure cap (like a Medicaid block grant long desired by Republicans), and states—like Tennessee and Utah—may not be willing to compromise on these points.

How Do States Expand Medicaid without Doing a Medicaid Expansion?

Political rhetoric around Medicaid has shifted over the lifespan of the program, often mirroring the social construction of the individuals eligible

5. We acknowledge the Rosenbaum and Sommers (2013) article which asked this same question regarding Arkansas's Private Option.

for the program (Olson 2010; Grogan 2011). Because earlier Medicaid reforms focused on expanding coverage to groups broadly considered deserving—children and pregnant women and infants—there was little debate about the recipients themselves (Tanenbaum 1995). Instead, the debate tended to focus on how state governments could redesign the Medicaid program to improve quality and access to care, and control (or decrease) Medicaid expenditures.

Actually, there was not much debate about redesigning the Medicaid program, since a broad consensus emerged by the mid-1990s that Medicaid managed care was the desired reform option (Grogan 1997). There was bipartisan agreement that contracting with private managed care organizations would be more efficient than relying on the traditional state-run fee-for-service Medicaid program and hopefully improve access and quality. As mentioned above, when the conservative backlash toward Medicaid expansions took hold during the SCHIP reauthorization period in 2008, the argument was twofold: first, that states had been allowed to expand Medicaid too far, so that conservatives questioned whether recipients were deserving of subsidized coverage; and second, an inefficient publicly run program was an inappropriate vehicle to use as a platform for expanding health coverage in America. Given these two concerns, it is not surprising that many Republican leaders spoke out strongly after 2010 against relying on Medicaid as the centerpiece for expanding coverage for America's uninsured.

Nonetheless, despite these major ideological concerns, the federal funding attached to the Medicaid expansion is a huge inducement, making outright rejection of expansion difficult even for Republican governors. Thus, as mentioned, the waivers present an opportunity for conservative leaders to reform the Medicaid program substantially enough to make a convincing argument that they are not utilizing a state-run public program to expand coverage to a group with questionable deservingness. How do they do this?

It's a Private Sector Approach, Not State-Run Medicaid—Arkansas, Iowa, and Michigan

Arkansas started the fight for a Medicaid expansion waiver in ways similar to states adopting Medicaid managed care in earlier years. The key argument initially put forward by Democratic governor Beebe in conservative Arkansas focused on the need to control Medicaid costs. He never questioned the deservingness of the uninsured to receive Medicaid coverage but argued that the private sector could do it better. In 2011 the Beebe administration did not shy away from arguing that Medicaid should remain intact, but agreed that it needed to be significantly reformed. However, as opposition in the Republican-controlled legislature increased in 2013, the administration strategically eliminated the term *Medicaid* from public statements, and only focused on the *private option*.

The intent of this framing was clearly to portray the waiver as distinct from Medicaid and not building on the traditional program. Republican representative Justin Harris's question to Arkansas's Medicaid Director, Andrew Allison, is illustrative of conservative attempts to link reform back to Medicaid: "You also made a comment earlier about . . . the private option being, private insurance. But is it not true . . . that *private insurance still has to act and resemble Medicaid*, is that not correct?" Allison's response insisted that incorporating private plans into the reform will make it distinct from Medicaid: "Neither the Health Care Independence Act, nor the Affordable Care Act, nor guidance that the Insurance Commissioners put out, nor this draft waiver says private insurance must now mimic Medicaid. It just doesn't" (Kauffman 2013).

Interestingly, many proponents of the private option in Arkansas argued that not only would the reform control health care costs—a claim that many supporters and opponents questioned because premiums on the exchange were typically more expensive than what states would pay Medicaid managed care plans—but it would improve access to care because more providers would participate in the exchange plans and the state did not have a robust Medicaid managed care market (Rosenbaum and Sommers 2013; Allison 2014). This argumentation is important, because desire to not only expand coverage but also improve access implicitly acknowledged the new enrollees' deservingness. When deservingness was explicitly acknowledged, the newly eligible were always referred to as the "working poor." For example, Governor Beebe said the following in his January 2013 State of the State Address:

> There is another important discussion to be had this session about a very different group of Arkansans than the elderly, the disabled, and the children who we currently insure under Medicaid. There are thousands of Arkansas families living in homes where one or both parents work, but where health insurance is not affordable. Very rarely do adults of working age qualify for Medicaid, and rising costs have led more companies to drop insurance coverage for their employees. These families and individuals are often referred to as "the working poor," and we have a real chance to provide them better access to health care. (Beebe 2013)

Although Beebe was clearly making a moral argument in support of their deservingness to receive publicly subsidized health insurance, it is important that deservingness is specifically attached to the "working poor." We see a very similar rhetoric take hold in the next two states that passed Medicaid waivers—Iowa and Michigan.

Similar to Arkansas, Iowa's Governor Branstad described the Medicaid program as broken and also pursued a private option approach where the state contracts with qualified health plans on the ACA exchange to provide coverage to new Medicaid enrollees (see table 2). However, although the Branstad administration described the waiver as providing a "commercial-like benefits package," surprisingly little rhetoric focused on this aspect of Iowa's reform. Instead, the discourse shifted in Iowa to a focus on "shared responsibility." As Branstad described it, "If you have no skin in the game, you spend more. . . . We want to give people incentives to make the right choice" (Noble 2013).

Iowa's waiver reforms go along with this rhetoric. Although Arkansas imposed cost-sharing mechanisms for its newly eligible at very low income levels (50–138 percent FPL), the state capped it at 2 percent of income. In contrast, Iowa's reform incorporated cost sharing, premiums, and health behavior incentives (see table 2). As mentioned before, these mechanisms are not new to the Medicaid program, but they had never been imposed on persons below the FPL prior to Iowa's waiver. Iowa asks for very little in premiums ($5 monthly premium for those at 50–100 percent FPL, and a $10 monthly premium for those at 101–138 percent FPL); however, the state imposes cost sharing on all those newly eligible (0–138 percent FPL) at up to 5 percent of quarterly income. This is quite a significant change. These are the "skin in the game" reforms that the Branstad administration emphasized.

However, the Branstad administration put equal emphasis on the healthy behavior reforms that allowed a more malleable discourse to emerge. As Branstad put it: "The carrots and sticks in the Iowa plan will not produce miracles. At the same time, there is a real 'declarative value' for promoting healthy behaviors" (Bruner 2013). This language allowed Democrats in Iowa to be supportive even though they were concerned with the premium and cost-sharing reforms being too harsh. Although they recognized that changing health behaviors, such as quitting smoking and losing weight, is difficult, they still believed it was the right direction to go in. At the same time, conservatives who demanded greater responsibility from the newly eligible could point to his calls for increased financial skin-in-the-game for the newly enrolled.

In sum, Branstad emphasized how the two sides of the responsibility coin in the Iowa plan—cost sharing and premiums on one side, and healthy behavior incentives on the other—would encourage *shared responsibility*.

Just a few months later, Michigan's waiver was approved, meaning the debate about their waiver proposals was happening at about the same time period. Despite important differences in their waiver proposals, the discourse over reform was almost identical. Specifically, Michigan did not include a "private option" approach. However, because the rhetoric focused almost entirely on personal responsibility in ways very similar to Iowa, one would be hard-pressed to know that this reform element was missing from Michigan but present in Iowa.

While Michigan's leaders used the term "personal responsibility" instead of "shared responsibility," the emphasis was primarily focused on healthy behaviors as evidenced by the reform's name: the "Healthy Michigan Plan." Similar to Iowa, Michigan included monthly premiums and cost sharing, as well as healthy behavior incentives. However, distinct from Iowa, it also included a health savings account component (see table 2). Although Michigan imposes "skin in the game" and also adopted a health savings account requirement to be used to pay for monthly premiums, its rhetorical framing of "personal responsibility" focused on responsibility for the individual to take care of themselves, to exercise, eat right, and ensure they are seeing their physicians regularly for checkups (Michigan Health & Wellness 2016). Governor Snyder's press release asserts that personal responsibility is the hallmark of the Healthy Michigan Plan (Governor Rick Snyder 2013), but also argues that "the Healthy Michigan Plan is providing hard-working Michiganders with the health care coverage they need to lead healthy, productive lives" (Governor Rick Snyder 2014a).

It is important to note that, similar to the discourse in Iowa and Arkansas, Governor Snyder and other proponents repeatedly call the new enrollees "hard-working Michiganders" (Governor Rick Snyder 2015). Snyder argued that most of the enrollees who would benefit from the program were already working, but have low earnings, putting them in danger of bankruptcy if they needed to receive any care. This group would be protected from bankruptcy and have healthier outcomes if they had health insurance. Snyder very explicitly framed the debate around expanding Medicaid as an economic argument, both for the individual and for the state of Michigan (Governor Rick Snyder 2014b).

By implementing cost sharing, premiums, and healthy behavior incentives, and by focusing on shared or personal responsibility, Iowa and

Michigan moved the personal responsibility lever further to the right, both in rhetoric and in the actual reforms. At the same time, the overall tone from both the Branstad and Snyder administrations was not overtly aggressive or harsh toward new enrollees. Governor Branstad would refer to the waiver's ability to provide needed services, such as mental health and disability services for many who were not previously eligible, and Governor Snyder highlighted the improvement in health and the quality of life for all of the new enrollees in the program (Governor Rick Snyder 2013; Governor Rick Snyder 2015). Nonetheless, by bringing the term *responsibility* to the fore, and emphasizing the *working* poor, they set the stage for more conservative states to move even further to the right.

It's Not a Medicaid Handout Because Only Paying Consumers are Deserving—Pennsylvania, Indiana, and Arkansas Again

As mentioned above, questions about whether "able-bodied" adults are deserving of subsidized public health insurance is an old and long-standing debate in America. Allowing states the option to expand to this very specific group, whose deservingness has always been questioned, meant that the cultural trope of 'individual responsibility' (Harvey 2005: 76; Wacquant 2010) could reemerge at any time. It did with a vengeance in the next two waiver states.

Pennsylvania under Republican governor Tom Corbett was the first state to actively pursue a work requirement in their waiver proposal. Requiring the newly enrolled to either be employed or seeking employment was a point of contention within the state and in negotiations with federal officials. The rhetoric in Pennsylvania pivoted on the work requirement even though the federal government ultimately did not approve this reform element, and the remaining reforms are almost identical to Michigan's reforms (cost sharing for 0–138 percent FPL up to 5 percent of income; monthly premiums for 101–138 percent FPL up to 2 percent of income; and healthy behavior incentives), but with no health savings account.

Initially, the discourse in favor of Pennsylvania's waiver was focused on the benefits provided by the private sector and the virtues of the free market. For example, Governor Tom Corbett (R) argued that the "Healthy Pennsylvania" plan would provide "high-quality, private sector health insurance within reach of all citizens, regardless of their means" (Governor Tom Corbett 2014). This part of Pennsylvania's rhetorical frame was surprisingly similar to Arkansas's discourse around the private option, and ironically so, given that Pennsylvania did not pursue a private option, but a Medicaid managed care approach instead (see table 2).

However, Corbett was also a firm and outspoken believer in connecting employment and eligibility for the Medicaid expansion waiver. In the Healthy Pennsylvania waiver proposal, any individual who was working less than twenty hours a week needed to demonstrate that they had completed twelve job search activities a month in order to remain eligible for coverage. For Corbett, the work requirement was essential to the entire waiver proposal. Jennifer Bransetter, Corbett's policy director, remarked that, for the governor, removing the employment criteria "breaks the plan as a whole" (Associated Press 2014).

Although some of the rhetoric of personal responsibility was similar to Iowa and Michigan because it also focused on encouraging healthy behaviors, there was often an oblique reference to work as well: "[Our plan] provides incentives for healthy behaviors and increased independence through greater access to employment opportunities" (Governor Tom Corbett 2013). In Pennsylvania, there was a more overt attempt to define who among the newly eligible would be deserving of Medicaid benefits—those that are working or trying to work.

Note that this moral claim is so important that even after significant pushback from the federal government, legislators, and interest groups in Pennsylvania, Corbett did not drop the work requirement but modified it instead to a voluntary work search under a one-year pilot program.

Indiana was having its Medicaid expansion waiver debate at the same time as Pennsylvania and the discourse was very similar. Much of the rhetorical focus of Indiana policy makers was in couching the discussion of deservingness in terms of those individuals who acted like good health care consumers rather than individuals receiving a handout. The components of the Healthy Indiana Plan (HIP 2.0) were patterned after earlier reforms the state implemented in 2009. Seema Verma, architect to both reforms, remarked that the structure of Indiana's reforms was meant to "promote the notion of consumerism," and that it "transforms Medicaid beneficiaries into consumers" (Roob and Verma 2008). This transformation led to the most complex structure of the Medicaid expansion in any waiver state. Indiana implemented four different benefits plans, premiums for all of the newly insured regardless of income, cost sharing for those below the poverty line, and an emphasis on healthy behaviors for all the newly enrolled. The central component to Indiana's plan—transforming the newly eligible into health care consumers—was the Personal Wellness and Responsibility (POWER) health savings account.

Fundamental to this belief in *transformation* is the logic that the newly eligible have to work to become consumers of health care. Although

Indiana did not propose a work requirement as Pennsylvania did, it focused instead on imposing severe consequences for failure to pay monthly premiums. In particular, individuals above the poverty line who neglect to make monthly premium payments into their POWER account are disenrolled from the program for six months. Individuals below the poverty line who cannot afford or choose not to make monthly premium payments are shunted from the HIP+ plan, with its extended benefit package and cost-sharing protections, to the HIP Basic plan with fewer benefits and more mandatory cost sharing for services. The monthly premium payment requirements, along with severe consequences for nonpayment, implicitly impose a tie to work as it is difficult to imagine how one could pay their monthly premium without earnings. While the policy design imposes an implicit work requirement, the policy goal was made explicit: Ryan Streeter, the policy director for Governor Mike Pence, remarked, "We want to make sure that the program is consistent with our efforts to get people to work" (Wall 2014).

The design of Indiana's expansion plan affirms a traditional conservative view of structuring public benefit programs. This view holds that public benefits, which are purely a handout, should by design be miserly, so as to not encourage dependency. Indiana policy makers argued that their Medicaid expansion plan sought to short-circuit dependency with a system designed to encourage consumerism and consumer behavior by increasing benefits for individuals who are willing and able to pay into the system, and by putting money into a health savings account to pay for premiums and cost sharing. Without these elements, proponents argued, their program just "turns into a regular Medicaid program" (Groppe 2013).

Arkansas's experience after the election of a new Republican governor offers additional insight into this shifting conservative frame of the Medicaid expansion. As a Republican, Asa Hutchinson was immediately in opposition to the private option that previous Democratic governor Beebe had created and implemented. Whereas Beebe avoided the term *Medicaid*, claiming that the private option was an entirely new program, Hutchinson strategically linked the private option with Medicaid and argued that expansion built on and grew the Medicaid program. In all of his public speeches and statements on the Medicaid expansion, Hutchinson never referred to the waiver as the "private option" without also calling it "Medicaid." It is noteworthy that in this context—a conservative state, which had just elected a Republican majority in both chambers of the General Assembly together with a Republican governor for the first time since Reconstruction—one central attack against private option reform was to simply call it "Medicaid." Presumably, Medicaid is so poorly perceived in the state that just using the word *Medicaid* is sufficient to suggest the reform is bad.

While Hutchinson's discourse denotes a dramatic shift from that employed by Beebe, it is remarkably consistent with the rhetorical patterns we observed above in Pennsylvania and Indiana. Following directly on the heels of more conservative reforms in Pennsylvania and Indiana, Hutchinson also raised questions about the deservingness of the newly enrolled in the private option and the need for improving personal responsibility and work as part of the program (Governor Asa Hutchinson 2015). John Selig, director of the Arkansas Department of Human Services under the Beebe and Hutchinson administrations, almost seemed to be stealing a script from Indiana when he said after Hutchinson took office, "We believe in consumerism, we think they'll (the newly eligible) use care more appropriately and get a sense of how insurance works" (Andrews 2014).

In a speech on healthcare and Medicaid reform in Arkansas, Hutchinson specifically said he "wanted to talk about the profile of those on the Private Option." In describing their profile, he began by stating that "there are unintended consequences to the Private Option. I don't know that anybody anticipated that parolees coming out of prison are put on the Private Option." After noting this "unintended" characteristic, he then discussed recipients' employment status:

> About 40 percent of the enrollees, at the time of application for the Private Option, showed no income. That means they were unemployed. Seventy percent of those on the Private Option were employed at some point in time, which tells me they were trying to get a job. That tells us that most are working but cannot find the steady work that is needed. Young people were more likely to have work than those who were over forty-five. Women were more likely to have work than men. This tells us that the older male population should be targeted for work. These might be men who've been laid off or who need to learn new skills to transition into another career. It's interesting that 10 percent of those on the Private Option are considered medically frail. And that population seems to me, if the Private Option were to end, would qualify for traditional Medicaid. This is all helpful information because it's the data that guides our debate. . . . I believe that there are some principles that should frame the debate. One of them is work and responsibility. I want our social programs in Arkansas to be an incentive for people to work as opposed to an incentive for people not to work. (Governor Asa Hutchinson 2015)

This long quote detailing the profile of the private option waiver recipient in Arkansas is significant because it reveals many important aspects of the conservative frame. First, not all recipients should be treated equally: ex-prisoners on parole should be treated differently from working families, for example. Second, and most explicitly stated, access to Medicaid should be tied to work. And third, Medicaid should return to its original intent—the medically frail should be kept separate in the traditional program as intended.

Not only does Hutchinson's rhetoric closely match Indiana and Pennsylvania's, but Arkansas's adoption of health savings accounts, called "health independence accounts," under its waiver reauthorization process also follows Indiana's lead. Similar to Indiana, Arkansas requires very poor people (with earnings between 50–99 percent FPL) to contribute $5 a month to a health savings account with consequences if they do not act as a consumer should. In particular, failure to pay would trigger co-pays (Andrews 2014).

More Consumer Skin in the Private Sector Game—New Hampshire and Montana

Similar shifts in rhetoric and framing took place in the later waiver expansion states of New Hampshire and Montana. The unique dynamic in these cases involved a Democratic governor trying to sell a conservative legislature on the waiver as an alternative to a straight ACA Medicaid expansion. In some ways the elements of these two waivers were less far-reaching than in other states, but much of the language was the same. Leaders emphasized the deservingness of the newly eligible and a shift toward participants as consumers rather than welfare recipients.

The debate over Medicaid in New Hampshire evolved throughout multiple rounds. Governor Maggie Hassan initially tried to get a straight expansion but was rebuffed by a legislature opposed to Obamacare. She ultimately negotiated a waiver with conservative leaders that included a premium assistance model similar to Arkansas's private option. Not all Republican policy makers were assuaged with the inclusion of the private option, claiming—similar to Hutchinson in Arkansas—that alone it did not go far enough to meet their concerns about a state-run program. Drawing on a conservative frame established in Indiana and Pennsylvania, and furthered at the same time in Arkansas, New Hampshire Republicans proposed strict cost sharing, large deductibles for enrollees below the poverty line, and a work requirement. Democrats controlling the state's house of representatives would not go that far, making New Hampshire the only waiver state after Arkansas to not require any premiums of the newly eligible, and only requiring cost sharing for those above the poverty line.

By the time New Hampshire was in the throes of its waiver negotiations in the beginning of 2015, the deservingness of the newly eligible was central to the debate. By this time, both proponents and opponents of Medicaid expansion heavily emphasized the deservingness (or un-deservingness) of potential enrollees when framing the legislation. Governor Maggie Hassan (D) made it a habit of including a list of the types of individuals who would benefit because of the expansion. Her list of beneficiaries included the "hard-working granite-staters" who already paid taxes and who worked as teachers' aides, construction workers, health care workers, and retail clerks (Governor Maggie Hassan 2014).

In contrast, Republican policy makers raised concerns about individuals who were not deserving of coverage benefiting from an unsustainable entitlement. For example, Representative Neil Kurk worried that the reform would allow able-bodied people to "stay at home on the hammock" without having to work. "Is that the situation, that simply because you are alive and poor you receive this health care and you don't have to do any work if you don't wish to?" (Bookman 2013). At the heart of these arguments in New Hampshire is a very old debate, but one that has been largely absent until recently, about whether Medicaid should be restricted to the "truly needy" or if the program should expand to include a larger group of deserving Americans.

Similar patterns of discourse emphasizing the role of deservingness and private markets occurred in Montana. Democratic governor Steve Bullock remarked at the signing of the expansion legislation that this was a victory for all of the hard-working Montanans who were one accident away from bankruptcy. Bullock stated that expanding Medicaid was about more than just improving health access in the state—it also provided a pathway out of poverty and up the economic ladder (Governor Steve Bullock 2015). Supportive policy makers continued this framing of the newly eligible. Representative Chuck Hunter stated that Medicaid expansion would help the "ranch hands and veterans and cooks and waiters and store clerks. They work in our motels, on our call centers. . . . They are often working two jobs to make ends meet. If we pass this bill . . . our families will be more healthy and more productive" (Dennison 2013a).

And similar to Democratic governor Beebe's original rhetoric for the private option in Arkansas, Montana policy makers from both political parties emphasized the strong role of the private sector and the lack of a role for the government in the administration of their Medicaid waiver. Bullock observed that Montana's expansion plan would not expand government services, but would mirror their Children's Health Insurance Program (CHIP), by using federal money to contract with a private third party administrator to manage the expansion (Dennison 2014). Again, stealing a songbook from Arkansas, Montana's chief architect of the expansion plan, Republican Senator Edward Buttrey, stressed that his bill was not a Medicaid expansion and that it would never expand Medicaid. Rather, it expands the "private-sector insurance exchange" (Dennison 2013b), and allows the newly eligible the opportunity to select their own insurance plans that fit their needs. Buttrey framed his expansion legislation as more far-reaching than merely expanding health benefits; rather, it focused on finding solutions to bringing hard-working taxpayers out of poverty, and into new jobs where they could learn new skills.

While proponents of the Montana waiver echoed Democratic frames in New Hampshire and Arkansas, opponents imitated the now familiar conservative Republican frame. Two themes rang out in Montana's oppositional framing: returning Medicaid to its original intent, and tying work to benefits while questioning the deservingness of the newly eligible. First, Republican policy makers argued that Medicaid should target the group of people that it was originally intended to serve; adding the higher-paying privately insured enrollees would hinder care for the "truly needy" who are the medically frail (Whitney 2015a). Second, in tying deservingness to work, they argued further that the newly eligible "have the ability to up your hours and do what you can to get above the FPL which is just $11,760, and then get insurance on the exchange. I mean, that's a reasonable solution for that individual" (Whitney 2015b).

Without a Work Requirement or the Block Grant, You Don't Get a Medicaid Waiver—Utah and Tennessee

Republican governors in Utah and Tennessee both tried and failed to get a Medicaid waiver approved by their Republican-controlled legislatures. Many of the same elements of reform were included in their proposed plans and much of the same rhetoric was used. Obviously, many political factors help to explain why waivers pass in some states and not others (Hertel-Fernandez et al., 2016), and we do not mean to imply in this article that the framing is directly related to passage or failure. However, in documenting the shifts in discourse over time among the waiver states, we note both what seems to become the expected conservative framing by 2015, and what may be new demands—even if not passed—and their associated rhetoric. The rhetoric used to explain why the waiver was not enough in Tennessee and Utah suggests that the needle on what conservatives say they require to comply with a Medicaid expansion may be shifting further to the right.

Following the lead of other Republican-dominated states, they sought to use the Medicaid expansion waiver to convince conservative legislators that their proposed reform was not a Medicaid expansion. Indeed, Tennessee governor Bill Haslam was explicit in describing this strategy: "What we have to come up with is a plan that says this is not really expanding Medicaid as contemplated by the Obama administration" (Farmer 2014). Explaining the political dilemma facing Republican legislators, he explained further, "I think the concern they have is 'if I get in a primary race and somebody says he voted for Obamacare . . . ' they want to be able to show the distinction and I think that's one of the things we'll work really hard over the summer to show here's why this is different" (Daniels 2015).

Governor Haslam ultimately released a waiver proposal called "Insure Tennessee," which contained many of the same elements used by other states, notably premiums, co-pays, and incentives for healthy behaviors, and employed the same rhetorical device emphasizing greater personal responsibility. Also, similar to Indiana and Arkansas, Haslam tied his reform to the importance of work through the use of required payments into health savings accounts.

However, the Haslam administration also included two new elements. First, people below 138 percent FPL could choose to either receive a defined contribution voucher to apply to their employer's health insurance plan, or receive vouchers through a redesigned component of the state's existing TennCare program (Governor Bill Haslam 2014). Proponents developed a slightly new frame to explain this reform element, arguing that Haslam's plan better "prepared participants for eventual transition to commercial health coverage" (Governor Bill Haslam 2014).

Second, Haslam's plan also involved an agreement from Tennessee hospitals to make up the difference in funding when the federal match phases from 100 percent to 90 percent. As a result, the state budget would not be directly affected. Tennessee attempted to up the ante in emphasizing an increased role for the private sector and limiting the role of the state to a defined contribution under which hospitals would pay the state share. This latter reform element is especially related to long-standing Republican concerns about fiscal sustainability.

Initially, the plan seemed to win over previously skeptical legislators, and these two new elements seemed to make a difference in how the plan was perceived. One Republican member of the state house of representatives commended the governor that "this is not some cut-and-paste plan that other states have tried to sell as unique" (Daniels 2015). Another

Republican senator said he decided to support the governor's plan once he became convinced that Haslam won conservative compromises from the Obama administration (Boucher 2015). Ultimately, Insure Tennessee did not receive enough support to advance through key legislative committees, despite the concessions in the waiver and a similar conservative framing.

And even Haslam's strong moral claim that the state has an obligation to help the poor, rather than moving other legislators, was largely countered with a very old conservative argument that people have an obligation to increase charity care, and that charity care is available for people in need. For example, a local news source reported that state representative Sheila Butt said that "the existence of facilities like the Hope Clinic show government intervention may not be needed. 'I can tell you from experience, that when constituents have called our office, we have found places like Hope Clinic,' she said. 'We can't depend on the government for every single answer to every single question'" (Sisk 2015).

Nonetheless, in Tennessee, Republican arguments that a Medicaid expansion—even a conservative waiver reform—would not be fiscally sustainable with no escape valve became a focal point. Despite Tennessee hospitals agreeing to pay the state share, Senator Brian Kelsey, chair of a key committee, explained, "I'm concerned that this will be like the Eagles' 'Hotel California,' where you can check in but never check out" (Sisk 2015).

Fiscal sustainability was a similar battle cry and sticking point in Utah as well. However, they were also rhetorically unwilling to compromise on the work requirement reform as Pennsylvania had, for example. Similar to governors in other waiver states, Utah governor Gary Herbert asserted that personal responsibility should be the guiding framework for any attempts to reform the health care system (Herbert 2012).

However, Utah house Republicans also wanted assurances that Medicaid would be returned to its "original intent" as specified under their "Utah Cares" plan, which called for using state general funds and the less generous federal matching rate to fund the program (Moulton 2015). Ironically, Utah Cares would have cost the state more money while only extending coverage to 100 percent of FPL with a more limited benefit package. But, proponents of Utah Cares argued that their program was focused on the truly vulnerable and deserving in their state. Speaker of the Utah House of Representatives Greg Hughes (R), a backer of the Utah Cares plan, stated that Governor Herbert's plan broadens Medicaid to include populations which were never intended to be covered by the original legislation, referring to the mostly single, able-bodied adults without dependent children which would be covered under the "Healthy Utah" plan. Policy makers aligned with Speaker Hughes against Governor Herbert argued that physicians would no longer accept the needy Medicaid patients because of low reimbursement rates, and that potential cost overrun in the governor's plan could lower the amount of funding for programs that served the truly vulnerable in society, including the developmentally disabled, and those in children's programs and nursing homes (Gehrke 2015; Davidson 2015).

Initially, Governor Gary Herbert (R) of Utah had identified a work requirement as an essential component of any waiver application from the state. During a meeting with President Obama, Herbert referenced the work requirement, remarking that he had not gotten everything that he wanted in his negotiations over expanding Medicaid. Obama stopped the meeting and called Secretary Burwell to see if there was any flexibility on this point. When Herbert returned from his trip to Washington, DC, he reported that federal officials agreed to a work effort reform, which would require that newly eligible Medicaid enrollees would be connected with job training and job enhancement services, but not require employment to be eligible for Medicaid (Moulton 2014).

But this was not enough for Utah house Republicans. As Speaker Hughes wrote to explain his opposition to the governor's waiver proposal, there were two main sticking points for which they were unwilling to compromise. "Our governor, Gary Herbert, sought to receive a federal waiver that would allow Utah to implement a work requirement [that tied eligibility to work instead of just job training and job enhancement services] for Medicaid expansion recipients. He was turned down. He also tried to structure a program with a cap in order to protect the state from serious cost overruns that could put our budget, and the ability to fund other needed programs, in jeopardy. Again, the federal government said no" (Hughes 2015).

A cap on expenditures (or what is more commonly referred to as a Medicaid block grant) is not a new Republican idea. It was first requested by Reagan in 1981 and pushed hard by the Gingrich Republican-controlled Congress in 1994, and was a Republican rallying cry again during the SCHIP reauthorization debate in 2008. However, until Utah Cares, this was not part of the waiver requests. Time will tell whether this becomes a common waiver request as the work requirement now is. Note, as of this writing, Arizona has a waiver proposal pending with the federal government that also includes a work requirement.

Summary: Patterns around Rhetoric and Reform

In an effort to distinguish between the diffusion of policy elements versus political rhetoric, we documented not only how the elements of waiver reforms have developed in these first adopter waiver states, but also how the reforms have been framed, and whether there is an interaction between reform elements and political discourse.

We presented a chronological evolution of framing in these waiver states, though we acknowledged that our timeline was short and the number of states was small. Our data are exploratory but suggest the possibility of some emerging rhetorical-reform patterns. Although the most common reform elements are similar to elements in non-waiver states, the rhetoric around and the use of the other reform elements make the waiver states distinct. In general, we found a strong link between overall framing and reforms proposed. In each stage, when the discourse significantly changes, it is associated with a specific demand for new reform elements. The first three states—Arkansas, Iowa, and Michigan—focused largely on the importance of embedding reform within the private sector and encouraging the "right healthy choices" through "shared responsibility"; whereas, the next set of states—Pennsylvania and Indiana—were steadfast that personal responsibility must encourage work behaviors where one is expected to pay for benefits received. This became the first real push to tie Medicaid reforms to work through the use of health savings accounts and a proposed work requirement (see table 3). This framing was carried forward by the next wave of states—New Hampshire and Montana—where it seemed commonplace for conservatives to claim that poor people must look for work and must have skin in the private sector game. And, the debate in the failed waiver states—Utah and Tennessee—largely hinged on their lack of ability to secure a work requirement.

We find a chronological pattern developing where each grouping of conservative states pushed for reforms further to the right of their predecessors, and its associated rhetoric remained in sync—questioning the deservingness of the newly eligible and seeking to return Medicaid to its original intent of only serving the truly needy. The framing of deservingness in the first three adopter states—Arkansas, Iowa, and Michigan—focused on the "working poor" and assumed most new recipients are "hard-working," and the frame was fairly similar to that used in non-waiver expansion states. However, the next set of adopters put a dagger in this assumption of deservingness. Pennsylvania and Indiana set the stage, and all remaining waiver states followed, by claiming that Medicaid deservingness should

Table 3 Discourse and Reform Elements by State

	Discourse								
	Arkansas September 2013	Iowa December 2013	Michigan December 2013	Pennsylvania August 2014	Indiana January 2015	Arkansas 2015	New Hampshire March 2015	Montana November 2015	Tennessee & Utah
Reform Element	"Private Option"	"Iowa Health and Wellness Plan"	"Healthy Michigan Plan"	"Healthy Pennsylvania Plan"	"Healthy Indiana Plan 2.0"	Reauthorization	"New Hampshire Health Protection Program Premium Assistance"	"Montana Health and Economic Livelihood Partnership Program"	No Passage
Cost-sharing	X	X	X	X	X	X	X	X	
Medicaid managed care	X	X	X	X	"High quality private" X	X	X	"Strong role for private to promote jobs" X	
Premiums		"Skin in the Game"; "Incentives for Right Choice"	"Shared Responsibility"	"Incentives for Healthy Behavior"	"Promote consumerism"				
Healthy behavior incentives									
Premium assistance to purchase QHPs on exchange	"Efficiency; Improved Access"	X				Private option not enough to induce "correct" behavior	X		
Health savings accounts			X		"Transform into health care consumer"	"Need incentive to work"**			

(continued)

Table 3 Discourse and Reform Elements by State (*continued*)

	Discourse								
Reform Element	Arkansas September 2013	Iowa December 2013	Michigan December 2013	Pennsylvania August 2014	Indiana January 2015	Arkansas 2015	New Hampshire March 2015	Montana November 2015	Tennessee & Utah
	"Private Option"	"Iowa Health and Wellness Plan"	"Healthy Michigan Plan"	"Healthy Pennsylvania Plan"	"Healthy Indiana Plan 2.0"**	Reauthorization	"New Hampshire Health Protection Program Premium Assistance"	"Montana Health and Economic Livelihood Partnership Program"	No Passage
Voluntary work incentives				"Independence through greater access to employment opportunities"**	Encourages work because need earnings to fulfill consumer requirements		Hard-working granite-staters vs. lazy unemployed		Work requirement essential
Deservingness frame and underlying assumptions	Working poor with assumption that most recipients fit this category			Currently working or trying to work with assumption that many do not	IN: Health care recipients with assumption that most need to be transformed into consumers		Both frames—deserving working poor and undeserving unemployed—present		Only the "truly needy" are deserving with assumption that others should be working and buying private insurance

Notes: X means the state adopted this reform element, but there was little to no discourse/discussion around that particular aspect of reform.
A blank cell means the state did not adopt the reform element and there was no discourse about it.
*Fought for work requirement with this language.
**Added during reauthorization process in 2015.

be tied to work. Under this frame, only the "truly needy," who are unable to work, should be given Medicaid benefits with no requirements attached (see last row of table 3).

Proponents of waivers in these conservative states all claim their reforms to be dramatically different from a traditional Medicaid expansion. While their most common reform elements are more similar than different from non-waiver states, our analysis of all the elements of reform, as well as the associated rhetoric, suggests that both the rhetoric and reforms are distinct in important and potentially consequential ways. The framing has resurfaced questions—some thought settled under the passage of the ACA—about who is deserving of Medicaid and whether so-called able-bodied adults should be left out. And, the elements of reform assert this deservingness frame: enrollees are required to pay for the benefits (e.g., premiums, co-pays), and they must have earnings to do so (e.g., health savings accounts, a work requirement or incentive).

Conclusion

The evolution of state 1115 waivers connected to the expansion of Medicaid is a fascinating example of reinvention throughout the policy diffusion process. The first states that expanded Medicaid with a waiver—Arkansas and Iowa—can either be thought of as late adopters who reinvented the innovation, or first adopters of a new innovation. Either way, this is a clear example that adopting a policy is not necessarily a simple dichotomous choice for a state. The terms of the debate changed with each subsequent waiver, influencing the range of options being considered and the way the reform was talked about.

While our focus has been on Medicaid policy, waivers have also played an important role in the development of social policy in the United States, particularly with education policy in the wake of "No Child Left Behind" and welfare policy in the 1990s. States have few options in the face of federally established rules and regulations. State policy makers can attempt to persuade a majority of members of Congress and the executive branch to modify existing rules and regulations, or they can withdraw from participating in the program. Waivers allow states to find a middle-ground approach between those two options and it is in a federal system where waivers are an important instrument for policy diffusion. Waivers allow modifications to federal policy to diffuse to interested states.

These waiver states are important because they may act as predictors of how far Medicaid may shift to meet conservative ideology, thus having the potential to put Medicaid on a distinctive path in waiver states. This is a crucial moment in the evolution of the Medicaid program. One would have thought that the ACA Medicaid expansion would further consolidate the Medicaid program, creating more equal treatment within states because categorical requirements were abandoned in favor of a simple means test,[6] and more equity across states because of the initial federal mandate to expand to 138 percent FPL. Of course, the Supreme Court upended this latter goal, but the waivers may upend the former as well. A handful of Republican-controlled states have used intense criticism of Medicaid to convince fellow conservatives to support their distinct version of a Medicaid expansion.

While the Obama administration and most state Democrats support a straight expansion, they have been willing to compromise and support waiver proposals under the logic that even restrictive coverage is better than no coverage. It appears as a win-win, since this approach has also enabled conservative legislators to say that they did not support Obamacare or a Medicaid expansion but an entirely new reform. Our tour through these conservative states with adopted or proposed waivers provides a window into the language used to thread this delicate needle. However, documenting the reality of the reforms adopted alongside this framing also provides a window into what is at stake.

While proponents both in Indiana and for Arkansas's reauthorization were explicit that "skin in the game" meant an implicit tie to work—since earnings are needed to meet the health savings account requirements used to allow recipients to act like "consumers" who pay the co-pay and premium share requirements—an implicit tie may not be enough for conservative states going forward. Debates surrounding Utah and Tennessee's failed waiver proposals, and Arizona's pending waiver, suggest conservative states will continue to push for a Medicaid work requirement and are also looking for ways to impose an expenditure cap (like a Medicaid block grant long desired by Republicans). And, if the wider Republican Party looks like it does in Tennessee and Utah (i.e., a strong Tea Party component, see Hertel-Fernandez et al., 2016), states may not be willing to compromise on these points.

It is not only conservative rhetoric around Medicaid that has shifted back toward a focus on the personal responsibility and deservingness of Medicaid enrollees. Conservative efforts to return the program to its so-called original intent—to reserve the program only for those who are "truly needy"—may be successful in these waiver states. Indiana's reform, for example, creates a very fragmented Medicaid program where each group is treated to a different set of rules and benefits according to group

6. There are also federal requirements for states to create streamlined enrollment processes.

characteristics (e.g., single adults) and ability to pay. In this sense, the reform begins to look a lot like a very old Medicaid program where the program contributed toward keeping the poor impoverished. Moreover, new cost-sharing reforms allowed for the very poor and enabled states to dis-enroll individuals who are unable to pay, which were never allowed previously, moving the program even further to the right of Medicaid's original design (and intent) because it arguably seeks to punish the poor.

In response to conservative claims that Medicaid has moved too far toward covering undeserving people of adequate means, Democrats have shied away from offering a robust defense of the virtues of expanding Medicaid to people of some means (or what some might call that completely ambiguous term, the "middle class"). Instead, Democrats have argued that Medicaid is vitally important for the "vulnerable" and for "hard-working" American families. Note, in both cases, their defense for expanding Medicaid ironically plays into a larger Republican frame of returning Medicaid to its original intent. First, using the term "vulnerable" primes one for a debate about who is truly vulnerable, and second, claiming that the newly eligible under a Medicaid expansion are deserving because they're "hard-working" suggests an underlying agreement about tying Medicaid deservingness to work. Although one would not expect a robust defense of Medicaid among Democrats in a predominantly conservative state, it is noteworthy that there is no readily apparent distinctive liberal frame for a transformative Medicaid expansion even in liberal expansion states.[7] Given the importance of political discourse to move a vision for larger reform forward, the silence of an alternative frame is deafening.

▪ ▪ ▪

Colleen M. Grogan is a professor in the School of Social Service Administration at the University of Chicago. Her broad areas of research interest include health policy and health politics. She has written several book chapters and articles, and coauthored a book on the political evolution and current politics of the US Medicaid program. A second area of research focuses on participatory processes and the role of nonprofits in civic society and the American welfare state. She is currently working on a book titled *America's Hidden Health Care State*, which examines the intent behind America's submerged health care state. Grogan is editor of the *Journal of Health Politics, Policy and Law*, and the academic director of the Graduate Program in Health Administration and Policy (GPHAP) at the University of Chicago.

7. We emphasize "readily apparent" in this sentence, since we have not done the discourse analysis in predominantly liberal expansion states to back up this claim.

Phillip M. Singer is a doctoral candidate in the Department of Health Management and Policy at the University of Michigan School of Public Health. His research interests include state health policy and health politics, the implementation of the Affordable Care Act, and Medicaid.

David K. Jones is an assistant professor in the Department of Health Law, Policy and Management at Boston University's School of Public Health. He is editor-in-chief of the *Public Health Post*. His research focuses on the politics of health policy. His forthcoming book with Oxford University Press examines how states made decisions about implementing the ACA's health insurance exchanges. He is working on a new book on health in the Mississippi Delta, retracing Robert Kennedy's steps in this region. He also studies Medicaid, CHIP, and health reform in France. His work has appeared in periodicals such as the *New York Times*, the *Washington Post*, the *Wall Street Journal*, and *Politico*. He was the winner of AcademyHealth's Outstanding Dissertation Award in 2015.

References

Allison, Andrew. 2014. "Arkansas's Alternative to Medicaid Expansion Raises Important Questions about How HHS Will Implement New ACA Waiver Authority in 2017." *Journal of Health Politics, Policy and Law* 39, no. 5: 1089–98.

Andrews, Michelle. 2014. "Arkansas Weighs Plan to Make Some Medicaid Enrollees Fund Savings Accounts." *Kaiser Health News*, July 22. khn.org/news/michelle-andrews-on-arkansas-plan-for-medicaid-savings-accounts/.

Associated Press. "Pennsylvania Awaits Ruling on Proposal to Link Work Requirements to Medicaid Benefits." *PBS NewsHour*, PBS, April 27, 2014.

Balla, Steven. 2001. "Interstate Professional Associations and the Diffusion of Policy Innovations." *American Politics Research* 29, no. 3: 221–45.

Beebe, Mike. (2013). Quoted in Project Vote Smart. "2013 Arkansas State of the State Address." votesmart.org/public-statement/759191/2013-arkansas-state-of-the-state-address#.WDxZb8njVCw.

Boehmke, Frederick. 2005. *The Indirect Effect of Direct Legislation: How Institutions Shape Interest Group Systems.* Columbus: Ohio State University Press.

Bookman, Todd. 2013. "Medicaid Expansion Plan Approved by Commission." *New Hampshire Public Radio*, October 8. nhpr.org/post/medicaid-expansion-plan-approved-commission.

Boucher, Dave. 2015. "Q&A: Insure Tennessee Legislative Supporters." *Tennessean*, April 20. www.tennessean.com/story/news/health/2015/04/18/insure-tennessee-legislative-support-question-answer/26017927/.

Boushey, Graeme. 2016. "Targeted for Diffusion: How the Use and Acceptance of Stereotypes Shape the Diffusion of Criminal Justice Policy Innovations in the American States." *American Political Science Review* 110, no. 1: 198–214.

Bruner, Charles. 2013. "Iowa View: Health Care Comes with Responsibility." *Des Moines Register*, December 15. www.desmoinesregister.com/story/opinion /columnists/2013/12/14/iowa-view-health-care-comes-with-responsibility/4025123/.

Case, Anne, Harvey Rosen, and James Hines Jr. 1993. "Budget Spillovers and Fiscal Policy Interdependence: Evidence from the States." *Journal of Public Economics* 52, no. 3: 285–307.

Commonwealth Fund. 2008. "Indiana First to Expand Medicaid Coverage via Health Accounts." New York: Commonwealth Fund. www.commonwealthfund.org /publications/newsletters/states-in-action/2008/feb/february-march-2008/snapshots –short-takes-on-promising-programs/indiana-first-to-expand-medicaid-coverage -via-health-accounts.

Corbett, Tom (2014). Quoted in Project Vote Smart. "Gov. Tom Corbett's 2014–15 Budget Speech." votesmart.org/public-statement/843890/gov-tom-corbetts-2014- 15-budget-speech/?search=Healthy%20Pennsylvania#.Wllqzn3jUIQ.

Daniels, Frank. 2015. "Governor, Time to Spend That Political Capital." *Tennessean*, April 22.

Davidson, Lee. 2015. "House Unveils Counter to Healthy Utah, Though with Few Details." *Salt Lake Tribune*, February 27. www.sltrib.com/home/2231335-155 /house-unveils-counter-to-healthy-utah.

Dennison, Mike. 2013a. "Broad, Deep Support for Medicaid Expansion Shows Muscle at Capitol." *Billings Gazette*, March 25. Retrieved from infoweb.newsbank .com/resources/doc/nb/news/145464FD6CF959F8?p=AWNB.

Dennison, Mike. 2013b. "Montana Senate Dems, Handful of Republicans Roll New Medicaid Program into 'Compromise' Bill." *Billings Gazette*, April 16. billingsgazette.com/news/state-and-regional/montana/montana-senate-dems -handful-of-republicans-roll-new-medicaid-program/article_dc799a9c-7ceb-5113 -8eee-c7bde4c4c7ce.html.

Dennison, Mike. 2014. "Bullock on Medicaid: 'More or Less a New Way, than Any Other State Has Taken.'" *Billings Gazette*, November 17. billingsgazette.com /news/state-and-regional/montana/bullock-on-medicaid-more-or-less-a-new-way -than/article_5e878c89-4289-55df-81cf-d375d1b5f82f.html.

Farmer, Blake. 2014. "Interview: Haslam on 'Threading the Needle' with Medicaid Expansion." *Nashville Public Radio*, December 3. nashvillepublicmedia.org/blog /2014/12/03/interview-haslam-threading-needle-medicaid-expansion/.

Gehrke, Robert. 2015. "Herbert Leaves Health Reform to a Legislature That Has Shunned Earlier Attempts." *Salt Lake Tribune*, October 15. www.sltrib.com/home /3064148-155/herbert-now-up-to-legislature-to.

Glick, Henry R., and Scott P. Hays. 1991. "Innovation and Reinvention in State Policymaking: Theory and the Evolution of Living Will Laws." *Journal of Politics* 53, no. 3: 835–50.

Governor Asa Hutchinson. 2015. *Transcript of Governor Asa Hutchinson's Health-care Speech.* governor.arkansas.gov/press-releases/detail/transcript-of-governor -asa-hutchinsons-healthcare-speech.

Governor Bill Haslam. 2014. *Haslam Announces Insure Tennessee Plan.* news.tn.gov /node/13336.

Governor Maggie Hassan. 2014. *State of the State Speech.* governor.nh.gov/media
/speeches/state-of-state-2014.htm.

Governor Rick Snyder. 2013. *Gov. Snyder Signs Healthy Michigan into Law, Bringing
Health Care to 470,000 Michiganders.* www.michigan.gov/snyder/0,4668,7-277
-57577_57657-312514–,00.html.

Governor Rick Snyder. 2014a. *Gov. Rick Snyder Says Healthy Michigan Plan Sur-
passes First-Year Enrollment Goal of 322,000.* www.michigan.gov/snyder
/0,4668,7-277-57577_57657-332691–,00.html.

Governor Rick Snyder. 2014b. *Gov. Snyder: Healthy Michigan Plan Reaches 85,761
Enrollees After One Week.* www.michigan.gov/snyder/0,4668,7-277-57577-325714
–,00.html.

Governor Rick Snyder. 2015. *Gov. Rick Snyder: Healthy Michigan Plan Has Enrolled
More Than 600,000 People in First Year.* www.michigan.gov/snyder/0,4668,7
-277-57577_57657-351257–,00.html.

Governor Steve Bullock. 2015. *Governor Steve Bullock Signs Montana HELP Act into
Law.* governor.mt.gov/Newsroom/ArtMID/28487/ArticleID/1313.

Grogan, Colleen M. 1997. "The Medicaid Managed Care Policy Consensus for
Welfare Recipients: A Reflection of Traditional Welfare Concerns." *Journal of
Health Politics, Policy and Law* 22, no. 3: 813–36.

Grogan, Colleen M. 2008. "Medicaid: Health Care for You and Me?" In *Health
Politics and Policy*, 4th ed., edited by James Morone, Theodor Litman, and Leonard Robins, 329–54. New York: Delmar Thompson.

Grogan, Colleen M. 2011. "You Call It Public, I Call It Private, Let's Call the Whole
Thing Off?" *Journal of Health Politics, Policy and Law* 36, no. 3: 401–11.

Grogan, Colleen M. 2013. "Medicaid: Designed to Grow." In *Health Politics and
Policy*, 5th ed., edited by James Morone and Daniel Ehlke, 142–63. Stamford, CT:
Cengage Learning.

Grogan, Colleen M., and Christina M. Andrews. 2011. "The Politics of Aging within
Medicaid." In *The New Politics of Old Age Policy*, edited by Robert B. Hudson.
Baltimore: Johns Hopkins University Press.

Grogan, Colleen M., and Elizabeth Rigby. 2009. "Federalism, Partisan Politics, and
Shifting Support for State Flexibility: The Case of the U.S. State Children's Health
Insurance Program." *Publius: The Journal of Federalism* 39, no. 1: 47–69.

Grogan, Colleen M., and Eric Patashnik. 2003. "Between Welfare Medicine and
Mainstream Program: Medicaid at the Political Crossroads." *Journal of Health
Politics, Policy and Law* 28, no. 5: 821–58.

Grogan, Colleen M., and Vernon K. Smith. 2008. "From Charity Care to Medicaid:
Governors, States, and the Transformation of American Health Care." In *A More
Perfect Union*, edited by Ethan G. Sribnick. Philadelphia: University of Pennsyl-
vania Press.

Groppe, Maureen. 2013. "Expanding Medicaid Tied to 'Personal Responsibility.'"
Indianapolis Star, December 5.

Grossback, Lawrence J., Sean Nicholson-Crotty, and David A. M. Peterson. 2004.
"Ideology and Learning in Policy Diffusion." *American Politics Research* 32, no. 5:
521–45.

Harvey, David. 2005. *A Brief History of Neoliberalism.* New York: Oxford University Press.

Hays, Scott P. 1996. "Patterns of Reinvention: The Nature of Evolution during Policy Diffusion." *Policy Studies Journal* 24 (1996): 551–66.

Herbert, Gary. 2012. "HERBERT: The Statehouse, Not White House, Should Lead on Health Reform." *Washington Times*, July 31. www.washingtontimes.com/news /2012/jul/31/the-statehouse-not-white-house-should-lead-on-heal/.

Hertel-Fernandez, Alexander Warren, Theda Skocpol, and Daniel Lynch. 2016. "Business Associations, Conservative Networks, and the Ongoing Republican War over Medicaid Expansion." *Journal of Health Politics, Policy and Law*, 41, no. 2: 239–86.

Hughes, Greg, Speaker of the Utah House of Representatives. 2015. "The Case for Reform and against Healthy Utah." Posted in *Policy Buzz*. February 25. utahpolicy .com/index.php/features/policy-buzz/4914-the-case-for-reform-and-against-healthy -utah.

Karch, Andrew. 2007. *Democratic Laboratories: Policy Diffusion among the American States.* Ann Arbor: University of Michigan Press.

Karch, Andrew, and Matthew Cravens. 2014. "Rapid Diffusion and Policy Reform: The Adoption and Modification of Three Strikes Laws." *State Politics and Policy Quarterly* 14, no. 4: 461–91.

Kauffman, Jacob. 2013. "Arkansas Committee Discusses Differences between Medicaid and Private Option." *UALR Public Radio*, June 27. ualrpublicradio.org/post /arkansas-committee-discusses-differences-between-medicaid-and-private-option #stream/0.

KFF (Kaiser Family Foundation). 2011. "Five Key Questions and Answers about Section 1115 Medicaid Waivers." Washington, DC: Kaiser Family Foundation.

KFF (Kaiser Family Foundation). 2016a. "Average Annual Growth in Medicaid Spending." Washington, DC: Kaiser Family Foundation.

KFF (Kaiser Family Foundation). 2016b. "Health Insurance Coverage of the Total Population." Washington, DC: Kaiser Family Foundation.

Kliff, Sarah. 2013. "Privatizing the Medicaid Expansion: 'Every State Will Be Eying This.'" *Washington Post Wonkblog*, March 8. www.washingtonpost.com/news/wonk /wp/2013/03/08/privatizing-the-medicaid-expansion-every-state-will-be-eying-this/.

Medicaid.gov. 2016a. "Demonstrations and Waivers." www.medicaid.gov/medicaid -chip-program-information/by-topics/waivers/waivers_faceted.html.

Medicaid.gov. 2016b. "Managed Care." www.medicaid.gov/medicaid-chip-program -information/by-topics/delivery-systems/managed-care/managed-care-site.html.

Michigan Health & Wellness. 2016. "A Healthier Michigan Will Be a Stronger Michigan." www.michigan.gov/healthymichigan.

Mintrom, Michael. 1997. "Policy Entrepreneurs and the Diffusion of Innovation." *American Journal of Political Science* 41, no. 3: 738–70.

Moulton, Kristen. 2014. "Utah Gov. Gary Herbert: We Have a 'Conceptual' Deal on Medicaid." *Salt Lake Tribune*, September 9. archive.sltrib.com/story.php?ref= /sltrib/news/58395005-78/utah-health-herbert-medicaid.html.csp.

Moulton, Kristen. 2015. "Panel Rejects Healthy Utah; Opts for House Alternative, Utah Cares." *Salt Lake Tribune*, January 28. www.sltrib.com/home/2249356-155 /panel-rejects-healthy-utah-opts-for.

Noble, Jason. 2013. "Branstad Promises Changes to IowaCare Program to Improve Health-Care Delivery." *Des Moines Register*, February 26. blogs.desmoinesregister .com/dmr/index.php/2013/02/26/branstad-promises-changes-to-iowacare-program -to-improve-health-care-delivery.

Olson, Laura Katz. 2010. *The Politics of Medicaid*. New York: Columbia University Press.

Plazas, David. 2015. "Haslam Counters Critics, Makes Case for Insure Tennessee." *Tennessean*, February 3. www.tennessean.com/story/opinion/2015/02/02/haslam -counters-critics-makes-case-insure-tn/22774731/.

Rogers, Everett M. 1983. *Diffusion of Innovations*. 3rd ed. New York: Free Press.

Roob, Mitchell, and Seema Verma. 2008. "Indiana: Health Care Reform amidst Colliding Values." *Health Affairs Blog*, May 1. healthaffairs.org/blog/2008/05/01 /indiana-health-care-reform-amidst-colliding-values/.

Rosenbaum, Sara, and Benjamin D. Sommers. 2013. "Using Medicaid to Buy Private Health Insurance – The Great New Experiment." *New England Journal of Medicine* 369, no. 1: 7–9.

Shipan, Charles R., and Craig Volden. 2006. "Bottom-up Federalism: The Diffusion of Antismoking Policies from U.S. Cities to States." *American Journal of Political Science* 50, no. 4: 825–43.

Shipan, Charles R., and Craig Volden. 2014. "When the Smoke Clears: Expertise, Learning, and Policy Diffusion." *Journal of Public Policy* 34, no. 3: 357–87.

Sisk, Chas. 2015. "Lawmakers Give Insure Tennessee Cold Shoulder." *Nashville Public Radio*, January 27.

Skocpol, Theda, Christopher Howard, Susan Goodrich Lehmann, and Marjorie Abend-Wein. 1993. "Women's Associations and the Enactment of Mothers' Pensions in the United States." *American Political Science Review* 87, no. 3: 686–701.

Sparer, Michael. 2012. "Medicaid Managed Care: Costs, Access, and Quality of Care." Princeton, NJ: Robert Wood Johnson Foundation.

Tanenbaum, Sandra, J. 1995. "Medicaid Eligibility Policy in the 1980s: Medical Utilitarianism and the 'Deserving' Poor." *Journal of Health Politics, Policy and Law* 20, no. 4: 933–54.

Thompson, Frank J. 2012. *Medicaid Politics: Federalism, Policy Durability, and Health Reform*. Washington, DC: Georgetown University Press.

Volden, Craig. 2007. "States as Policy Laboratories: Emulating Successes in the Children's Health Insurance Program." *American Journal of Political Science* 50, no. 2: 294–312.

Wacquant, Loic. 2010. "Crafting the Neoliberal State: Workfare, Prisonfare, and Social Insecurity." *Sociological Forum* 25, no. 2: 197–220.

Wall, J. K. 2014. "The Most Likely Conflict Zone between Pence, Obama." *Indianapolis Business Journal*, August 7. www.ibj.com/blogs/12-the-dose/post/48956 -the-most-likely-conflict-zone-between-pence-obama.

Whitney, Eric. 2015a. "Medicaid's Western Push Hits Montana." *Kaiser Health News*, January 6. khn.org/news/medicaids-western-push-hits-montana.

Whitney, Eric. 2015b. "Why Montana Hospitals Back Bullock's Medicaid Expansion Plan." *Montana Public Radio*, March 3. mtpr.org/post/why-montana-hospitals -back-bullocks-medicaid-expansion-plan.

The Seeds of Policy Change: Leveraging Diffusion to Disseminate Policy Innovations

Frederick J. Boehmke
University of Iowa

Abigail Matthews Rury
University of Iowa

Bruce A. Desmarais
Pennsylvania State University

Jeffrey J. Harden
University of Notre Dame

Abstract We conduct a series of simulations to compare how various strategies for seeding a policy in the American states affect the rate at which that policy spreads. Using empirically derived parameters of the policy diffusion process, we simulate the diffusion of a hypothetical policy after seeding the policy in just a handful of states. We compare these strategies to seeding the ten states the RWJF monitored during the states' implementation of the Affordable Care Act of 2010. We attempt to mimic the choices that policy advocates make when deciding which states to target with their resources. Our results indicate that focusing on innovative states, that is, those that tend to adopt new policies faster, offers a valuable boost in the speed of diffusion. Even better, though, is a strategy that targets policy leaders.

Keywords policy diffusion, policy advocacy, networks

Introduction

Should policy advocates spread their efforts equally across governing units, or focus on a few key jurisdictions? Faced with limited resources, advocates typically choose to pursue their case in a limited number of forums. Yet, they ultimately wish to influence policy as broadly as possible by seeding a cascade of policy adoption across jurisdictions beyond the

The authors would like to thank participants at the 2015 Robert Wood Johnson Foundation Conference on Diffusion of ACA Policies Across the American States and comments received from the anonymous referees. This research was supported in part by National Science Foundation Grants SES-1558661, SES-1619644, SES-1637089, CISE-1320219. Any opinions, findings, and conclusions or recommendations are those of the authors and do not necessarily reflect those of the sponsor.

Journal of Health Politics, Policy and Law, Vol. 42, No. 2, April 2017
DOI 10.1215/03616878-3766728   © 2017 by Duke University Press

initial advocacy targets. For example, if the Robert Wood Johnson Foundation discovered an effective means to increase states' implementation of the ACA, it could target a small number of key states to maximize its implementation efforts. Wishing to understand the best way to target their resources and maximize return on their budget while maximizing policy impact, policy advocates could use this information to guide future campaigns.

Researchers have provided a body of knowledge on which to base these calculations through an extensive literature that seeks to explain the diffusion of policy innovations across countries, states, or cities. Typically, this research examines the timing of adoption for a single innovation as it spreads across a set of jurisdictions. For example, studies analyze why some states adopt antismoking bans much sooner than other states (Shipan and Volden 2006; Pacheco 2012). This literature has led to an increasingly refined theoretical understanding of the mechanisms that drive policy change, an empirical understanding of states' features that correlate with adoption, and the accumulation of substantively motivated diffusion studies of a wide variety of individual policies. While their findings may hold lessons for those supporting a new policy innovation, they do not necessarily offer immediate insight into a crucial question facing advocates: How can we best target our limited resources to maximize the chance that states adopt our policy?

And the answer matters, since advocates face this situation whether they explicitly confront it or not. Consider some examples. Advocates for bans on same-sex marriage found success in two states before taking a more comprehensive national approach targeting eleven states for ballot measures to adopt constitutional bans in 2004. Four states have approved recreational use of medical marijuana since 2012, with national groups such as the Marijuana Policy Project, NORML, and the Drug Policy Alliance playing an important role. The Marijuana Policy Project says it was targeting five more states for adoption in 2016 (Gurciullo, Mawdsley, and Campbell 2015). Similarly, after a successful campaign to ban affirmative action in California in 1996, Ward Connerly and his group followed up with attempts to do the same in Colorado, Florida, Washington, Michigan, and other states (Boehmke 2005: 39). Finally, the Robert Wood Johnson Foundation (RWJF) wished to support the implementation of the Patient Protection and Affordable Care Act (ACA) of 2010. Its program connects researchers and policy makers to monitor and track the implementation and effects of the ACA (Corlette, Lucia, and Keith 2012).

The academic literature contains important information about how to shape the course of policy diffusion. We seek to relate this evidence to the question posed above by identifying and evaluating strategies for policy advocates. Specifically, we draw from the policy diffusion literature to extract information about which states may serve as the most effective seeds for policy change. By seeds, we mean the states on which advocates might best focus their first efforts. Given the consistent finding in the literature that adoption in one state directly influences adoption in other states, the identity of the initial policy seeds will shape the future spread of the policy across all states. Advocates can leverage these flows to identify the features that make an individual state or an ensemble of states the most effective target for their efforts.

We draw from extant findings in the policy diffusion literature on the multiple pathways through which policies spread between states. Combining these pathways with various internal features of states known to influence policy innovation allows us to identify a parsimonious set of features that explains the timing of states' adoptions of a new policy. We then estimate the parameters of an event history model using data on the diffusion of a large number of policies and use these results to explore how different combinations of seeds influence the speed of policy diffusion. We identify four strategies for choosing seed states and evaluate their effectiveness and compare them to the states with whom the RWJF collaborated.

Our results indicate that the choice of seeding strategy greatly affects the rate of diffusion. Picking the states with the most contiguous neighbors to maximize spillover effects offers little to no advantage over just picking states randomly. Choosing policy leaders, though, reduces the time to adoption by other states by up to 40 percent. The top policy leaders—identified using Desmarais, Harden, and Boehmke's (2015) measure of states most copied by other states—have a widespread and quick influence on other states, which facilitates quick diffusion. Interestingly, if we treat the states supported by the RWJF during implementation of the ACA as seeds, it performs quite well, losing out only to the strategies that include the top policy leaders.

Policy Innovations and the ACA

The ACA requires significant state effort, and states vary in the way in which they approach implementing the ACA's provisions. Passage of the ACA created an occasion to study the effects of the ACA on individuals' health. The new law also produced an opportunity to analyze the way in which states adopt the ACA's policies. Seeing a chance to pair policy practitioners and academics, the RWJF sponsored a program to examine the implementation and effects of the ACA as it spread across the fifty states (Corlette, Lucia, and Keith 2012). The program, which began in May 2011, monitors and tracks ACA policies in ten states: Alabama, Colorado, Maryland, Michigan, Minnesota, New Mexico, New York, Oregon, Rhode Island, and Virginia.[1]

States play a prominent role in implementing the ACA. For example, the health insurance exchanges, only one aspect of the ACA, can be effected in a number of ways. States may elect to run their own exchange, they can collaborate with the federal government, or states can surrender the entire exchange to the federal government (Jones, Bradley, and Oberlander 2014). How a state goes about selecting its exchange is an area ripe for exploration. Potential barriers to enacting these reforms are also important considerations.

The ACA's provisions, although distinct, share one important commonality: states must adopt and implement the policies. We are interested in discovering what unites the ACA's policies individually, as well as policies generally, to answer the question that motivates many of us in this issue: How can we maximize the rate of policy adoption? We explore the degree to which the ensemble of starting states selected—the seeds—affects the number of eventual adoptions.

Sources of Diffusion between the American States

The study of the diffusion of innovations has been traced back to Rogers's (1962) work on the spread of hybrid corn seed, but was recast to public policies shortly thereafter with Walker's (1969) work on state policy innovativeness. Walker argued that states adopt policies to address their own internal public policy issues, but also in response to what states see happening among their peers. Legislators must make policy across a dizzying array of domains with countless alternatives for addressing each social or economic problem. The policies adopted in other states serve as shortcuts and templates in a potentially intractable information environment. A state's internal characteristics and resources for learning about new policies, as well as the actions of other states in their peer network, shape the likelihood of policy innovation.

While Walker laid the groundwork for the study of the diffusion of policy innovations, the field only really took off two decades later when Berry and Berry (1990) introduced the method of event history analysis (EHA) as a way to capture the influences of both internal and external

---

1. We subsequently learned that Illinois was later added as an eleventh state (Pacheco and Maltby, 2017), but our simulations use the original ten states from Corlette, Lucia, and Keith (2012).

influences on policy adoptions. EHA allows researchers to study the choice of whether to adopt the policy on a year-to-year basis while properly capturing changes in state characteristics each year. EHA also captures peer effects by incorporating information about which states have already adopted. Scholars have applied this technique in hundreds of studies to understand the spread of a wide variety of policies, including health policies such as the Children's Health Insurance Program (Volden 2006), antismoking policies (Pacheco 2012), pain management policies (Imhof and Kaskie 2008), and the ACA itself (Pacheco and Maltby 2017).

While EHA policy diffusion studies have developed and tested a wide variety of theoretical mechanisms influencing policy adoption, as well as examined the various empirical determinants of adoption for different policies, our interest lies in identifying common factors on which to build our simulation. To that end, we focus on the common distinction between internal and external determinants. For the former, we wish to identify a parsimonious set of predictors that work across a wide range of policies. This sets the baseline on which we will examine the influence of external factors that play the most interesting part in our simulation of the success of various strategies for choosing seed states.

In identifying general internal determinants of policy innovation, researchers have drawn on Walker's (1969) notion of "slack resources." These facilitate the time and ability it takes for states to identify, study, and possibly implement new policies. States with greater slack resources innovate more quickly while states deficient in them tend to lag behind, waiting to identify what works in the more innovative states. Slack resources include access to professional staff and funding sources that allow legislators the time to identify and research new policies (e.g., Shipan and Volden 2006). They also include broader characteristics of the state such as the size and diversity of its population, which tend to increase the scope of its potential public policy needs and therefore motivate innovations.

More interesting for our question of how to seed states, though, is the role of external determinants. Meaningful diffusion, rather than sequentially unrelated adoption, occurs as states react to what other states have enacted (Simmons, Dobbin, and Garrett 2006). The presence of diffusion generally means that the identity of who adopts matters since it shapes which states will follow the initial adopters.

A look to external factors, and specifically to the interstate networks through which policies diffuse, aligns our current research question with the rapidly growing body of work on maximizing marketing influence in social networks (e.g., Hartline, Mirrokni, and Sundararajan 2008; Chen, Wang, and Yang 2009; Chen et al. 2011; Van Eck, Jager, and Leeflang

2011; Bhagat, Goyal, and Lakshmanan 2012). These studies follow a similar design and research question to ours. The central question is, given a network structure connecting consumers and a set of assumptions regarding the determinants of product adoption and spread across the network, what is the set of first adopters on which the marketer should focus in order to maximize long-run adoption, subject to a marketing budget constraint? We can draw on insights from the literature on policy diffusion to formulate a model of individual states' adoption propensities, as well as the dynamics of diffusion across the states.

Theories of diffusion in the American states typically rely on one of three mechanisms: emulation, learning, and competition (Gilardi 2016). Emulation occurs when states somewhat blindly follow other states' lead and adopt a policy because others have done so merely to avoid being left behind. Learning happens when states see the benefit of a policy for other states and realize that they, too, could benefit (Volden 2006; Volden, Ting, and Carpenter 2008; Gilardi 2010). Competition occurs when the policy creates spillover effects, such as with tax rates or environmental protection legislation, that lead to positive or negative feedback cycles (Boehmke and Witmer 2004; Berry and Baybeck 2005).

While none of the mechanisms points directly to a specific set of peer states to consider, scholars have focused on geographic contiguity. This captures many important forms of economic competition since residents in one state can evade or acquire taxes or goods by driving across a nearby border (Berry and Berry 1990; Berry and Baybeck 2005). Contiguous states also do a reasonable job of capturing states' peer networks, which may be regional in nature given the tendency for neighboring states to be similar. Thus, the number or proportion of neighboring states sharing a border often predicts policy adoption in other states (Berry and Berry 1990; Mooney 2001).

Limiting diffusion to occur only between contiguous neighbors rules out the vast majority of possible pathways. Yet, considering all possible pairs of states also creates challenges. Scholars have tackled this problem in two different ways. Some have modeled the path of diffusion between all pairs of states within a single policy area using observed variables (Volden 2006). Thus, if states adopt a policy shortly after similar states have adopted it, this suggests learning and emulation as possible mechanisms. Others have taken a less structured approach by identifying patterns of the timing of adoption across more than one hundred policies (Desmarais, Harden, and Boehmke 2015). If state A repeatedly adopts policies just a few years after state B, and is less likely to adopt a policy that state B has not previously adopted, then state A likely views state B as one of its peers.

Methods for Simulating Policy Diffusion

In the following two subsections, we outline the steps that we took to identify the influence that the identity of initial adopters has on policy diffusion. In short, we identified the parameters of a "typical" policy diffusion episode by examining the pattern across nearly one hundred different policies. We then used these parameters to simulate the diffusion of a new policy, varying the characteristics of the first adopters to see how subsequent diffusion pattern varies. Those interested in the results can skip straight to the next section, "Simulation Results."

Estimating the Parameters of the Diffusion Model

In this subsection we draw from the extant literature on policy diffusion to construct an EHA model to provide reasonable parameter estimates for a policy diffusion episode. Our task deviates from the standard approach in a couple of ways that inform our model. These both follow from our goal of identifying "typical" parameter values for our simulation that relate internal and external characteristics to the probability of adoption; we do not want our simulation to be tailored too specifically to the parameters of an EHA for a single policy.

First, we utilize a large number of polices that diffused across the American states in order to identify "typical" parameter values since they will form the basis for our simulation. By estimating the influence of internal and external factors across many policies, we avoid having our results be sensitive to the parameters from a single policy. To obtain these estimates we apply a relatively new technique to jointly estimate a single event history model for multiple policies. Known as Pooled Event History Analysis (PEHA), this approach stacks the data from multiple EHA models for a collection of policies and then estimates them in a single model (Boehmke 2009; Kreitzer and Boehmke 2016). This framework permits a wide variety of flexibility when viewed as a multilevel, or mixed, model with the policies or states viewed as the levels.

Our collection of policies comes from Boehmke and Skinner's (2012b) database of 137 policies that diffused across the American states (see also Boehmke and Skinner 2012a). The included policies draw from a variety of policy areas, such as health, corrections, taxes, welfare, etc. The policies began diffusing as early as 1912 and as late as 2007, with the last observed adoption occurring in 2009. In order to include all fifty states and to produce results more relevant for the current era, we only consider policies that began diffusing in or after 1960, which results in eighty-seven policies. While we include all policies to obtain the most general estimates, our results do not change much if we use only the twenty-one remaining health policies, suggesting that health policy diffusion does not differ much from the spread of other policies.

Our second deviation involves estimating a parsimonious model of policy diffusion. In a typical single policy EHA, scholars will include the kinds of internal and external influences we described above, but they will also add a selection of variables to assist in explaining adoption of the specific policy. Because we use nearly one hundred policies, collecting such information for all of them would prove difficult and, just as importantly, would compromise the generalizability of our simulation. We therefore include a handful of independent variables commonly used in the policy diffusion literature to explain innovation. Motivated by Walker's (1969) notion of slack resources, we include total state population and real personal income from the Bureau of Labor Statistics, and a measure of state legislative professionalism (Squire 2007). Further, we account for citizen ideology with a continuous measure of citizen opinion liberalism (Berry et al. 1998) and partisan control of state government (Klarner 2003), via separate indicators of unified Democratic and Republican government control. Finally, to control for other differences across the states, we include fixed effects for each state.

To capture external diffusion forces, we utilize two different networks of interdependence. First, we start with the ubiquitous contiguity network that has been the focal point of most of the work on interstate policy diffusion (e.g., Mooney 2001). A variety of studies finds that policies diffuse between neighboring states due to economic competition (Berry and Berry 1990; Boehmke and Witmer 2004; Berry and Baybeck 2005) or learning (Mooney 2001; Volden 2006; Volden, Ting, and Carpenter 2008; Pacheco 2012). We therefore include a count of the number of states that share a land border and that have adopted the policy before the current year.

Second, we draw on Desmarais, Harden, and Boehmke's (2015) estimates of the latent policy diffusion network. This study uses recent developments in latent network inference (Gomez-Rodriguez, Leskovec, and Krause 2010), combined with Boehmke and Skinner's (2012a) data on policy adoptions to estimate a dynamic, latent diffusion network from 1960 to 2009. Unlike contiguity networks, this approach allows for connections between all pairs of states and uses the data to identify which states influence a state's decision to adopt a new policy. The procedure uses three quantities to determine whether there is a policy diffusion tie from state

A to state B. First, how frequently does state B adopt a policy shortly after state A? Second, how frequently does state B adopt a policy that state A has not previously adopted? Third, how many other states regularly adopt in the interim between the adoptions of states A and B that could be used to explain the adoptions of state B? If these quantities are, respectively, high, low, and low, then state A is likely to be deemed a *source* for state B—a state emulated by state B. Analysis of these source states shows that they differ greatly from the network of contiguous states, reflect patterns of leadership and homophily, and that controlling for the count of adoptions in source states in an event history analysis explains adoption just as well as adoptions in contiguous states (Desmarais, Harden, and Boehmke 2015).

We make one modification to the previous calculation of this variable. The original study accounts for the role of this latent network by including the count of a state's sources that have adopted each policy prior to the current year (Desmarais, Harden, and Boehmke 2015). The latent network estimation strategy, however, assumes that the effect of adoptions by source states decays over time. Specifically, they include an exponential decay to capture the probability that a prior adoption by state A influences adoption today in state B if the latter counts the former among its sources. Using their identified value of 0.5 for the decay parameter, which constitutes an average time of two years for a policy to diffuse, we calculate the contribution in the current year from state i's source states in year t, $S_i(t)$, based on the source states' years of adoption, t_j, as

$$Sources_{it} = \sum_{j \in S_i(t)} 0.5 \exp\left(\frac{-(t - t_j)}{0.5}\right). \tag{1}$$

This means, for example, that a source state that adopts in the prior year has seven times as great an effect as a source state that adopted two years ago. The effect therefore decays quite quickly and effectively vanishes just four years after adoption.

With these variables in place, we now move to estimating our PEHA of state policy innovations in our sample of eighty-seven policies. As described above, we stack the data for each of the separate policies using the same value for each of the six variables measuring internal character-istics in the corresponding year. We include policies starting in the first year in which they begin to diffuse and then treat any remaining states that have yet to adopt as right censored in the last year of an observed adoption. Our dependent variable then marks whether a state adopts a policy in a given year and it excludes states once they have adopted the policy. For each

Table 1 Pooled Logit EHA of Policy Diffusion, 1960–2009

	Coefficient	Standard Error
Lagged sources adoptions	8.5267*	0.4382
Lagged neighbors adoptions	0.3928*	0.0223
Personal income	0.5738*	0.0748
Total population	0.0905*	0.0283
Legislative professionalism	−1.0890	0.6872
State citizen ideology	0.0098*	0.0035
Unified Republican control	−0.0204	0.0760
Unified Democratic control	0.0629	0.0664
Time	−0.1354*	0.0176
Time squared	0.0072*	0.0014
Time cubed	−0.0001*	0.0000
Constant	−5.4113*	0.2779

Notes: $N = 44{,}457$. Fixed effects for states included but not reported. Standard errors clustered on each combination of state and policy.
* Indicates that the associated coefficient achieves significance at the .01 level.

policy, we calculate our two external diffusion measures based on lagged adoptions by neighbors or sources. To account for within policy time trends, we include a cubic polynomial of time, measured since the year of first adoption for each policy (Carter and Signorino 2010). Finally, we include state fixed effects to capture any remaining, constant variation across states in their propensity to adopt policies quickly or slowly.[2]

Table 1 reports the results of our model. Overall, our parsimonious model of policy diffusion recovers a variety of statistically and substantively notable effects. With the exception of the legislative professionalism and two unified government control variables, all of the reported coefficients are statistically different from zero at conventional levels. Larger, wealthier states adopt faster, as the slack resources interpretation would suggest. States that are more liberal also tend to adopt sooner, though this result likely depends to some extent on the mix of policies that we use. We also find strong evidence of diffusion between states, with the lagged neighbors' variable producing its typical positive and statistically significant effect. Further, the decayed sources variable also produces a positive and statistically significant effect. Note that the magnitude exceeds that for the

2. Note that we exclude fixed (or random) effects for each policy. Since we wish to obtain estimates for a generic policy, including such effects would then require us to pick one specific effect (or average across multiple specific effects) to use for our simulation. By omitting these terms, we effectively recover the average across policies.

coefficient on neighbors' adoptions since the decayed variable takes on much smaller values; substantive effects calculations show that a change from standard deviation below the mean to one above it increases the probability of adoption by about 0.075 for contiguous neighbors and just below 0.05 for decayed sources.

Simulating Diffusion

To simulate the diffusion of new policy innovation across the American states, we start with the estimates in table 1. We treat these estimates as the parameters of a logit EHA model governing the spread of a hypothetical policy across the American states.[3] We use them to generate adoption data in year t for state i according to the following formula:

$$y_{it}^* = X_{it}\beta + u_{it}, \tag{2}$$

where X_{it} represents the value of the observed covariates in state i at time t used in our EHA model in table 1, β represents the estimated coefficients reported in that table, and u_{it} follows a logistic distribution.[4]

We start our policy diffusion process in 1989 and let it run through 2009 since by then all fifty states had usually adopted. When y_{it}^* exceeds zero we code that state as adopting, $y_{it} = 1$, and treat that adoption as fixed in all future time periods. We assume no adoptions in 1989 other than those we explicitly seed and then generate data for 1990 according to Equation 2. We do this one year at a time in order to update our lagged diffusion variables each year. For each year, we record the number of states that adopt the policy that year.[5]

We repeat this process 1,000 times and then calculate the average number of states that have adopted by each year as well as corresponding confidence intervals.[6] At its baseline, of course, this process will merely

---

3. We recognize, of course, that our sample limits the generalizability of our estimates to the entire universe of potential policies, especially since our sample excludes policies that do not diffuse widely.

4. Alternatively, we could have simulated values of the independent variables into the future to start our simulation in some hypothetical future world, but using the recent past seemed like the most realistic approach and introduced less randomness into our model since we would have needed to generate a stream of hypothetical values of state population, income, the latent sources network, etc. (Hanmer and Ozan Kalkan 2013).

5. Note that we set our time variables to start with $t=0$ in 1989 since that marks the first year of our hypothetical policy's diffusion process.

6. Note that, due to its nonpartisan legislature, Nebraska has no data for the unified government measures and therefore gets omitted from our EHA model in table 1. In order to avoid its absence from interfering with our diffusion simulation, we set these two variables to zero for the simulation procedure.

summarize the information in our empirical model. By selectively seeding an initial set of adopters, however, we can begin to discern how different advocacy strategies influence the speed with which a policy spreads through the system.[7]

Strategies for Choosing Seed States

In this subsection, we describe strategies for choosing ensembles of policy seeds. We base these strategies off relatively simple heuristics since complex interdependencies in the system make it difficult to identify the optimal set of seeds ex ante. For example, do we seed innovative states or assume they will adopt quickly on their own and seed less innovative states? Do we seed states connected to lots of other states to maximize spread up front or focus on states that are more isolated since they are harder to reach through diffusion networks? We focus on identifying seeding strategies through heuristics based on theoretical concepts such as policy leadership and connectedness, though we discuss the results of a guided brute force approach in the discussion section. To draw a connection to the diffusion of the ACA, we also consider the ten states chosen for the RWJF's ACA monitoring program and proceed as if the RWJF had treated them as seed states rather than merely supporting their adoption.

We start with the two variables in our analysis that capture external influences. Previous adoptions by neighbors and decayed sources both have a clear, positive effect on adoption in connected states in our PEHA estimates, indicating that increasing the number of sources or neighbors that have adopted a policy increases the probability that a state will follow suit. Thus, we can choose seed states to influence the greatest number of other states as sources or neighbors.

Our first approach to identifying an ensemble of seed states therefore considers the states that serve as sources for the greatest number of other states. If we wish to spread a policy as quickly as possible, then it makes sense to target the most widely followed states first. For example, according to Desmarais, Harden, and Boehmke (2015), California serves as a source for anywhere between three and forty-one states between 1960 and 2009. Since 1990, at least nineteen states view it as a source in every year. New York serves as a source for an average of 24.6 states (compared to 19.4 for

---

7. Given its assumptions (which match those of the standard EHA model), our model implies that every state will eventually adopt the policy, so we focus on the cumulative proportion adopting each year rather than on the total number of adopters since that will ultimately always be fifty.

CA) per year between 1960 and 2009, though it has dropped from over thirty prior to 1990 to under ten since the mid-1990s. Since the first adoption by a source state increases the probability of adoption by a follower state by 3.9 percent according to our estimates, getting just one of the more frequently identified source states to adopt would have a widespread effect on the course of adoption by other states. At the other extreme, Oklahoma serves as a source for just 1.4 states per year over this five-decade period. Thus, the one-period effect of seeding a policy in New York exceeds that in Oklahoma by a factor of eighteen.

Our second approach follows the same logic by targeting states with the most contiguous neighbors. Consider the difference between seeding a policy in Maine with one neighbor (to say nothing of Alaska or Hawaii), or states with two neighbors such as Florida or Washington, and seeding it in states such as Missouri or Tennessee with eight neighbors, or Kentucky or Colorado with seven neighbors. While not as dramatic a difference as we see in the most and least frequent source states, choosing states with the most neighbors still influences three to four times as many states as choosing more geographically isolated states. And, according to our estimates, the first adoption by a neighboring state increases the probability of adoption by a follower state by 2 percent.

Our third approach moves beyond connectivity to identify innovative states based on their prior history of policy adoptions. Here we utilize Boehmke and Skinner's (2012a) measure of policy innovativeness. If policy innovativeness means adopting policies early on, then this list will identify the states that do so most often. While this third strategy does not focus on interstate diffusion specifically, it seems an intuitive and attractive approach: by getting widely viewed policy leaders to adopt early on, other states may likely follow.

Our final simulation strategy comes directly from the case of the ACA. In seeking to help states develop programs within the context of the ACA, the RWJF partnered with ten states in its ACA monitoring program: Alabama, Colorado, Maryland, Michigan, Minnesota, New Mexico, New York, Oregon, Rhode Island, and Virginia. We evaluate the hypothetical effect of seeding a policy in these states to see how the RWJF's choice fares when contrasted to the three above. The RWJF's states did not necessarily adopt all of the ACA's provisions, but rather the RWJF supported these states' efforts to adopt the ACA.

In order to provide a baseline against which to compare our four seed strategies, we take two approaches. In the first we seed no states, while in the second we seed five random states for each draw. The former indicates how policies diffuse in the absence of advocacy in seed states, while the latter provides a more direct comparison to an arbitrary seed strategy in that it does not begin with a five-state deficit.

To identify the most innovative states or the top source states, we take the average for each over the last ten years' worth of data (1980–1989). We use this approach since advocates would need to work off available data at the beginning of their attempt to spread a policy. We identify the top five states for each variable—most contiguous neighbors, top sources, and most innovative—and set them as having adopted the policy in 1989. We then run the diffusion process as described above across the forty-five remaining states. To compare the effectiveness of our strategies to that taken by the RWJF in the context of the ACA, we repeat our simulations with the top and bottom ten states. We chose five states for our main results since this seems a more reasonable target for an advocacy group than seeking to get ten states to adopt in the first year.

In selecting these strategies, we hope to identify how each shapes the spread of a proposed new policy innovation. Using real-world values of state characteristics and diffusion networks complicates our ability to isolate the distinct effects of each strategy, though, since these characteristics often overlap. For example, as we show in the next section, highly innovative states tend to be sources for more states, whereas states with many contiguous neighbors are not necessarily top sources. Thus, our results must be interpreted as illustrating the empirical and real-world differences between various strategies for seeding new policies rather than isolating the theoretical contributions of different mechanisms of diffusion. We turn to these issues in more detail in the following section.

Simulation Results

In this section, we report on the performance of our four seeding strategies. As detailed in the previous section, this involves starting our hypothetical policy diffusion processes by seeding five states that adopt the policy in year one and then tracing out the rate of adoption among the other forty-five states. We consider four strategies. The first seeds policy leaders—those states whose adoptions influence the greater number of other states based on Desmarais, Harden, and Boehmke's (2015) estimates. Second, we consider states with the most contiguous geographic neighbors since that forms the other primary pathway of policy diffusion. Third, we consider a strategy that combines these two to identify the states with the largest combined effect of the two. Finally, we seed the five most innovative states as identified by Boehmke and Skinner (2012a).

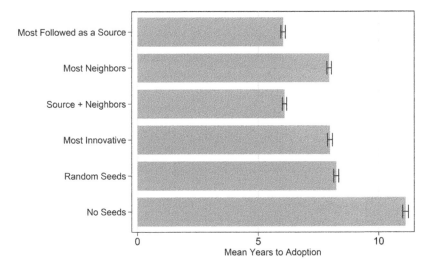

Figure 1 Expected Years to Adoption, by Seed Ensemble Type
(Five Seeds)

Notes: Bars represent the average years to adoption. We calculated these by taking the average years to adoption within each draw and then averaging across draws. The black capped lines represent 95 percent confidence intervals for the average years to adoption based on the standard error of the mean across all 1,000 draws.

Each simulation produces a diffusion sequence over the fifty states consisting of the year of adoption for each state. These produce the familiar S-curve of cumulative adoptions explored in the literature, but with differences in how quickly the policy spreads across seeding strategies. Rather than present the average adoption curve along with standard errors, we focus more on succinct metrics to capture the relative speed of each seeding strategy. Our first chart presents the average years until a state adopts the policy along with a 95 percent confidence interval. To calculate this, we took the average years to adoption within each draw and then averaged and calculated the standard error of the mean across all 1,000 draws.

The bars in figure 1 show that having no seeds is, not surprisingly, the slowest strategy, with an average of just over eleven years until a state adopts. This mostly sets the stage for interpreting the efficacy of the other strategies, all of which start out with a built-in advantage from the five states that we seed in year one. Two strategies emerge as the most effective according to figure 1: seeding the top five sources or seeding the top five combinations of sources and neighbors. These both result in an

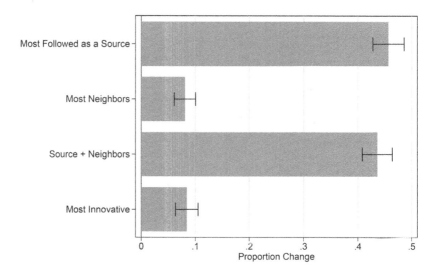

Figure 2 Proportion Increase in Probability of Adoption per Year
Relative to Random Seed Strategy, by Seed Ensemble Type (Five Seeds)

Notes: Bars represent the average proportion reduction in the probability of adoption for each strategy relative to the random seed strategy. We calculated these using the average probability of adoption for each strategy within each draw and then calculating the proportion improvement relative to random seeds within each draw. We then averaged across draws. The black capped lines represent 95 percent confidence intervals for the average improvement based on the standard error of the improvement across all 1,000 draws.

average adoption time of just over six years, nearly half the time for no seeds. Perhaps a more appropriate comparison lies with seeding five randomly selected states each draw. The average time here is 8.2 years, still substantially faster than seeding no states. Relative to a random seeding strategy, the two best strategies offer a 26 percent reduction in time to adoption. Interestingly, seeding the top five states in terms of contiguous neighbors, or the five most innovative states, produces almost no gain relative to five random states.

Figure 2 offers a different perspective on the results. Rather than focus on years to adoption, it turns to the average probability of adoption per year. Further, we focus more explicitly on relative performance by comparing the reduction in the probability of adoption for each strategy to the random seeds strategy. Random seeds offers a fairer comparison than no seeds since the latter does not start out with five adoptions in year one. We estimate the improvement by calculating the average probability of adoption for each strategy and then calculating the proportion reduction of

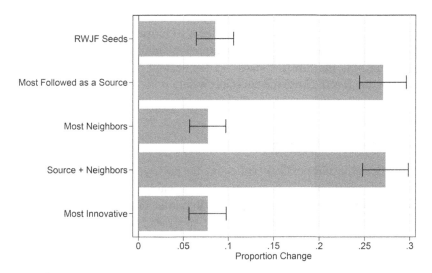

Figure 3   Comparison of RWJF Seed Ensemble to Alternatives Relative
to Random Seeds (Ten Seeds)

Notes: Bars represent the average proportion reduction in the probability of adoption for each strategy relative to the random seed strategy. We calculated these using the average probability of adoption for each strategy within each draw and then calculating the proportion improvement relative to random seeds within each draw. We then averaged across draws. The black capped lines represent 95 percent confidence intervals for the average improvement based on the standard error of the improvement across all 1,000 draws.

each relative to random seeds. As before, we do this for each draw and then take the average improvement and the standard deviation of the average across draws. These results correspond to those presented in the previous figure in terms of ordering the strategies. Top sources and top sources plus neighbors offer about a 44 percent improvement over a random seeding strategy. Most innovative offers an 8.4 percent gain while most neighbors produces an 8.1 percent increase.

Finally, we repeat the simulation process to compare the effectiveness of the ten states supported by the RWJF for the adoption and implementation of the ACA. As noted earlier, for the purpose of comparison we run our simulation using the top or bottom ten states for each strategy. Figure 3 displays the results by repeating the previous plot of the proportion improvement against random seeds. The general pattern of our previous results holds. Notably, the top ten states in terms of contiguous neighbors performs worse than the random seed strategy. Of particular interest, though, is that seeding the ten RWJF states emerges as the second best strategy with an 8.5 percent improvement relative to random seeds, which is greater than the improvement from the top innovators or the most neighbors strategies, about one-third the improvement of the top sources strategy, and puts the RWJF "seeds" as the second best strategy. Thus, it appears the RWJF chose the ten states wisely if the goal was to maximize influence on other states.

Discussion and Conclusion

It is infeasible and possibly ineffective for policy entrepreneurs to lobby directly every policy maker and/or policy-making body. Given that an advocate will have to select targets, two important questions should inform the composition of the initial target (i.e., seed) set. First, how likely are the targets to respond to the efforts of the advocate and adopt the policy? Second, how will the targets' adoptions influence the propensity for other policy makers to support the policy? We have shown that the policy diffusion literature can be used to integrate answers to both of these questions into a comprehensive data-driven strategy for policy advocacy. We show that careful selection of the seed set can increase the speed with which a policy spreads through the states by over 40 percent relative to a random strategy, and even more relative to a poorly chosen strategy.

While the combinatorics makes it impractical to check all possible combinations of states, we find that choosing the top policy sources over the last few years offers the greatest improvement in the speed of diffusion. Recall that sources are states that other states tend to follow in the adoption of new policies. So if, for example, an entrepreneur persuades New York or Florida or California to adopt a new policy, then over two dozen other states will be more likely to adopt that policy in the next year or so. And, while this may sound obvious—getting leader states to adopt will increase adoption among other states—our other results indicate it is not. Consider our finding for contiguity, the other primary source of interstate diffusion. Seeding the states with the most neighbors barely performs better than a random seeding strategy in terms of average years to adoption.

These results underscore the fact that the effectiveness of a seeding strategy depends on a fairly complex interaction of features within the system of fifty states and how they evolve over the course of a diffusion. For example, we speculate that the findings for neighbors occurs because, while states with lots of neighbors will influence many other states up front, they also have more pathways of inward influence, whereas states with few neighbors have only one or two pathways of influence. Starting with the easy-to-reach states that maximize short-term influence does not offer much advantage over starting with the hard-to-reach states and letting them propagate outwards to the easy-to-reach states. In this light, it is not obvious that seeding the five most influential states produces the fastest diffusion across all states. A variety of characteristics of the seed ensemble matter. In addition to the geographic spread, the underlying probability of adoption of its member states also matters. For example, if California is very likely to adopt in year one or two, then targeting it may be a wasted effort compared to seeding a state that would be much less likely to adopt otherwise. Further, seeding California and Oregon may not make sense since they border each other.

While our results indicate that seeding top sources offers a very effective strategy, we have not fully explored the interdependence of states within an ensemble. We have, however, attempted to explore the issue a little bit to see if we can improve on the top sources approach. Briefly, we tried to identify likely candidate states by running fifty simulations with each state as the single seed. We identified the top ten states and then ran all 252 five-state combinations of the top ten individual states based on fastest diffusion times when they are seeded. These results largely confirmed what we found already, since the top combinations all involved states ranked very highly as sources. In fact, the top five source states emerged as the second and fifth best strategies (two states are tied for the fifth most frequent source), and the differences among these top strategies were minuscule. Similar results emerge when we identify the best state on its own, then identify the best state to pair it with, then the best third state to add, and on to the best fifth state.

Overall then, these results seem to support the notion that a strategy for seeding policies that targets the most frequent sources will fare quite well. Of course, the identity of the most frequent source states changes over time. Table 1 in Desmarais, Harden, and Boehmke (2015) shows that New York, for example, ranks as the most frequent source state for all five of the five-year intervals from 1960 through 1984, then drops to number two for the next two intervals and to number five from 1995 through 1999 before dropping out of the top fifteen after 2000. Washington, in contrast, does not make the top fifteen for 1970–1995 but then moves into the top five from 2000 through 2004 and again from 2004 through 2009. Thus, to seed the top sources, one has to know who they are at any given point in time. And, while we do not have sufficient data to know for sure, we suspect that the identity of those policy leaders varies across policy areas as well.

Policy advocates appear to follow a strategy that overlaps somewhat with our approach, though they clearly place an important premium on identifying states in which they perceive a high chance of success. While that conclusion may be premature without a more comprehensive study to evaluate advocates' choice of seed states, it appears to match the strategies chosen in many of the cases we outlined previously, though perhaps not the one selected by the RWJF in support of the ACA. The RWJF appears to have sought out more geographic and ideological diversity than the groups working on legalizing recreational marijuana, anti–affirmative action policies, or same-sex marriage bans. The Marijuana Policy Project effectively acknowledges the importance of receptivity when Rob Kampia, the group's executive director, called efforts to legalize marijuana in Michigan, Missouri, and Ohio "outlier initiatives" and "premature" due to their low chance of success (Gurciullo, Mawdsley, and Campbell 2015).

This suggests an important line of inquiry for future investigations of advocacy strategies. Our approach assumes that advocates can successfully lobby states to adopt their policy, whereas the reality clearly indicates that failure may be more common than success and that it may take years to persuade potential seeds to adopt. This likely helps explain advocates' apparent focus on early successes rather than on choosing states to maximize the future spread of their policy. Such successes help build momentum and facilitate fundraising and membership recruitment going forward. Yet, our results show that the spillover effects of securing adoption in a desirable seed state—in particular, one of the top source states—offers benefits of its own by increasing the chance of adoption in other states that might outweigh the additional up-front cost of advocacy in that state. While further simulations could explore the cost-benefit tradeoff more explicitly, the consistent emergence of the most frequent sources as the most effective targets suggests that one might rank states by expected influence by multiplying the probability of adoption by the number of states that count the target among their sources.

■ ■ ■

Frederick J. Boehmke is a professor of political science and director of the Iowa Social Science Research Center at the University of Iowa. He received his PhD from Caltech in 2000 and was a Robert Wood Johnson Scholar in Health Policy Research at the University of Michigan from 2005 to 2007. His research focuses on state politics, policy diffusion, and political methodology.

Abigail Matthews Rury is a PhD candidate in the Department of Political Science at the University of Iowa. Her research focuses on judicial politics, network analysis and the law, policy diffusion, and quantitative data analysis.

Bruce A. Desmarais is an associate professor in the Department of Political Science and Institute for CyberScience at Pennsylvania State University. In his research, he focuses on the development and application of research methods for understanding the complex interdependence that underlies the formation and implementation of law and public policy.

Jeffrey J. Harden is an assistant professor in the Department of Political Science at the University of Notre Dame. His areas of specialty are American politics and political methodology. His research agenda in American politics focuses on political representation, public policy diffusion, and state politics. His methodology interests include the interpretation and communication of statistical models, network inference, and simulation.

References

Berry, Frances Stokes, and William D. Berry. 1990. "State Lottery Adoptions as Policy Innovations: An Event History Analysis." *American Political Science Review* 84, no. 2: 395–415.

Berry, William D., and Brady Baybeck. 2005. "Using Geographic Information Systems to Study Interstate Competition." *American Political Science Review* 99, no. 4: 505–19.

Berry, William D., Evan J. Ringquist, Richard C. Fording, and Russell L. Hanson. 1998. "Measuring Citizen and Government Ideology in the American States, 1960–93." *American Journal of Political Science* 42, no. 1: 327–48.

Bhagat, Smriti, Amit Goyal, and Laks V. S. Lakshmanan. 2012. "Maximizing Product Adoption in Social Networks." In *Proceedings of the Fifth ACM International Conference on Web Search and Data Mining*, 603–12. New York: ACM.

Boehmke, Frederick J. 2005. *The Indirect Effect of Direct Legislation: How Institutions Shape Interest Group Systems*. Columbus: Ohio State University Press.

Boehmke, Frederick J. 2009. "Approaches to Modeling the Adoption and Modification of Policies with Multiple Components." *State Politics and Policy Quarterly* 9, no. 2: 229–52.

Boehmke, Frederick J., and Paul Skinner. 2012a. "State Policy Innovativeness Revisited." *State Politics and Policy Quarterly* 12, no. 3: 303–29.

Boehmke, Frederick J., and Paul Skinner. 2012b. "State Policy Innovativeness Scores V1.1." hdl.handle.net/1902.1/18507, Harvard Dataverse, V4.

Boehmke, Frederick J., and Richard Witmer. 2004. "Disentangling Diffusion: The Effects of Social Learning and Economic Competition on State Policy Innovation and Expansion." *Political Research Quarterly* 57, no. 1: 39.

Carter, David B., and Curtis S. Signorino. 2010. "Back to the Future: Modeling Time Dependence in Binary Data." *Political Analysis* 18, no. 3: 271–92.

Chen, Wei, Alex Collins, Rachel Cummings, Te Ke, Zhenming Liu, David Rincon, Xiaorui Sun, Yajun Wang, Wei Wei, and Yifei Yuan. 2011. "Influence Maximization in Social Networks When Negative Opinions May Emerge and Propagate." In *Proceedings of the 2011 SIAM International Conference on Data Mining (SDM 2011)*, 379–90. Mesa, Arizona, April 2011.

Chen, Wei, Yajun Wang, and Siyu Yang. 2009. "Efficient Influence Maximization in Social Networks." In *Proceedings of the Fifteenth ACM SIGKDD International Conference on Knowledge Discovery and Data Mining*, 199–208. New York: ACM.

Corlette, Sabrina, Kevin Lucia, and Katie Keith. 2012. "Cross-Cutting Issues: Monitoring State Implementation of the Affordable Care Act in Ten States: Rate Review." Technical Report, Urban Institute. www.urban.org/research/publication /monitoring-state-implementation-affordable-care-act-10-states-rate-review/view /full_report.

Desmarais, Bruce A., Jeffrey J. Harden, and Frederick J. Boehmke. 2015. "Persistent Policy Pathways: Inferring Diffusion Networks in the American States." *American Political Science Review* 109, no. 2: 392–406.

Gilardi, Fabrizio. 2010. "Who Learns from What in Policy Diffusion Processes?" *American Journal of Political Science* 54, no. 3: 650–66.

Gilardi, Fabrizio. 2016. "Four Ways We Can Improve Policy Diffusion Research." *State Politics and Policy Quarterly* 16, no. 1: 8–21.

Gomez-Rodriguez, Manuel, Jure Leskovec, and Andreas Krause. 2010. "Inferring Networks of Diffusion and Influence." In *Proceedings of the Sixteenth ACM SIGKDD Conference on Knowledge Discovery and Data Mining*, 1019–28. ACM: New York.

Gurciullo, Brianna, Karen Mawdsley, and Katie Campbell. 2015. "Weed Rush: The Marijuana Legalization Movement Begins in the States." *Center for Public Integrity*, August 16.

Hanmer, Michael J., and Kerem Ozan Kalkan. 2013. "Behind the Curve: Clarifying the Best Approach to Calculating Predicted Probabilities and Marginal Effects from Limited Dependent Variable Models." *American Journal of Political Science* 57, no. 1: 263–77.

Hartline, Jason, Vahab Mirrokni, and Mukund Sundararajan. 2008. "Optimal Marketing Strategies over Social Networks." In *Proceedings of the Seventeenth International Conference on World Wide Web*, 189–98. New York: ACM.

Imhof, Sara L., and Brian Kaskie. 2008. "Promoting a 'Good Death': Determinants of Pain- Management Policies in the United States." *Journal of Health Politics, Policy and Law* 33, no. 5: 907.

Jones, David K., Katharine W. V. Bradley, and Jonathan Oberlander. 2014. "Pascal's Wager: Health Insurance Exchanges, Obamacare, and the Republican Dilemma." *Journal of Health Politics, Policy and Law* 39, no. 1: 97–137.

Klarner, Carl. 2003. "The Measurement of the Partisan Balance of State Government." *State Politics and Policy Quarterly* 3, no. 3: 309–19.

Kreitzer, Rebecca J., and Frederick J. Boehmke. 2016. "Modeling Heterogeneity in Pooled Event History Analysis." *State Politics and Policy Quarterly* 16, no. 1: 121–41.

Mooney, Christopher Z. 2001. "Modeling Regional Effects on State Policy Diffusion." *Political Research Quarterly* 54, no. 1: 103–124.

Pacheco, Julianna. 2012. "The Social Contagion Model: Exploring the Role of Public Opinion on the Diffusion of Antismoking Legislation across the American States." *Journal of Politics* 74, no. 1: 187–202.

Pacheco, Julianna, and Elizabeth Maltby. 2017. "The Role of Public Opinion—Does It Influence the Diffusion of ACA Decisions?" *Journal of Health Politics, Policy and Law* 42, no. 2, 309–40.

Rogers, Everett M. 1962. *Diffusion of Innovations*. New York: Free Press.

Shipan, Charles R., and Craig Volden. 2006. "Bottom-up Federalism: The Diffusion of Antismoking Policies from U.S. Cities to States." *American Journal of Political Science* 50, no. 4: 825–43.

Shipan, Charles R., and Craig Volden. 2008. "The Mechanisms of Policy Diffusion." *American Journal of Political Science* 52, no. 4: 840–57.

Simmons, Beth A., Frank Dobbin, and Geoffrey Garrett. 2006. "Introduction: The International Diffusion of Liberalism." *International Organization* 60, no. 4: 781–810.

Squire, Peverill. 2007. "Measuring State Legislative Professionalism: The Squire Index Revisited." *State Politics and Policy Quarterly* 7, no. 2: 211–27.

Van Eck, Peter S., Wander Jager, and Peter S. H. Leeflang. 2011. "Opinion Leaders' Role in Innovation Diffusion: A Simulation Study." *Journal of Product Innovation Management* 28, no. 2: 187–203.

Volden, Craig. 2006. "States as Policy Laboratories: Emulating Success in the Children's Health Insurance Program." *American Journal of Political Science* 50, no. 2: 294–312.

Volden, Craig, Michael M. Ting, and Daniel P. Carpenter. 2008. "A Formal Model of Learning and Policy Diffusion." *American Political Science Review* 102, no. 3: 319–32.

Walker, Jack L. 1969. "The Diffusion of Innovations among the American States." *American Political Science Review* 63, no. 3: 880–99.

The Role of Public Opinion—Does It Influence the Diffusion of ACA Decisions?

Julianna Pacheco
University of Iowa

Elizabeth Maltby
University of Iowa

Abstract We consider two ways that public opinion influenced the diffusion of ACA policy choices from 2010 through 2014. First, we consider the policy feedback mechanism, which suggests that policy decisions have spillover effects that influence opinions in other states; residents in the home state then influence the decisions of elected officials. We find that both gubernatorial ACA announcements and grant activity increased support for the ACA in nearby states. Consistent with our expectations, however, only gubernatorial announcements respond to shifts in ACA support, presumably because it is a more salient policy than grant activity. Second, we test for the opinion learning mechanism, which suggests that shifts in public opinion in other states provide a signal to elected officials about the viability of decisions in their own state. We find evidence that states are more likely to emulate other states with similar ACA policy preferences when deciding about when to announce their decisions. Our results suggest that scholars and policy makers should consider how shifts in public support influence the spread of ideas across the American states.

Keywords public opinion, Affordable Care Act, policy diffusion

Does public opinion in one state influence the policy decisions of other states? While there is general agreement that policy makers consider the opinions of their own residents (Konisky 2007), few scholars offer theoretical advancements for understanding how or when public opinion matters for the *spread* of ideas. Instead, scholars focus on elite-driven

This work has been supported (in part) by award #94-16-05 from the Russell Sage Foundation. Any opinions expressed are those of the author(s) alone and should not be construed as representing the opinions of the foundation.

Journal of Health Politics, Policy and Law, Vol. 42, No. 2, April 2017
DOI 10.1215/03616878-3766737   © 2017 by Duke University Press

mechanisms of diffusion, arguing that policies are adopted either because policy makers emulate or learn from states with "successful" policies or because states compete to gain an economic advantage. Of the 117 articles published on policy diffusion in the American states since Walker (1969), only 65 consider the influence of public opinion. The majority of these authors are concerned with public opinion in the home state, noting that policy makers should be responsive to their own citizens. Government officials are seeking reelection; therefore, preferences of state residents should be related to policy adoption in the home state (e.g., Berry and Berry 1992).[1] Yet, missing in our theories of policy diffusion is the possibility that public opinion plays a more central role in the spread of policy ideas, not just the adoption of policy in the home state.

To better incorporate the ways that public opinion in one state both influences and is influenced by other states' policy decisions, it is important to have accurate measures of citizens' attitudes toward specific policies. Methodologically, scholars often measure public opinion indirectly via demographics (e.g., percentage of Evangelicals) or reelection factors (e.g., competitiveness). Yet, there is no guarantee that demographics or reelection factors proxy for specific policy preferences. For example, the correlation between the changes in the percentage of adult smokers and preferences toward smoking bans in restaurants is a mere −.06 (Pacheco 2012). Scholars who rely on direct measures of public opinion tend to use ideology (Taylor et al. 2012) or state culture (Crowley 2004). These broad measures of opinion, however, do not provide a clear understanding about the role of public opinion because (1) they are stable over time, preventing inferences about how changes in opinion influence the diffusion process; and (2) it is unclear exactly how broad measures of ideology or culture should be linked to actual policy choices (e.g., Matsusaka 2001; Lax and Phillips 2012). Empirically, research that considers the role of public opinion is best suited to include direct measures of preferences that are specific to policy choices.

We contribute to our understanding about the role of public opinion on state policy making by looking at policy choices on the Affordable Care Act from 2010 through 2014. First, we consider *the policy feedback mechanism*, which suggests that policy decisions have spillover effects

---

1. We started with Graham, Shipan, and Volden's (2013) list of articles on policy diffusion and updated it through 2014. We then read each article to determine if and how public opinion was included in the analyses as well as in the theoretical discussions. We include only articles that looked at policy diffusion in the American states. Graham, Shipan, and Volden's (2013) original list is broad with studies that mention diffusion but do not focus on how or why policies are adopted; these were also not included in our final list of articles.

that influence opinions in other states; residents in the home state then influence the decisions of elected officials. We find that both gubernatorial ACA announcements and grant activity exhibit spillover policy effects; that is, both types of decisions increased support for the ACA in nearby states. Consistent with our expectations, however, only gubernatorial announcements respond to shifts in ACA, presumably because it is a more salient policy than grant activity. Second, we test for *the opinion learning mechanism*, which suggests that shifts in public opinion in other states provide a signal to elected officials about the viability of decisions in their own state. We find evidence that states are more likely to emulate other states with similar ACA policy preferences when deciding about the timing of gubernatorial announcements but do not consider similarity in ACA policy preferences when making decisions about less visible policies, such as grant activity.

The results suggest that public opinion is more than an internal factor that influences policy adoption. Instead, public opinion is a potential lever that accelerates the diffusion process; it also explains the geographic patterns of policy adoption. Scholars and policy makers are encouraged to consider how shifts in public support influence the spread of ideas, particularly those related to health care decisions, across the American states.

Public Opinion and Policy Diffusion: Two Mechanisms of Influence

We consider two mechanisms that account for the influence of opinion on policy diffusion. *The policy feedback mechanism* suggests that policy decisions have spillover effects that influence opinions in other states; residents in the home state then influence the decisions of elected officials. *The opinion learning mechanism* suggests that shifts in public opinion in other states provide a signal to elected officials about the viability of decisions in their own state. We describe both mechanisms and their applicability to the ACA below.

The Policy Feedback Mechanism

The policy feedback mechanism suggests that the public plays a major role in the diffusion process by reacting to policy choices in other states and then pressuring their own officials to make similar decisions.[2] The policy feedback mechanism has two components. First, policy preferences are

2. Pacheco (2012) refers to this mechanism as the "social contagion model."

shaped by policy choices *in other jurisdictions*. While there is evidence that policies influence mass preferences (Soss and Schram 2007; Pacheco 2014), less is known about spillover policy effects. The most compelling evidence comes from Pacheco (2012), who finds that public support for smoking bans in restaurants increased after enactment of antismoking legislation in neighboring states. Pacheco's (2012) work builds on other studies that show that individual behaviors are influenced by policy decisions in nearby states. For instance, residents travel to other states to purchase lottery tickets (Berry and Baybeck 2005), buy cigarettes (Hyland et al. 2005), and obtain abortions (Althaus and Henshaw 1994).

While there is empirical support for the first component of the policy feedback mechanism, it is unlikely to apply to all policies. Policies that are proximate and visible are most likely to shape public opinion (Soss and Schram 2007). Policies that are highly proximate, such as smoking bans or seatbelt laws, are those that individuals have direct and recurrent experiences with, while less proximate policies—including many redistributive policies—are largely hidden from citizens' daily lives. Highly visible policies are those that receive large amounts of media and electoral attention. Distinguishing policies based on proximity and visibility is important because these characteristics may determine how policies influence mass preferences. Proximate policies influence mass opinions through implementation (Soss 1999), while visible policies influence preferences through the information environment (Brewer 2003), which includes information transmitted via social networks and overlapping media markets (Zukin and Snyder 1984). We would expect the same pathways to apply to spillover policy effects. Spillover policy effects are most likely to occur when residents living near the borders of states have ample opportunities for direct policy experience or policy learning through the information environment.

Applied to the ACA, visibility is most applicable. However, not all decisions within the ACA are equally visible. Some decisions, such as choosing a structure for the online health insurance marketplace, are highly visible both to residents of the state and to residents in neighboring states. Citizens are less likely to be aware of other decisions, such as applying for federal funding. This leads to our first hypothesis:

H1 ACA state policy decisions that are highly visible influence policy preferences in nearby states.

The second component of the policy feedback mechanism is the policy responsiveness of elected officials to changing constituent opinions. State preferences are highly related to policy choices, regardless of whether scholars focus on broad measures of public opinion (Erikson, Wright, and McIver 1993) or specific policies (e.g., Hill, Leighley, and Hinton-Andersson 1995; Mooney and Lee 2000; Gray, Lowery, and Godwin 2007). More recent evidence using time series analyses finds evidence of dynamic policy responsiveness. *Shifts* in public support for governmental spending correspond to changes in state spending (Pacheco 2013), and an increase in support for antismoking legislation increases the probability that states adopt smoking bans (Pacheco 2012). Presumably, it is precisely because state officials are interested in reelection that they actively gauge and respond to shifts in public opinion in their home state (Erikson, MacKuen, and Stimson 2002). We would expect the same dynamics to apply to ACA policy decisions, which leads to our second hypothesis:

> H2 *Policy makers respond to shifts in support for the ACA among their constituents.*

The Opinion Learning Mechanism

The opinion learning mechanism focuses on the reaction of elected officials to changing opinions in like-minded states. Berry and Berry (1992: 400), for instance, argue that adoptions in nearby states can counteract public opinion against a policy or intensify pressures to adopt a policy in a state where the public favors it. There is also evidence that states are more likely to emulate states that are ideologically similar (Volden 2006), suggesting that elected officials learn about viable policies from states that are similar in their policy preferences. Changes in national sentiment, particularly on salient policies (Nicholson-Crotty 2009), speed up or slow down the diffusion process as elected officials learn about the political gains or losses of policy enactments. According to the opinion learning model, when policy preferences between two states are similar, it provides a signal to elected officials about the viability of policies in their own state. Policy diffusion is, therefore, a product of elected officials responding to policy preferences elsewhere, as opposed to legislators learning about policy successes in other jurisdictions.

A crucial component of the opinion learning mechanism is the monitoring of external opinion by elected officials. While political officials often catch wind of shifting preferences among their constituents (Erikson, MacKuen, and Stimson 2002), there is also evidence that gauging shifts in policy preferences, especially on issues that are not salient (Burstein 2003), is burdensome for political officials (Weaver 2000; Manza and Cook 2002). While the rapid growth of public and private opinion polling has increased the amount and quality of information available to political actors (Geer

1996), it is also likely that poll respondents are somewhat unrepresentative of the broader constituency (Berinsky 1999). Given the difficulties in opinion monitoring, it is reasonable for elected officials to look elsewhere, and especially at those states that are similar, for information about their own residents.

State policy makers may have additional incentives to look at policy preferences elsewhere that have little to do with responding to constituent preferences. Instead, elected officials may look to states with similar ideological or partisan leanings in order to learn about how to "craft" their policy stances and "win" public support for what they desire (Jacobs and Shapiro 2000). According to this view, politicians are uncertain about public opinion, but believe that it is susceptible to change and malleable enough to support their preferred positions (Jacobs and Shapiro 2000). Elected officials rely on three techniques to change public opinion, including tracking public opinion, managing press coverage, and priming the public to support certain policies (Jacobs and Shapiro 2000). It is reasonable to assume that state officials use similar strategies to promote policy decisions and that the external monitoring of similar states is part of that strategy.

Recent work by Pacheco (2013) provides direct evidence that state legislators respond to public opinion outside their borders, although there is no explanation for whether officials are looking elsewhere due to sincere or strategic motives. Pacheco (2013) finds that legislators in less professional states respond to changes in national policy sentiment when deciding on expenditures instead of state-specific opinions, presumably because these states lack the necessary resources to gauge opinion shifts among their constituents.

Regardless of whether the opinion learning mechanism is a result of sincere or strategic motives, we might expect elected officials to pay the most attention to external opinion shifts on policies that are particularly salient. If opinion learning is sincere, then policy makers may have more uncertainty about how their constituents will respond in the next election to policy decisions on salient issues. If opinion learning is strategic, it is the highly partisan issues that increase competition among policy makers who then promote their favored positions via campaigns and counter-campaigns (Jacobs and Shapiro 2000). In both scenarios, we would expect the following as it applies to the ACA:

H3 States are more likely to emulate the highly visible decisions of the ACA from states with similar levels of ACA support.

The Diffusion of Affordable Care Act Decisions

The underlying design and structure of the ACA relies on the cooperation of the fifty states (Greer 2011), and states have significant leeway to tailor reform to the tastes of their residents (Jacobs and Skocpol 2012). We concentrate on two components of the ACA that we believe allow us to test our hypotheses regarding the policy feedback mechanism and the opinion learning mechanism. The first component is the timing of gubernatorial decisions regarding the new health insurance marketplace. While every state is required to have a health insurance marketplace, states may choose how much control they have in creating the marketplace. States can control all aspects of their marketplace (state marketplace), share control of the marketplace with the federal government (partnership marketplace), or cede all power in marketplace creation to the federal government (federal marketplace).

Governors, as the most powerful persons in state government (Rosenthal 1990; Beyle 2004), were instrumental in determining which option their state would take. By announcing the marketplace structure for their state, governors play a critical role in legitimizing the ACA by signaling to the public that health care reform in their state will move forward. We expect, then, that public support toward the ACA should increase following gubernatorial announcements in nearby states.

The second decision that we focus on is the timing of grant applications. The federal government offered grants for those states that were making progress toward establishing a marketplace. States choose when to apply for funding based on their needs and planned expenditures. Level 1 establishment grants (awarded to thirty-seven states, although states can apply for this grant multiple times) are available for states that are making progress in establishing a marketplace through a step-by-step approach. Level 2 establishment grants (awarded to fourteen states) are available for states that are moving ahead with their state-based marketplace at a faster pace. Here, we look at the timing and frequency of states' grant applications, rather than the amount of money states requested from the federal government, because we believe that these decisions signal willingness to implement the ACA (see Rigby 2012 for a similar argument).[3]

3. It is possible that the frequency with which states apply for grants reflects the amount of money states were awarded. For example, states that initially asked for money may not need to apply for future grants, while others need more funding. However, we think it unlikely that this is the case. States which were awarded less money for their first grant were not more likely to apply for later grants. For example, Alabama, which was awarded over $8 million for their first grant, did not apply for future funding. But Colorado, which received close to $40 million from their initial grant, applied for three more grants during this time period. To ensure that states' previous grant awards do not drive our results, we ran models which included the amount of money awarded for the previous grant. Our results remain unchanged.

We picked these two decisions for empirical and substantive reasons.[4] First, as described below, these decisions have ample variation over time, allowing us to explain how shifts in opinion influenced the dynamics of state policy making. Additionally, information regarding the timing of both policy decisions is readily available for us to code. Substantively, these two policy decisions vary on visibility and saliency, allowing us to test *H1* and *H3*. Gubernatorial announcements and the implementation of the health insurance marketplaces received high media attention at both the national and local levels (Gollust et al. 2014), and decisions regarding the ACA are highly salient to the American public (Blendon, Benson, and Brulé 2012). Unlike decisions about the marketplace, grant activity received relatively less media coverage, likely because state health departments rather than politicians applied for these grants. This may also explain why less visible policy decisions are not as responsive to public opinion. Because bureaucrats are often not elected, they may feel less beholden to public preferences.

We anticipate the policy feedback mechanism and the opinion learning mechanism to be particularly influential for the timing of marketplace decisions and less so for the timing of grant applications. Given the salience and media coverage of the ACA, we anticipate that gubernatorial announcements will influence policy preferences in nearby states (*H1*). Similarly, because governors are sensitive to preferences in like-minded states, we expect changes in policy preferences toward the ACA in nearby states to influence gubernatorial announcements in the home state (*H3*). While both decisions are likely to be related to public opinion in the home state, we suspect that grant applications will be less related to changing preferences since these decisions are largely hidden from the public (*H2*).

Finally, while much is known about the determinants of state-level decision making regarding the *types* of marketplaces (federal, state-based, or partnership) (e.g., Jones, Bradley, and Oberlander 2014), scholars know relatively less about the timing of decisions related to gubernatorial announcements as well as the determinants of grant activity. Thus, our article not only contributes to the extensive literature on policy diffusion, but also has implications for health policy scholars.

---

4. States' decisions on Medicaid expansion was another highly visible policy choice in implementing the ACA. Due to data limitations, we chose not to study this policy. We expect, however, that the role of public opinion in diffusing states' Medicaid expansion decisions is similar to gubernatorial announcements about marketplace structure since both decisions were very public.

Table 1 Types of Marketplace Exchanges and Date of Announcement by State, Collected from the Kaiser Family Foundation Policy Briefs

State-Based Marketplace	State-Federal Partnership Marketplace	Federal Marketplace
CA, 9/30/2010	AR, 12/12/2012	AL, 11/13/2012
CO, 6/1/2011	DE, 7/2012	AK, 6/17/2012
CT, 6/1/2011	IL, 7/2012	AZ, 11/28/2012
HI, 7/11/2011	IA, 12/14/2012	FL, 12/2012
ID, 11/11/2012	MI, 11/16/2012	GA, 11/16/2012
KY, 7/17/2012	NH, 2/13/2013	IN, 7/2012
MD, 4/4/2011	WV, 2/15/2013	KS, 11/9/2012
MA, 4/12/2006		LA, 7/2/2012
MN, 3/20/2013		ME, 11/16/2012
NV, 6/16/2011		MS, 12/2012
NM, 3/28/2013		MT, 11/6/2012
NY, 4/12/2012		NE, 11/15/2012
OR, 7/17/2011		NJ, 12/7/2012
RI, 9/19/2011		ND, 11/2012
SD, 9/26/2011		OH, 11/16/2012
VT, 5/26/2011		OK, 11/19/2012
WA, 5/11/2011		PA, 12/12/2012
		SC, 11/15/2012
		TN, 12/14/2012
		TX, 7/9/2012
		UT, 5/10/2013
		VA, 12/14/2012
		WI, 11/16/2012
		WY, 11/14/2012

Measuring State ACA Policy Decisions

We rely on policy briefs from the Kaiser Family Foundation to measure the month and year in which governors announced their marketplace decisions starting in 2010. States differ significantly in both the type of marketplace exchanges as well as the timing of gubernatorial announcements as shown in table 1. California was the first state to announce the structure of its marketplace in September 2010. By May 2013, all fifty states had announced their marketplace structure.

Data on the timing decisions of grant applications come from various reports by the Centers for Medicare and Medicaid Services. Table 2 shows differences across the states in the type of grants and timing of applications. States were eligible to apply for grants roughly once every quarter,

Table 2 State Applications to Federal Grants by Type and Quarter, Collected from the Centers for Medicare & Medicaid Services

Quarter	States Applying to Level 1 Grants	States Applying to Level 2 Grants
1/2011 – 3/2011	IN, RI, WA	
4/2011 – 6/2011	CA, CT, IL, KY, MD, MN, MO, MS, NC, NV, NY, OR, WV	
7/2011 – 9/2011	AL, AZ, DE, HI, IA, ID, ME, MI, NE, NM, TN, VT	RI
10/2011 – 12/2011	AR, CO, KY, MA, MN, NJ, NV, NY, PA, TN	
1/2012 – 3/2012	IL, NV, OR, SD, TN	WA
4/2012 – 6/2012	CA, HI, IA, NY	CT, MD, NV, VT
7/2012 – 9/2012	AR, CO, KY, MA, MN	
10/2012 – 12/2012[1]	CT, DE, IA, MI, MN, NC, NH, UT, VA, VT	CA, KY, MA, NY, OR
1/2013 – 3/2013	AR, IL, NH, RI	HI
4/2013 – 6/2013	NM, NV, VA, VT, WV	CO
7/2013 – 9/2013	AR, CT, IA, ID, RI	MN
10/2013 – 12/2013	AR, DE, MS, NH, NM, NV, RI, UT, WA	
1/2014 – 3/2014	NH, NY, RI, UT	
4/2014 – 6/2014		
7/2014 – 9/2014	MA, RI, VA	
10/2014 – 12/2014[1, 2]	CT, IL, MA,[3] MD, NH, NY, RI, VT, WA	AR, ID

[1]During this quarter, there were two application dates for both L1 and L2 grants.
[2]This quarter is not included in the analysis.
[3]Massachusetts applied to two L1 grants during this quarter.

but were allowed to apply in multiple funding cycles. While the majority of states applied for one grant during each cycle, table 2 shows that Massachusetts applied for two L1 grants during the last quarter of 2014. Additionally, more states applied for L1 grants compared to L2 grants. Given that L2 grants were relatively rare, the analyses below uses a measure that combines grant activity for L1 and L2 grants.

Measuring State ACA Support over Time

We rely on the Kaiser Family Foundation Health Tracking Polls to measure state opinion toward the ACA over time. Support for the ACA was asked for forty-seven consecutive months using the following question, "As of right now, do you generally support or generally oppose the health care proposals being discussed in Congress?" Respondent answers ranged from strongly support to strongly oppose. As the ACA became law, the question stem changed slightly to, "As you may know, a new health reform bill was signed into law."[5]

To estimate state opinion toward the ACA, we will rely on multilevel modeling, imputation, and post-stratification (referred to as MRP), developed by Gelman and Little (1997) and extended by Park, Gelman, and Bafumi (2004; 2006). MRP produces accurate estimates of public opinion by state (Lax and Phillips 2009) and congressional district (Warshaw and Rodden 2012), and over time (Pacheco 2011; 2013).

As described in the appendix, we model survey responses as a function of gender, race, age, education, region, state, and state presidential vote share. These are standard predictors of MRP and perform quite well (Lax and Phillips 2009). We use the population frequencies obtained from the public use micro data samples in 2010 supplied by the census bureau for post-stratification.

Adding a Time Component

We add a time component by pooling surveys across a small time frame. We use a three-quarter moving average to estimate quarterly opinion toward the ACA. For instance, to get point estimates for Q1 in 2011 using a three-quarter pooled window, we combine estimates from Q4 in 2010, Q1 in 2011, and Q2 in 2011, and then perform the MRP technique on this pooled dataset. The MRP process is repeated for each quarter after moving the time frame up a quarter at a time. By pooling and taking the median estimate, the first and last quarters are missing. Pacheco (2011) shows that while there is a trade-off between the reliability of estimates and sensitivity to very short-term shocks, the efficiency benefits of pooling over a small time period outweigh the costs of biasedness.

The use of multilevel modeling and post-stratification overcomes two major problems that arise when trying to measure state opinion from national

5. Few questions ask about insurance marketplaces (only five over the time period), and none capture preferences on grant activity. We follow the lead of others (Brace et al. 2002; Plutzer and Berkman 2005), and assume these questions capture a broader ideology about the ACA. Validity analyses largely confirm this assumption. Five surveys asked respondents about general opinions toward the ACA and insurance marketplaces. The correlation between these opinions is modest ($r = .51$). More important, in results available on request, both outcomes are predicted by similar covariates. For the most part, the same individual characteristics that predict support for the ACA also predict support for state marketplaces.

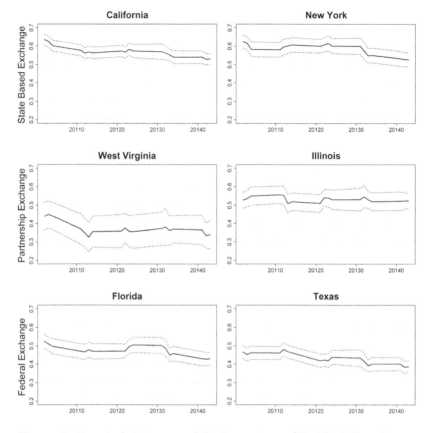

Figure 1 Quarterly Measures of the Percentage of Residents Favoring the ACA from Quarter 2 in 2010 to Quarter 3 in 2014

Note: 20110 = Quarter 1 in 2011.

surveys. Multilevel modeling increases the reliability of less populous states via "shrinkage towards the mean."[6] Indeed, the MRP approach has been shown to be superior to the aggregation method in terms of reliability, particularly when sample sizes are small, for instance, when N is less than 2,800 across all states (Lax and Phillips 2009). Post-stratification corrects

---

6. As pointed out by a reviewer, the MRP strategy may create more similarity in opinion for certain states, particularly the less populated states, which may falsely provide evidence of spread in opinion. This concern is precisely why we include few state-level covariates and rely mostly on individual demographic factors to estimate opinion in the first stage of the MRP strategy. We also add that the strategy creates similarity among states based on their sample sizes, not based on factors that we believe influence the spread of opinion such as contiguity or ideological similarity. We would be more concerned if the least populated states were in the same geographic area. Finally, we reanalyze the error correction models in table 3 but drop the ten least populated states that are at the highest risk of contaminating the results. Inferences from these models are nearly identical to the models reported in the manuscript.

for non-representativeness due to sampling designs by adjusting estimates so that they are more representative of state populations.

Figure 1 shows quarterly estimates of the percentage of state residents who are "very" or "somewhat" favorable toward the ACA from Q2 in 2010 to Q3 in 2014 for select states.[7] While not exhaustive, figure 1 gives a descriptive glimpse into the dynamic properties of state opinion toward the ACA. State favorability toward the ACA is generally low; on average across the United States and during this time period, only 46 percent of residents view the ACA favorably, which corroborates with previous research. This national estimate, however, ignores significant variation across and within states; 73 percent of the variance in ACA favorability is across states and 28 percent is within states. In some states (e.g., California), a majority of residents favor the ACA, while in others (e.g., West Virginia) support is much lower than the national average. As shown in figure 1, there is also movement in ACA favorability with some states declining in support and others experiencing bouts of increased support.[8]

Empirically Testing the Policy Feedback Mechanism

We begin by testing whether ACA policy decisions have spillover policy effects on ACA preferences. Recall that we expect state policy decisions that are highly visible to influence policy preferences in nearby states; more specifically, we expect the timing of gubernatorial announcements, but not the timing of ACA grant applications, to influence shifts in support elsewhere. To test for spillover policy effects, we employ traditional time series methods. More specifically, we use an error correction model (ECM). An ECM allows for the estimation of both short- and long-term effects of independent variables and tells us how quickly the system returns to equilibrium or the overall mean after being disrupted. The dependent variable captures the *changes* in opinion toward the ACA. A lagged dependent variable is included to account for time dependence. For all time varying covariates, we include both the differenced independent variable ($[\Delta X]_t$) and the lagged independent variable ($X_{(t-1)}$) to account for both short- and long-term effects.

The main independent variables are the proportion of neighboring states in which the governor has announced an ACA decision and applied for grant applications. We control for a number of other factors that may influence changes in ACA preferences. First, we control for policy

7. See table A1 in the appendix for full text of the question wording and dates of the survey.
8. The appendix provides additional information about the estimation strategy as well as validation checks.

decisions in the home state with the expectation that there may be some policy feedback effects. Specifically, we include measures of whether the governor in the home state has already announced the ACA decision and grant activity. We also include a measure of the type of exchange that a state announced since those that defaulted to the federal government are generally less supportive of the ACA (Jones, Bradley, and Oberlander 2014). Finally, we include fixed unit effects (e.g., state dummies) to account for unit heterogeneity and fixed time effects (e.g., quarter/year dummies) to account for systemic factors. We also include panel corrected standard errors as suggested by Beck and Katz (2011).

Results are shown in table 3. The coefficient on the lagged dependent variable gives the error correction rate with a value closer to zero, indicating a slow return to equilibrium. As shown in Model 1 in table 3, the coefficient on the lagged dependent variable for state ACA support is −.46, suggesting that opinion is relatively quick to return to equilibrium when disrupted.

Consistent with the first part of the policy feedback mechanism, the model suggests that, as the proportion of neighboring states announce their ACA decisions, ACA support in the home state increases in the short run, but not the long term. The coefficient on the differenced proportion of neighboring states variable gives the short-term effect of policy adoption on state public opinion. To get the estimated effect of a unit change in X, we simply multiply this effect with the coefficient. For instance, a .35 increase in the proportion of neighboring states that announce the ACA decision (which is roughly two standard deviations above the mean change) *increases* public support for the ACA in the next quarter by about 1 percent (e.g., $.35 \times .02$). Although this effect is small, it is large if changes in neighboring policies occur in consecutive quarters.

Surprisingly, neighboring grant activity also has a statistically significant effect on public support for the ACA in the short term. For instance, the model predicts that if the number of grants applied for by neighboring states increased by two (which is roughly two standard deviations above the mean change), public support for the ACA also increased by about 2 percent (e.g., $2 \times .009$) in the next quarter.

If the policy feedback mechanism is true, then opinion should influence the probability of state ACA decisions; state officials should respond to the preferences of state residents. To test the second component of the policy feedback mechanism, we employ event history analysis. The dependent variable in these models is the probability that state i will either announce their marketplace structure or apply for a federal grant in quarter t. For gubernatorial announcements, this variable takes a value of one in

Table 3 Testing the Policy Feedback Mechanism: Error Correction
Model Predicting Changes in Public Support for the ACA ($N = 768$)

Percentage favor ACA (t–1)	–.46***
	(.07)
Proportion neighbors that announced ACA decision (t–1)	.0003
	(.01)
Δ Proportion neighbors that announced ACA decision	.02**
	(.01)
Average number of grants applied for by neighbors (t–1)	.008
	(.007)
Δ Average number of grants applied for by neighbors	.009*
	(.005)
Home state announced ACA decision (t–1)	.01**
	(.003)
Δ Home state announced ACA decision	.01*
	(.004)
Home state applied for grants (t–1)	.00
	(.004)
Δ Home state applied for grants	–.003
	(.003)
Partnership exchange	–.03***
	(.01)
Federal exchange	–.08***
	(.01)
Constant	.22***
	(.04)

Note: Panel-corrected standard errors in parentheses. Significance levels: * .10, ** .05, *** .01 with a two-tailed test. Quarter/year and state dummies are also included in the model, but not shown due to space.
Δ = change.

the quarter that the governor in state i announces the state's marketplace structure and a zero in all quarters prior to announcement. Observations are dropped in the quarters after a state has declared the structure of their marketplace since the state is no longer "at risk" of innovating; this is the conventional coding scheme for event history analysis (Berry and Berry 1990). For grant activity, the dependent variable takes a value of one in all quarters that a state applied for either an L1 or L2 grant and a zero otherwise. Because states may apply for multiple grants and are, thus, "at risk" of another grant application in every quarter, cases are not dropped once a state has applied for their first grant. In the case of multiple or repeated events, it is important to control for a state's previous decisions (Beck, Katz, and Tucker 1998: 1272). Accordingly, we include a count of the previous number of grant applications for each state.[9] Since the dependent variables are dichotomous, we employ logistic regression. To account for potential problems of non-independence of observations and of heteroskedasticity, we rely on the cluster procedure where observations are clustered by state.

The main independent variable is state support for the ACA, as described in the previous section. According to *H2*, as support increases, the probability for announcement and grant activity should also increase. We include the proportion of neighbors that have announced their ACA decisions and neighboring grant activity to account for the influence of other states. Some states are highly involved in grant activity, and we expect for states with more resources to be particularly well suited to apply for federal grants. We include a binary variable which captures whether the home state belongs to the RWJF's State Network (1) or not (0). States that belonged to the Robert Wood Johnson Foundation's (RWJF) State Health Reform Assistance Network likely had assistance in applying for grants.[10]

We also control for a number of other determinants of state health policy making. We control for gubernatorial partisanship using a binary measure which takes the value of one if the governor is a Republican and zero otherwise. The ACA is a highly partisan issue and Republican-led states may take longer to announce their marketplace structures or be less likely to apply for grants. States with a larger uninsured population may be more proactive in implementing the ACA by announcing their marketplace structure early or may have greater need for federal funding assistance. To control for this, we include a measure of the percentage of uninsured state residents. We include several demographic measures that are often used in diffusion studies such as the natural log of the state's population size and the median income in the state. We also include time and time squared.[11]

---

9. This modeling strategy has the benefit of keeping all states in the analysis after the initial grant application, but assumes that all grant applications are predicted by the same covariates (see Boehmke 2009a: 236–37), which may not be realistic. As a robustness check, we ran separate models for the first grant application, second grant application, and so on. This strategy is not ideal since many observations are dropped from the analysis, and is inefficient since many of the covariates have the same effect for all grant applications. The results from these models are largely similar to the models shown.

10. With the goal of helping to expand health insurance coverage, the RWJF created the State Network in order to provide technical assistance to states as they worked to implement the ACA. State network members include Alabama, Colorado, Illinois, Maryland, Michigan, Minnesota, New Mexico, New York, Oregon, Rhode Island, and Virginia.

11. Inferences regarding the influence of public opinion are nearly identical when quarter/year dummy variables are included. We decided to include linear and squared versions of time since there were many quarters where no state announced its marketplace.

Table 4 Testing the Policy Feedback Mechanism:
Event History Analysis Predicting Gubernatorial Announcement
and Grant Activity

	Gubernatorial Announcements ($N=414$)	Grant Applications ($N=816$)
Δ ACA support	12.51	−4.36
	(11.17)	(5.03)
ACA support (t–1)	11.96**	−3.11
	(5.45)	(2.56)
Republican governor	−.15	−.31
	(.59)	(.34)
Natural log of population size	−.15	.02
	(.29)	(.14)
Median income	.00002	.00001
	(.00)	(.00)
Percent uninsured	.07	−.01
	(.08)	(.05)
Proportion neighbors that announced ACA decision (t–1)	2.42*	
	(1.38)	
Δ Proportion neighbors that announced ACA decision	3.54***	
	(1.09)	
Partnership exchange	−2.64***	−.33
	(.94)	(.21)
Federal exchange	−1.82***	−1.86***
	(.74)	(.43)
RWJF state network	−1.18	.18
	(.77)	(.29)
Total number of grant applications (t–1)		−.16
		(.16)
Proportion neighbors that applied for grants (t–1)		.39
		(.26)
Δ Proportion neighbors that applied for grants		.34
		(.44)
Time	−.65	.68***
	(.43)	(.13)
Time squared	.08*	−.03***
	(.04)	(.01)
Constant	−7.31	−3.07
	(4.59)	(2.15)

Note: Robust standard errors clustered by state in parentheses. Significance levels: * .10, ** .05, *** .01 with a two-tailed test.
Δ = change.

Results are shown in table 4. As shown in table 4, ACA support influences gubernatorial announcements, but not state grant activity. More specifically, the model predicts that a state that has the highest level of support for the ACA at time $t-1$ has a probability of announcing the ACA decision that is twenty points higher than states with the lowest level of support for the ACA in the previous year. It is interesting to note that including the public opinion measures does not completely account for the influence of neighboring states on gubernatorial announcements; states are also more likely to announce their decisions if neighboring states have already announced. This suggests the possibility that additional mechanisms of policy diffusion, besides the policy feedback mechanism, may be present. Turning to state-level grant activity, the majority of variables do not have a statistically significant influence. We do find that states with a federal exchange were less likely to apply for grants. Consistent with our expectations, however, public opinion does not influence state-level grant activity.

Overall, our results suggest modest support for the policy learning mechanism of diffusion. While we find that gubernatorial announcements and grant activity exhibit spillover effects that increased support for the ACA in neighboring states, public opinion is only significantly related to gubernatorial announcements in the home state. This generally conforms to our expectations that public opinion matters more for the diffusion of highly visible policy decisions, such as gubernatorial announcements of the ACA, compared to less salient policies, such as state-level grant activity.

Empirically Testing the Opinion Learning Mechanism

To test whether states are responsive to external public opinion on salient issues, as suggested by the opinion learning mechanism, we use directed dyad-quarter event history analysis where the dependent variables reflect increased similarity in policy decisions between two states in a dyad (Gilardi and Füglister 2008: 415). For gubernatorial announcements, we use a dichotomous measure that is coded one if the governor in State A announces that it will adopt the same marketplace that has already been announced by State B's governor in a previous quarter, and zero otherwise. For the time periods after State A has announced its marketplace structure, the dependent variable is set to missing since State A is no longer at risk of moving closer to State B's policy decision. For grant applications, our dependent variable takes a value of one if State A applies for a grant in quarter t that moves it closer to the number of grants that State B has applied for by quarter $t-1$. As with the previous grant application model, there is a possibility for repeated events whereby State A may apply for multiple grants which move its total number of grant applications closer to State B's total number of grant applications. It is important in cases of multiple or repeated events to control for the number of prior events, so we include a count of the previous instances of State A emulating State B's grant activity as suggested by Beck, Katz, and Tucker (1998: 1272).[12]

Dyadic analyses of policy diffusion are at risk for potential "emulation bias" whereby states appear to imitate another state, but, in reality, there is simply a trend for states to adopt the policy (Gilardi and Füglister 2008: 426–27; Boehmke 2009b). As a solution, Boehmke (2009b) suggests that researchers condition on whether states have the opportunity to be influenced by others by removing cases where $\Pr(y_{ijt}=1)=0$. Accordingly, in the gubernatorial announcement models, we exclude observations where State B has not yet declared their marketplace structure. In the grant application models, we exclude cases if State B has never applied for any grants or if State B has applied for the same number or fewer grants than State A.

According to the opinion learning mechanism, policy makers will consider the level of policy support in another state, at least in relation to their own citizens' policy support, when making policy decisions. Therefore, our independent variable of interest is the similarity in public support for the ACA in the dyad. More specifically, we measure the similarity in ACA support by taking the absolute difference between ACA support in State A and ACA support in State B from the previous quarter. We expect policy makers in State A will use ACA preferences in State B when deciding to announce the marketplace structure (*H3*). Since ACA decisions are more salient than grant activity, however, we do not expect to find the same effect for the timing of grant applications.

We also control for several factors that may affect the similarity in state decisions. First, we include measures of similarity in demographic characteristics. Population ratio is the ratio of the larger state in the dyad to the smaller. We also control for the absolute difference in median income between the two states in the dyad, the absolute difference in liberal ideology in the two states,[13] and the absolute difference between the

---

12. Volden (2006) also uses this strategy to control for the repeated nature of this type of dependent variable. As a robustness check, we also separately model the first instance of State A emulating State B's grant application activity, second instance, and so on. These models produce largely similar results.

13. We use Pacheco's (2014) measure of state ideology.

percentages of the population in each state that are uninsured. Same region is a binary measure which captures whether states belong to the same region (1) or not (0). Same party governor is a dichotomous variable which takes the value of one if the governors of both states in the dyad belong to the same political party. We also include a measure of whether State B was in the RWJF state network with the expectation that policy makers may view state network members as well-informed about the ACA and are therefore more likely to make similar decisions.

Last, we have specific controls for each policy decision. In the gubernatorial announcement models, we include a series of dummy variables for State B's marketplace structure. In the grant application models, we include a series of dummy variables for State A's marketplace structure, since states with federal or partnership marketplaces may be less likely to apply for federal funding. States that have previously applied for grants may find it easier to apply in the future, so we include a count of State A's previous grant applications.

Since our dependent variables are dichotomous, we use logistic regression models with standard errors clustered by dyad.[14] To account for a potential change in the baseline hazard across time, we include fixed time effects (e.g., quarter/year dummies).[15]

Results are shown in table 5. As suggested by the opinion learning mechanism, the absolute difference in ACA support is negative and statistically significant in the gubernatorial announcement model. When both states in a dyad have similar policy preferences, State A is more likely to announce the same marketplace structure that State B announced. As expected, the absolute difference in ACA support between two states is not statistically significant for grant activity. For policy decisions that are not as visible to the public, such as applying for federal funding, states do not consider the policy preferences of other states.

Figure 2 shows the predicted probability of State A announcing the same type of marketplace as State B across a range of absolute differences in ACA support.[16] The probability that State A announces the same type of marketplace as State B when citizens of both states have the same level of support for the ACA (the absolute difference = 0) is 0.17. This probability decreases to .05 if the difference in ACA support is large (0.4). These

14. Each pair of states is included twice in each quarter. When we cluster by dyad (not directed-dyad), each cluster includes both pairs of dyads. However, clustering by directed-dyad does not significantly change the results.

15. We also replicated the models using *time*, *time²*, and *time³* as suggested by Carter and Signorino (2010). This does not significantly change the results.

16. All other variables held constant at their mean or modal values.

Table 5 Testing the Opinion Learning Mechanism:
Directed Dyad-Quarter Event History Analysis

	Gubernatorial Announcements ($N = 2,016$)	Grant Applications ($N = 10,541$)
|ACA support (A) – ACA support (B)|$_{(t-1)}$	–3.70**	–.67
	(1.62)	(.89)
Same region	.49***	.04
	(.18)	(.09)
Same party governor	1.46***	.09
	(.18)	(.08)
Same exchange type		–.25***
		(.09)
Population ratio	.02**	–.01**
	(.01)	(.01)
|Median income (A) – median income (B)|	–.00001	.00000
	(.00)	(.00)
|Liberal ideology (A) – liberal ideology (B)|	–5.94***	.99
	(2.30)	(1.12)
|% Uninsured (A) – % uninsured (B)|	.02	–.04***
	(.03)	(.01)
State B in state network	.16	–.08
	(.23)	(.08)
State B partnership exchange	.50	
	(.36)	
State B federal exchange	1.67***	
	(.23)	
State A partnership exchange		–.47***
		(.11)
State A federal exchange		–2.68***
		(.11)
Total number of State A grant applications$_{(t-1)}$		–.10
		(.07)
Total cases of grant learning		.21**
		(.09)
Constant	–1.10***	.49*
	(.42)	(.26)

Note: Robust standard errors clustered by dyad in parentheses. Significance levels: * .10, ** .05, *** .01 with a two-tailed test. Quarter/Year dummies are also included in the model but not shown due to space.
    \| = absolute difference.

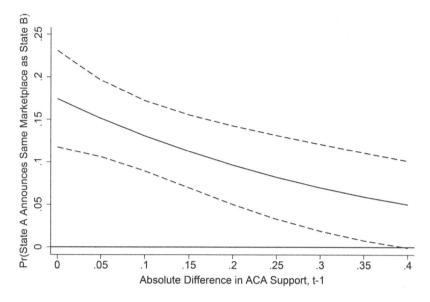

Figure 2 Probabilities that States Make Similar Policy Decisions across Levels of Similarity in Public Opinion: Gubernatorial Announcement of Same Marketplace

findings indicate that states may use similarity in policy preferences as a way to learn about policy decisions, at least for more visible policies.

Other factors also influence a state's decision to pursue similar policy actions. States are more likely to mirror the marketplace structures of other states when governors belong to the same political party. This effect may be unsurprising given the politics surrounding the ACA, but the finding does indicate that policy makers may have looked for partisan cues when making ACA-related decisions. Ideology, population ratio, and the type of marketplace exchange influence similarity in gubernatorial announcements. State similarities in population, and the percentage of uninsured matter for grant activity, and states are less likely to emulate the grant activity of other states with similar marketplace structures. Finally, we find that states with state-federal partnership marketplaces or federal marketplaces are less likely to apply for a grant to move the state closer to State B's grant activity compared to states with state-based marketplaces. This effect is likely due to the fact that states with state-based marketplaces are simply more likely to apply for federal funding. States are also more likely to apply to mirror another state's grant activity if they have previously copied State B's grant activity. This may reflect states' likelihood to apply for multiple grants once they see that other states have successfully applied for several grants.

Conclusion

Our results suggest that public opinion played a modest role in the diffusion of ACA gubernatorial announcements and state-level grant activity. While we find that gubernatorial announcements and grant activity exhibited spillover effects that increased support for the ACA in neighboring states, public opinion is only significantly related to gubernatorial announcements in the home state. Additionally, we find that states are more likely to announce their ACA decisions when other states with similar levels of ACA support take action. This suggests that states may use similarity in policy preferences as a way to learn about policy decisions—at least for more visible policies such as marketplace structures.

   These findings have larger implications for the political process. Research elsewhere suggests that governments react to the decisions of other governments by either learning from the policy experiments of others (Volden 2006) or by gaining an economic advantage over proximate states (Shipan and Volden 2008). Neither explanation places much weight on the influence of ordinary citizens. Our findings suggest that individuals play at least some role in the diffusion of policies—perhaps more so on policies that are highly visible. The influence that policy design and implementation has on policy preferences do not stop at the borders. Instead, policies have the potential to influence individuals elsewhere who may then pressure their own officials to adopt similar designs.

   In addition, we find evidence that state legislators use external shifts in policy support as cues about how to make policy decisions, regardless of the level of saliency. Public opinion then may be a potential lever that advocates use to accelerate the diffusion process—either by actively framing the policy debate in ways that are favorable toward their policy or by advising state legislators about public support in similar states. Future research should consider whether external public opinion monitoring is due to sincere or strategic motives as we discussed above.

   Finally, our results have implications for the future of the ACA. While public support for the ACA is not reacting as positively or as quickly as predicted (Blendon, Benson, and Brulé 2012), the slow movement of support for the ACA nationally may be partially attributed to differences in the timing of state-level decisions. As implementation progresses, however, we should see ACA support increase as components of the ACA continue to exhibit spillover policy effects. Moreover, as residents become more supportive of the ACA and its various components, we might likely see state legislators responding in more expansive ways.

■ ■ ■

Julianna Pacheco is associate professor of political science at the University of Iowa. She received her PhD from Penn State University in 2010 and was a Robert Wood Johnson Health and Society Scholar at the University of Michigan from 2010 to 2012. Her research explores political behavior, public opinion, state and local politics, and health policy. She has published in journal outlets such as the *Journal of Politics, Political Research Quarterly, State Politics and Policy Quarterly, Public Opinion Quarterly*, and *Political Behavior*. She is currently working on a project (with Elizabeth Maltby), funded by the Russell Sage Foundation, on state opinion toward the ACA and policy feedback effects.

Elizabeth Maltby is a PhD candidate in political science at the University of Iowa. Her research explores public policy, racial and ethnic politics, and political behavior in the United States. Her subfields of interest include policy feedback, criminal justice policy, immigration policy, and policy diffusion. Her paper (with Rene Rocha), "New Policy Creates New Politics: How Punitive Outcomes Structure Racial Threat among Latinos and Anglos," received an award for the best paper presented in the Race, Ethnicity, and Politics section of APSA in 2015.

References

Althaus, Frances A., and Stanley K. Henshaw. 1994. "The Effects of Mandatory Delay Laws on Abortion Patients and Providers." *Family Planning Perspectives* 26: 228–33.

Barrilleaux, Charles, and Carlisle Rainey. 2014. "The Politics of Need: Examining Governors' Decisions to Oppose the 'Obamacare' Medicaid Expansion." *State Politics and Policy Quarterly* 14: 437–60.

Beck, Nathaniel, and Jonathan N. Katz. 2011. "Modeling Dynamics in Time-Series-Cross-Section Political Economy Data." *Annual Review of Political Science* 14: 331–52.

Beck, Nathaniel, Jonathan N. Katz, and Richard Tucker. 1998. "Taking Time Seriously: Time-Series-Cross-Section Analysis with a Binary Dependent Variable." *American Journal of Political Science* 42: 1260–88.

Berinsky, Adam J. 1999. "The Two Faces of Public Opinion." *American Journal of Political Science* 43: 1209–30.

Berry, Frances Stokes, and William D. Berry. 1990. "State Lottery Adoptions as Policy Innovations: An Event History Analysis." *American Political Science Review* 84: 395–415.

Berry, Frances Stokes, and William D. Berry. 1992. "Tax Innovation in the States: Capitalizing on Political Opportunity." *American Journal of Political Science* 36: 715–42.

Berry, William, and Brady Baybeck. 2005. "Using Geographic Information Systems to Study Interstate Competition." *American Political Science Review* 99: 505–19.

Berry, William D., Evan J. Ringquist, Richard C. Fording, and Russell L. Hanson. 1998. "Measuring Citizen and Government Ideology in the American States, 1960–93." *American Journal of Political Science* 42: 327–48.

Beyle, Thad L. 2004. "The Governors." In *Politics in the American States*, 8th ed., edited by Virginia Gray, Russell L. Hanson, and Herbert Jacob, 194–231. Washington, DC: CQ.

Blendon, Robert J., John M. Benson, and Amanda Brulé. 2012. "Understanding Health Care in the 2012 Election." *New England Journal of Medicine* 367, no. 17: 1658–61.

Boehmke, Frederick J. 2009a. "Approaches to Modeling the Adoption and Diffusion of Policies with Multiple Components." *State Politics and Policy Quarterly* 9: 229–52.

Boehmke, Frederick J. 2009b. "Policy Emulation or Policy Convergence? Potential Ambiguities in the Dyad Event History Approach to State Policy Emulation." *Journal of Politics* 71, no. 3: 1125–40.

Brace, Paul, Kellie Sims-Butler, Kevin Arceneaux, and Martin Johnson. 2002. "Public Opinion in the American States: New Perspectives Using National Survey Data." *American Journal of Political Science* 46: 173–89.

Brewer, Thomas L. 2003. "The Trade Regime and the Climate Regime: Institutional Evolution and Adaptation." *Climate Policy* 3: 329–41.

Burstein, Paul. 2003. "The Impact of Public Opinion on Public Policy: A Review and An Agenda." *Political Research Quarterly* 56, no. 1: 29–40.

Carter, David B., and Curtis S. Signorino. 2010. "Back to the Future: Modeling Time Dependence in Binary Data." *Political Analysis* 18: 271–92.

CMS (Centers for Medicare and Medicaid Services). n.d. The Center for Consumer Information and Insurance Oversight. "Creating a New Competitive Health Insurance Marketplace." www.cms.gov/CCIIO/Resources/Marketplace-Grants /index.html (accessed on December 18, 2015).

Crowley, Jocelyn Elise. 2004. "When Tokens Matter." *Legislative Studies Quarterly* 29: 109–36.

Erikson, Robert S., Gerald C. Wright, and John P. McIver. 1993. *Statehouse Democracy: Public Opinion and Policy in the American States*. Cambridge: Cambridge University Press.

Erikson, Robert S., Michael B. MacKuen, and James A. Stimson. 2002. *The Macro Polity*. Cambridge: Cambridge University Press.

Geer, John Gray. 1996. *From Tea Leaves to Opinion Polls: A Theory of Democratic Leadership*. New York: Columbia University Press.

Gelman, Andrew, and Thomas C. Little. 1997. "Poststratification into Many Categories Using Hierarchical Logistic Regression." *Survey Methodology* 23, no. 2: 127–35.

Gilardi, Fabrizio, and Katharina Füglister. 2008. "Empirical Modeling of Policy Diffusion in Federal States: The Dyadic Approach." *Swiss Political Science Review* 14: 413–50.

Gollust, Sarah E., Colleen L. Barry, Jeff Niederdeppe, Laura Baum, and Erika Franklin Fowler. 2014. "First Impressions: Geographic Variation in Media Messages during the First Phase of ACA Implementation." *Journal of Health Politics, Policy and Law* 39: 1253–62.

Graham, Erin R., Charles R. Shipan, and Craig Volden. 2013. "The Diffusion of Policy Diffusion Research in Political Science." *British Journal of Political Science* 43: 673–701.

Gray, Virginia, David Lowery, and Erik K. Godwin. 2007. "The Political Management of Managed Care: Explaining Variations in State Health Maintenance Organization Regulations." *Journal of Health Politics, Policy and Law* 32: 457–95.

Greer, Scott L. 2011. "The States' Role under the Patient Protection and Affordable Care Act." *Journal of Health Politics, Policy and Law* 36: 469–73.

Hill, Kim Quaile, Jan E. Leighley, and Angela Hinton-Andersson. 1995. "Lower-Class Mobilization and Policy Linkage in the U.S. States." *American Journal of Political Science* 39: 75–86.

Hyland, Andrew, Cheryl Higbee, Qiang Li, Joseph E. Bauer, Gary A. Giovino, Terry Alford, and K. Michael Cummings. 2005. "Access to Low-Taxed Cigarettes Deters Smoking Cessation Attempts." *American Journal of Public Health* 95: 994.

Jacobs, Lawrence R., and Robert Y. Shapiro. 2000. *Politicians Don't Pander: Political Manipulation and the Loss of Democratic Responsiveness.* Chicago: University of Chicago Press.

Jacobs, Lawrence R., and Theda Skocpol. 2012. *Health Care Reform and American Politics: What Everyone Needs to Know.* New York: Oxford University Press.

Jones, David K., Katharine W. V. Bradley, and Jonathan Oberlander. 2014. "Pascal's Wager: Health Insurance Exchanges, Obamacare, and the Republican Dilemma." *Journal of Health Politics, Policy and Law* 39: 97–137.

KFF (Kaiser Family Foundation). 2013. "State Marketplace Profiles." kff.org/health-reform/state-profile/state-exchange-profiles.

KFF (Kaiser Family Foundation). 2015. "Kaiser Family Foundation Poll: January 2010–January 2015" (dataset). Princeton Survey Research Associates International (producer). Storrs, CT: Roper Center for Public Opinion Research, RoperExpress (distributor).

Konisky, David M. 2007. "Regulatory Competition and Environmental Enforcement: Is There a Race to the Bottom?" *American Journal of Political Science* 51: 853–72.

Lax, Jeffrey R., and Justin H. Phillips. 2009. "How Should We Estimate Public Opinion in the States?" *American Journal of Political Science* 53: 107–21.

Lax, Jeffrey R., and Justin H. Phillips. 2012. "The Democratic Deficit in the States." *American Journal of Political Science* 56: 148–66.

Manza, Jeff, and Fay Lomax Cook. 2002. "A Democratic Polity? Three Views of Policy Responsiveness to Public Opinion in the United States." *American Politics Research* 30: 630–67.

Matsusaka, John G. 2001. "Problems with a Methodology Used to Evaluate the Voter Initiative." *Journal of Politics* 63: 1250–56.

Mooney, Christopher Z., and Mei-Hsien Lee. 2000. "The Influence of Values on Consensus and Contentious Morality Policy: U.S. Death Penalty Reform, 1965–82." *Journal of Politics* 62: 223–39.

Morehouse, Sarah M., and Malcolm E. Jewell. 2004. "States as Laboratories: A Reprise." *Annual Review of Political Science* 7: 177–203.

Nicholson-Crotty, Sean. 2009. "The Politics of Diffusion: Public Policy in the American States." *Journal of Politics* 71: 192–205.

Pacheco, Julianna. 2011. "Using National Surveys to Measure State Public Opinion over Time: A Guideline for Scholars and an Application." *State Politics and Policy Quarterly* 11, no. 4: 415–39.

Pacheco, Julianna. 2012. "The Social Contagion Model: Exploring the Role of Public Opinion on the Diffusion of Antismoking Legislation across the American States." *Journal of Politics* 74: 714–34.

Pacheco, Julianna. 2013. "The Thermostatic Model of Responsiveness in the American States." *State Politics and Policy Quarterly* 13, no. 3: 306–32.

Pacheco, Julianna. 2014. "Measuring and Evaluating Changes in State Opinion across Eight Issues." *American Politics Research* 42: 986–1009.

Park, David K., Andrew Gelman, and Joseph Bafumi. 2004. "Bayesian Multilevel Estimation with Poststratification: State-Level Estimates from National Polls." *Political Analysis* 12: 375–85.

Park, David K., Andrew Gelman, and Joseph Bafumi. 2006. "State-Level Opinions from National Surveys: Poststratification Using Mulitilevel Logistic Regression." In *Public Opinion in State Politics*, edited by Jeffrey E. Cohen, 209–28. Stanford, CA: Stanford University Press.

Plutzer, Eric and Michael B. Berkman. 2005. "The Graying of America and Support for Funding the Nation's Schools." *Public Opinion Quarterly* 69: 66–86.

Rigby, Elizabeth. 2012. "State Resistance to 'Obamacare.'" *Forum* 10, no. 2: 1–16.

Rosenthal, Alan. 1990. *Governors and Legislatures: Contending Powers*. Washington, DC: CQ.

RWJF (Robert Wood Johnson Foundation). n.d. "About State Network." state-network.org/about/ (accessed November 21, 2016).

Shipan, Charles and Craig Volden. 2008. "The Mechanisms of Policy Diffusion." *American Journal of Political Science* 52, no. 4: 840–57.

Soss, Joe. 1999. "Lessons of Welfare: Policy Design, Political Learning, and Political Action." *American Political Science Review* 93: 363–80.

Soss, Joe, and Sanford F. Schram. 2007. "A Public Transformed? Welfare Reform as Policy Feedback." *American Political Science Review* 101: 111–27.

Taylor, Jami K., Daniel C. Lewis, Matthew L. Jacobsmeier, and Brian DiSarro. 2012. "Content and Complexity in Policy Reinvention and Diffusion: Gay and

Transgender–Inclusive Laws against Discrimination." *State Politics and Policy Quarterly* 12: 75–98.

Volden, Craig. 2006. "States as Policy Laboratories: Emulating Success in the Children's Health Insurance Program." *American Journal of Political Science* 50: 294–312.

Walker, Jack L. 1969. "The Diffusion of Innovations among the American States." *American Political Science Review* 63: 880–99.

Warshaw, Christopher, and Jonathan Rodden. 2012. "How Should We Measure District-Level Public Opinion on Individual Issues?" *Journal of Politics* 74: 203–19.

Weaver, R. Kent. 2000. *Ending Welfare as We Know It?* Washington, DC: Brookings Institution.

Zukin, Cliff, and Robin Snyder. 1984. "Passive Learning: When the Media Environment is the Message." *Public Opinion Quarterly* 48: 629–38.

Appendix A The Role of Public Opinion—Does it Influence The Diffusion of ACA Decisions? Multilevel Regression and Post-stratification (MRP)

To estimate state opinion toward the ACA, we will rely on multilevel modeling, imputation, and post-stratification (referred to as MRP) developed by Gelman and Little (1997) and extended by Park et al. (2004; 2006). MRP produces accurate estimates of public opinion by state (Lax and Phillips 2009) and congressional district (Warshaw and Rodden 2012) and over time (Pacheco 2011; 2013).

MRP can be divided into three steps: (1) estimation of a multilevel regression with predictors; (2) imputation; and (3) post-stratification (see also Park et al. 2004, 2006; Lax and Phillips 2009). We begin with a multilevel model to estimate opinion for individuals given demographic and geographic characteristics. Individual responses are explicitly modeled as nested within states and state-level effects capture residual differences. I model survey responses as a function of gender, race, age, education, region, state, and state presidential vote share. These are standard predictors of MRP and perform quite well (Lax and Phillips 2009).

The next step is imputation. We define each combination of demographic and geographic characteristics (for instance, a non-black female, aged 18–29, with a high school degree from Connecticut) as a "person-type." Each of the 3,264 person-types has an associated probability of supporting a particular policy, which is modeled in the multilevel regression as a function of individual and state covariates. Imputation is conducted on each person-type even if absent from the sample.

The final stage is post-stratification. Post-stratification corrects for differences between state samples and state populations by weighting the predicted values of each person-type in each state by actual census counts of that person-type in a state. We use the population frequencies obtained from the public-use micro data samples in 2010 supplied by the census bureau for post-stratification. The imputed opinion of each person-type is then weighted by the corresponding population frequencies. In the final step, we calculate the average response over each person-type in each state and summarize to get point predictions and uncertainty intervals.

Adding a Time Component

We add a time component by pooling surveys across a small time frame; in the example below, we use a three-quarter moving average to estimate quarterly opinion toward the ACA. For instance, to get point estimates for Q1 in 2011 using a three-quarter pooled window, we combine estimates from Q4 in 2010, Q1 in 2011, and Q2 in 2011 and then perform the MRP technique on this pooled dataset. The MRP process is repeated for each quarter after moving the time frame up a quarter at a time. By pooling and taking the median estimate, the first and last quarters are missing. Pacheco shows that while there is a tradeoff between the reliability of estimates and sensitivity to very short-term shocks, the efficiency benefits of pooling over a small time period outweigh the costs of biasedness.

The use of multilevel modeling and post-stratification overcomes two major problems that arise when trying to measure state opinion from national surveys. Multilevel modeling increases the reliability of less populous states via "shrinkage towards the mean." Indeed the MRP approach has been shown to be superior to the aggregation method in terms of reliability, particularly when sample sizes are small, for instance, when N is less than 2,800 across all states (Lax and Phillips 2009). Post-stratification corrects for nonrepresentativeness due to sampling designs by adjusting estimates so that they are more representative of state populations.

Validity Check

State opinions toward the ACA, if valid as we have measured them, should correlate with other variables that attempt to measure the same concept. There are two state surveys that asked residents about ACA favorability (see Appendix A.2): The Kentucky Health Issues Poll (KHIP) 2010–2014 and the Ohio Health Issues Poll (OHIP) 2011. Both surveys were conducted by the Institute for Policy Research at the University of Cincinnati and funded by the Foundation for a Healthy Kentucky and the Healthy Foundation of Greater Cincinnati.[1] When used with proper weights, aggregate estimates from KHIP and OHIP are representative of state populations. A key difference between the KFF polls and KHIP and OHIP is that the latter are yearly surveys, while the estimates from KFF shown in Figure 1 are quarterly. Additionally, recall that our estimates are based off a small moving average, which introduces additional error, albeit to improve reliability. Given this, it would be unlikely for our estimates to correspond exactly with measures from KHIP or OHIP. Nonetheless, we

---

1. The sample size for KHIP varies across time, but averages around 1,500 with statewide estimates being accurate to plus/minus 2.5 percent. See www.healthy-ky.org for more information. The sample size for the 2011 OHIP survey is 908; statewide estimates will be accurate to plus/minus 3.3 percent. For more information, see www.healthyfoundation.org/ohip.html.

can still get a sense of how well MRP performs by comparing my estimates with those obtained from KHIP and OHIP.

Appendix A.2 shows the percentage of Kentucky/Ohio residents who support the ACA according to KHIP/OHIP compared to the MRP estimates. While the MRP estimates are not exactly the same as those from KHIP or OHIP, there are substantial similarities. Moreover, the correlation between the MRP estimates and the estimates from KHIP is a healthy .92, if the most dissimilar estimate in 2010 is excluded. If anything, MRP seems to underestimate shifts in opinion toward the ACA in Kentucky, no doubt due to the multilevel regression that pulls state averages toward the national mean in order to increase reliability. This suggests that it will be more difficult to obtain statistical significance in dynamic analyses that use these estimates, providing a more stringent test of the hypotheses outlined in the article.

Appendix A.1

Question Text from Kaiser Family Foundation Surveys

Topic	Question Text	Dates Available
ACA Favorability	As you may know, a health reform bill was signed into law in 2010. Given what you know about the health reform law, do you have a generally favorable or generally unfavorable opinion of it?	monthly from 1/10–12/10[1], monthly 2/11–11/12[2], monthly 2/13–4/13, 6/13, monthly 8/13–8/14, monthly 10/14–1/15

[1]From 1/10–3/10, the survey read: "As of right now, do you generally support or generally oppose the health care proposals being discussed in Congress? Is that strongly support or somewhat support?" From 4/10–12/10, the survey read: "As you may know, a health reform bill was signed into law earlier this year. Given what you know about the health reform law, do you have a generally favorable or generally unfavorable opinion of it?"

[2]From 2/11–12/11, the survey read "As you may know, a health reform bill was signed into law early last year. Given what you know about the health reform law, do you have a generally favorable or generally unfavorable opinion of it?"

Appendix A.2

Percentage of Residents Favoring the ACA in Kentucky and Ohio

	2010	2011	2012	2013	2014
KHIP	36	47	41	39	49
	(33.5, 38.5)	(44.5, 49.5)	(38.5, 43.5)	(36.5, 41.5)	(46.5, 51.5)
MRP	45	43	40	39	42
	(43.1, 47.6)	(42.0, 43.5)	(38.3, 40.6)	(36.6, 41.7)	(41.5, 43.3)

	2010	2011	2012	2013	2014
OHIP		36			
		(32.6, 39.4)			
MRP	49	44	45	42	40
	(47.5, 50.4)	(42.6, 45.3)	(43.2, 46.6)	(39.7, 44.7)	(39.5, 41.1)

Framing, Engagement, and Policy Change: Lessons for the ACA

Andrew Karch
University of Minnesota

Aaron Rosenthal
University of Minnesota

Abstract Supporters of the Patient Protection and Affordable Care Act (ACA) sometimes speculate that public attitudes toward the law will shift if proponents succeed in focusing attention on its more popular components, but the scholarly literature on framing effects provides ample reason to question their assertion. This article contends that engagement, an alternative rhetorical strategy where advocates address the same policy dimensions as their opponents, is a more promising approach. Extending the engagement literature to the elite context in which most ACA-related decisions are made, it argues that elite-level engagement necessitates the additional task of linking policy change to opponents' broader philosophical and policy goals. Current debates surrounding the application of sales taxes to electronic commerce—a policy arena that seems far removed from health care policy but overlaps with the ACA in ways that make it an appropriate source of lesson drawing—illustrate the potential of an engagement strategy. Recently, many conservative lawmakers who previously opposed policy change have instead embraced online sales taxes as a mechanism for additional tax cuts. Analogous connections may facilitate the diffusion of ACA provisions that presently receive hostile receptions in Republican-leaning states.

Keywords policy diffusion, health care reform, rhetorical strategies

Public attitudes toward the Patient Protection and Affordable Care Act (ACA) epitomize the partisan polarization that characterizes contemporary American politics. Opinions of the law vary sharply by party, with most Democrats reporting a favorable view and most Republicans reporting an unfavorable view (DiJulio, Firth, and Brodie 2015). Dig a little deeper, however, and interesting patterns emerge. For instance, several provisions

Journal of Health Politics, Policy and Law, Vol. 42, No. 2, April 2017
DOI 10.1215/03616878-3766746 © 2017 by Duke University Press

of the ACA have received consistent majority support even though Americans remain divided in their general opinions. This pattern has led some ACA supporters to speculate that public attitudes may shift in a positive direction if the appealing features of the law are emphasized. In a recent interview with the *Washington Post*, for example, US Secretary of Health and Human Services Sylvia Burwell pledged to work harder to help Americans understand the ACA's many provisions, noting that "Obamacare isn't connected to the actual substance [of the law]" (Sun 2015). Stronger public support, in turn, might facilitate the diffusion of the ACA, leading to the widespread adoption of its more controversial provisions.

The strategy of emphasizing certain features of the ACA and downplaying others resonates with the scholarly literature on *framing effects*. Framing can affect public attitudes toward health care; experimental studies suggest that support for universal access depends partly on the extent to which appeals emphasize the individual behavioral causes of illness versus biological or systemic factors (Gollust and Lynch 2011). Are framing effects powerful enough to spur policy change, however? There is reason to be skeptical. Public policies often do not correspond to majority opinion, and the groups to whom elected officials are most responsive tend not to alter their views in response to shifting frames.

In contrast, advocates of policy change can pursue a different rhetorical strategy called *engagement* in which they focus on their opponents' considerations (Jerit 2008). Engagement implies that, rather than talking past one another using competing frames, competitors will converge on the same dimension. Existing research on engagement focuses on electoral campaigns and mass publics, however, and offers little insight into how this strategy may work in the elite setting in which most ACA-related decisions are made. In this article, we apply the engagement framework to elite-level communications, arguing that policy change is unlikely to occur if decision makers focus on the same consideration but offer competing claims. Instead, our notion of engagement implies an additional rhetorical task. Advocates must address their opponents' concerns *and* explain how their proposal helps opponents achieve their broader philosophical and policy goals. In the context of the ACA, this formidable task involves linking health care reform to Republican objectives such as cutting taxes or expanding the role of the private sector in government programs.

The main objective of this article is to evaluate the strengths and limitations of framing and engagement, applying these lessons to health care reform. Under what conditions will a framing strategy or an engagement strategy facilitate the diffusion of the ACA, and what can advocates do to take advantage of these windows of opportunity? After reviewing existing research on framing effects and engagement, it turns to a substantive policy arena—the application of sales taxes to electronic commerce—that seems far removed from health care policy but overlaps in ways that make it a good source of lesson drawing. Recent developments suggest that an engagement strategy is more likely to overcome the current hurdles to ACA diffusion. While engagement is certainly no cure-all for the partisan polarization that has enveloped health care reform, it may nevertheless prove to be a way for advocates to facilitate the widespread adoption of some of the law's components.

Opinion Change and Policy Change

Political issues, and the policy solutions that address them, can be viewed through many lenses. Policies are inherently multidimensional, serving several purposes and invoking many considerations. Public opinion scholars leverage this multidimensionality to study framing effects, which "occur when (often small) changes in the presentation of an issue or event produce (sometimes large) changes of opinion" (Chong and Druckman 2007: 104). Framing can "suggest how politics should be thought about, thereby encouraging citizens to understand events and issues in particular ways" (Kinder 2007: 156). Is the goal of education policy to promote economic development or equality of opportunity? Is abortion policy about women's rights, social justice, or protecting human life? Framing directs attention toward certain aspects of an issue and away from others, affecting how problems are defined, causes are diagnosed, moral judgments are reached, and remedies are identified (Entman 1993: 52).

Sometimes framing affects public attitudes. A common illustration of its power is the wide discrepancy between support for programs that assist the poor and support for "welfare" (Rasinski 1989). Legislative entrepreneurs and other stakeholders therefore invest considerable energy in developing frames that have the greatest impact on the "audience whose support they see as vital to bringing about their preferred outcomes" (Jones 1994: 195). Their ultimate objective is to shift the terms of debate onto favorable terrain, such that they are more likely to achieve their policy goals. For ACA supporters, research on framing effects suggests that they might generate stronger public support for the law by emphasizing its most popular components.

Most framing research assesses whether and how individuals' attitudes change in response to messages from politicians, media outlets, interest groups, and other elite sources. These studies use a "situational framing" approach (Jacobs and Mettler 2011), relying on experimental research designs during which subjects are exposed to varying frames. This approach greatly enhances our understanding of the psychological processes through which individuals form opinions about policy issues. Implicit in many individual-level studies of framing effects, however, is the bolder claim that framing-induced shifts in public attitudes also generate concomitant shifts in public policy. Some analysts make this assumption explicit. Based on experimental evidence, for instance, a recent study concludes that "advocates and public officials who frame children's issues in economic terms are likely to enjoy greater political success than those who do not" (Gormley 2012: 98).

Such definitive statements overstate the influence of framing effects on policy outcomes, partly because framing is an inherently competitive process (Chong and Druckman 2013). Elites generally lack control over the information that reaches the public, and citizens receive multiple and competing messages. Policy entrepreneurs can try to direct public attention toward certain considerations, but their opponents may emphasize a different set of arguments, images, and frames. As a result, the two sides might "talk past" one another by focusing on entirely different considerations. This is an important shortcoming of relying on laboratory settings to investigate framing effects: "By ensuring that frames reach their intended audience, experiments may exaggerate their power" (Kinder 2007: 157).

Moreover, two scholarly literatures offer reason to question whether framing effects spur policy change. The first is the extensive scholarly literature on democratic responsiveness. Most studies that find a correspondence between public opinion and public policy in the United States rely on highly aggregated measures of Americans' preferences (Stimson, MacKuen, and Erikson 1995). The subtle changes investigated in individual-level research on framing may not translate into system-level change. In addition, several recent studies demonstrate that government policy does not always correspond to public opinion. Lax and Phillips (2012) identify a "democratic deficit" in the states, finding that policy is consistent with majority will only half the time. Similarly, national policies and senatorial votes are more responsive to the views of the affluent and the organized than the preferences of the majority of Americans (Bartels 2008; Gilens and Page 2014). Importantly, the affluent tend to have more informed and consistent attitudes on political subjects (Delli Carpini and Keeter 1997). Framing effects therefore seem unlikely to alter the relatively crystallized views of the groups to whom elected officials are most responsive.

Indeed, the second research tradition that casts doubt on the potential connection between frames and policy decisions is, ironically, the literature on framing effects. Translating public opinion into policy outputs typically occurs in legislatures, lawmaking bodies that determine the timing and content of policy change. Legislators use distinct rhetorical strategies to shape the relevant lines of conflict (Mucciaroni 2011; Ferraiolo 2013). However, cataloging competing frames is not the same as demonstrating that the prominence of a particular frame has an independent effect on policy outcomes. In an era of partisan polarization, where even local officials' willingness to gather information about new policies is shaped by their ideological proclivities (Butler et al. 2015), it seems unlikely that rhetorical sparring will alter elite views on controversial topics such as health care. If key decision makers are impervious to framing effects, we should be circumspect about their causal force. As Jacobs and Mettler (2011: 926) explain, "Individuals who have experience or training related to the area of debate or are strongly motivated by its subject are less susceptible to framing." This caveat seems especially likely to apply to the officials who ultimately make the policy decisions in which we are interested.

In light of the preceding concerns, advocates of policy change may rely on an alternative rhetorical strategy known as *engagement*. Whereas framing suggests that competitors highlight what they view as favorable issues and avoid those emphasized by their rivals, engagement leads advocates to focus on the considerations of their opponents (Jerit 2008). In short, framing implies avoidance and engagement implies overlap. Recent research on elections illustrates the significance of this distinction, as competing parties and candidates tend to converge on the same issues (Sigelman and Buell 2004; Sides 2006; Green-Pedersen and Mortensen 2015). An identical dynamic can occur during policy discussions. In a study of the early 1990s health care reform debate, Jerit (2008) finds that proponents of policy change received increased public support when they engaged their opponents in a dialogue.

Engagement may be an especially appealing rhetorical strategy in a legislative setting where most protagonists are familiar with the arguments for and against certain courses of action. It may take a distinct form at the elite level, however. While there are exceptions, many contemporary policy debates pit Democrats and Republicans against each other. As a result, engagement efforts typically target partisan opponents. Well-informed elites are unlikely to be convinced by a clever reframing of an issue, and simply talking about the same considerations probably will not be sufficient to win them over. If supporters and opponents of policy change focus on the same dimension of the debate but make incompatible claims, the underlying impasse is liable to persist.

Advocates' success therefore may depend on their ability both to engage their opponents on the same dimension *and* link their preferred course of action to opponents' other goals. Those who want to alter the policy status quo must complete two rhetorical tasks. In addition to advancing their own claims, they also must defend their proposal against attack (Riker 1996). One way to defuse opposition is to convince skeptics that the proposal will allow them to achieve their broader objectives.[1] Individuals can support the same policy for different reasons, and building diverse coalitions is crucial in a legislative context. Thus, by redirecting the study of engagement from efforts to sway mass opinion to the study of elite-to-elite communication, it becomes necessary to identify instances of, and evaluate the impact of, a specific type of rhetorical claim. The empirical implication of the preceding discussion is that partisan logjams can be broken, contributing to policy change, when advocates engage their opponents on the same dimension and demonstrate that the proposal aligns with opponents' overarching ideals.

In the next section of this article, we turn to a policy arena—sales taxes and electronic commerce—where advocates confronted a political context similar to the one currently faced by ACA supporters. Frustrated by a lack of progress, supporters of applying sales taxes to online purchases had to decide whether and how to alter their rhetorical approach. Based on an overview of recent developments, we argue that they used engagement to try to achieve their goals. They linked their preferred solution to their opponents' larger objectives to try to broaden their coalition, or at least to encourage their rivals to fight change less vociferously. In addition to illustrating how an elite-level engagement strategy can operate, we assess the conditions under which it can facilitate policy change. Our evaluation of engagement's strengths and limitations offers valuable lessons for ACA supporters.

Sales Taxes and Electronic Commerce: Framing, Engagement, and Policy Change

In 2012 state governments collected $242.7 billion in general sales and gross receipts tax revenue and the average state depended on this source for

---

1. The engagement dynamic resonates with a growing social psychology literature on "moral framing" which suggests that framing efforts will be more persuasive if they connect to the moral foundations of their target audience (Day et al. 2014; Feinberg and Willer 2015; Wolsko, Ariceaga, and Seiden 2016).

30.5 percent of its total tax collections (O'Sullivan et al. 2013). However, this funding stream is at risk due to the rise of electronic commerce, the buying and selling of goods and services over the Internet. Online retail sales grew from $15 billion in 1999 (0.5 percent of all retail sales) to $261 billion in 2013 (5.8 percent).[2] The Supreme Court has ruled that state governments can only require out-of-state sellers to collect sales taxes if there is a "nexus" between the state and the remote vendor. Its 1992 decision in *Quill Corporation v. North Dakota* (504 U.S. 298 [1992]) made it possible for the states to begin asking Congress to allow them to collect sales taxes on online transactions (Nugent 2009; Lunder and Pettit 2013), but Congress has not acted. As a result, local vendors have to collect sales taxes for the state at the point of sale, but Internet retailers do not. Online purchasers are responsible for paying the tax, but compliance is low and enforcement is essentially nonexistent. Some analysts argue that e-commerce therefore "heralds some of the most difficult challenges ever to state taxing authority" (Scheppach and Shafroth 2008: 63).

State officials have responded to these challenges in several ways, both lobbying Congress and taking independent action. Twenty-three states are full members of the Streamlined Sales and Use Tax Agreement (SSUTA), an interstate compact that seeks to simplify, modernize, and synchronize state sales tax laws "so all types of vendors—from traditional retailers to those conducting trade over the Internet—could easily collect and remit sales taxes" (Maguire 2013: 9). Nineteen states have adopted "click through" laws,[3] which require local affiliates of online retailers to collect sales taxes on the transactions that they facilitate.[4] Several states negotiated deals with Amazon that require the online retailer to collect sales taxes (CanagaRetna 2012). Traditional "brick-and-mortar" retailers support these efforts. Working through professional associations such as the Retail Industry Leaders Association (RILA) and alliances such as the Marketplace Fairness Coalition, they argue that failing to collect sales taxes on online purchases effectively subsidizes online-only retailers.

Today, there is greater openness to the idea that state governments should be permitted to collect sales taxes on electronic commerce than there was

2. The US Census Bureau publishes an annual report that estimates e-commerce activity in key sectors of the economy. Called "E-Stats," the reports are available at www.census.gov/estats.
    3. The list of nineteen states can be found at trustfile.avalara.com/blog/which-states-collect -sales-tax-for-click-through-nexus/.
    4. The term "local affiliate" refers to individuals or businesses that pass customers onto online retailers like Amazon through their own websites. When the customer makes a purchase, the affiliate earns a referral fee or percentage of the sale. For one example, see affiliate-program .amazon.com/.

when the issue first emerged in the 1990s. At both the state and national levels, however, advocates confront a partisan divide that has caused their progress to stall (Karch and Rosenthal 2016). Many Democrats support initiatives to alter the status quo, but Republican support is mixed. This split is evident in the congressional trajectory of the Marketplace Fairness Act of 2013, which was endorsed by the Democrat-controlled Senate in a 69–27 vote[5] but made virtually no progress in the Republican-controlled House. It is also evident at the state level. The pace at which states have joined the SSUTA and adopted click-through laws has slowed, and many holdouts are under Republican control.[6]

Of course, there are several significant differences between the ACA and online sales taxation that prevent these cases from being equivalent. The ACA is a historically large social welfare expansion, the object of a heated national partisan debate, one of the most redistributive policies in generations, and a signature part of President Barack Obama's legacy. In contrast, electronic commerce has received far less attention from elected officials and the media, and it will undoubtedly have comparatively less powerful effects on the country. While electronic commerce lacks the political salience and economic impact of the ACA, however, the partisan dynamics described above suggest important areas of overlap. A partisan divide influences state policy choices about sales taxes and electronic commerce, just as partisanship affects state health care reform decisions (Jacobs and Callaghan 2013; Rigby and Haselswerdt 2013; Jones, Bradley, and Oberlander 2014). Indeed, many states that have not taken action on e-commerce have neither embraced the Medicaid expansion nor developed a state-level exchange.[7] This partisan split helps explain the speed of adoptions in the two policy areas, another key similarity. In both contexts, a large number of states embraced policy change immediately and then the pace of adoptions slowed to a trickle. Consider the SSUTA, which thirteen states joined when it came online in 2005. Only three states, all with Republican governors, joined the compact between 2011 and 2013.

5. Of the fifty-three members of the Democratic caucus who voted, forty-eight supported the Marketplace Fairness Act; only twenty-one of forty-three Republicans voted for it.

6. An event history analysis of the fourteen adoptions that occurred through 2013 confirms that, all else equal, Republican-led states are less likely to adopt a click through law. The results of this analysis are available on request.

7. For instance, seven states (Alabama, Florida, Idaho, Mississippi, South Carolina, Texas, and Virginia) have not joined the SSUTA, adopted a click through law, or endorsed the Medicaid expansion. This comparison should not be taken too far, however, since many ardent opponents of e-commerce taxation come from states that lack a sales tax (Alaska, Delaware, Montana, New Hampshire, and Oregon).

Similarly, only two of the five most recent states to adopt the Medicaid expansion had a Democratic governor. Most important for the purposes of this article, in both contexts advocates of policy change attempted to generate additional Republican support by trying to shift policy discussions onto more favorable terrain. Many ACA proponents have argued that framing can accomplish this task, but during the e-commerce debate advocates have used both framing and engagement strategies. By comparing the relative efficacy of these efforts, we can illuminate the prospects for similar ACA-related campaigns. We must be circumspect in interpreting our results given the important differences between the two policies. However, we believe that these differences do not outweigh the benefits we gain from using the electronic commerce taxation debate as an analytical tool for contemplating the future of the ACA.

In addition to offering potential lessons for proponents of health care reform, our examination of the e-commerce taxation debate has broader implications for the study of policy diffusion. Diffusion research tends to emphasize various background conditions that make adoption more or less likely, an approach that says relatively little about the public elected officials who make the decisions in which we are interested. Turning to the rhetorical strategies embraced by supporters and opponents of a specific reform therefore points the study of diffusion in a new and potentially constructive direction. Not only is it possible to examine the geographic spread of the rhetorical strategies themselves; it also becomes possible to assess whether, how, and under what conditions these strategies facilitate the consideration or even the adoption of policy innovations in jurisdictions that seem like unfavorable political terrain.

Our e-commerce case study draws on numerous qualitative data sources, including interest group publications, congressional testimony, national and state media coverage, and interviews with interest group officials, state lawmakers, and state-level bureaucrats. This triangulation strategy ensures greater internal validity by enabling us to identify idiosyncratic statements and giving us greater confidence in our conclusions (Yin 1989).

E-Commerce and Framing Effects

The first serious congressional foray into Internet-related tax policy led to passage of the Internet Tax Freedom Act (ITFA) in 1998. The ITFA established a three-year moratorium during which state and local governments could not impose "multiple or discriminatory taxes on electronic commerce," meaning consumers could not be taxed specifically for purchasing goods online.[8] State and local governments also could not levy new taxes on Internet access. During congressional hearings on the ITFA, proponents of online sales taxation argued that it did not represent a new tax but rather was the collection of a tax that was already due.[9] ITFA supporters nonetheless claimed that they were preventing a tax hike. As an interest group official explained, "Early on, the biggest argument and the easiest argument for [online sales tax opponents] to make . . . was to say this is a tax increase."[10]

The ITFA passed with strong bipartisan support,[11] leading to frustration among state-level bureaucrats and elected officials. Their disappointment eventually led to the creation of the Streamlined Sales Tax Project (SSTP) in March 2000, when forty-three states came together in an attempt to simplify their sales tax laws so that online sales taxes could be remitted more easily. In 2001, forty-two governors sent Congress a letter that invoked arguments about fairness in pressing for policy change. They argued that national officials would end the moratorium if they cared "about a level playing field for Main Street retail businesses" (Geewax 2001).[12]

The fairness frame has been ubiquitous since the 1990s, with supporters of policy change arguing that the status quo unfairly disadvantages brick-and-mortar retailers. Its prominence is reflected in the titles of congressional bills such as the Sales Tax Fairness and Simplification Act of 2005 and the Marketplace Fairness Act of 2015. Moreover, the rhetorical debate surrounding this issue has featured a contest between a fairness frame and a tax increase frame, as media coverage illustrates. When Oklahoma debated whether to collect an online sales tax in 2003, supporters said "it would level the playing field between local businesses and Internet retailers" (Carter 2003). A 2005 editorial in the *New York Times* argued that an online sales tax "would also help level the playing field between local and online retailers," while acknowledging that opponents would claim that "sales taxes online . . . represent a tax increase" (*New York Times* 2005). In 2009,

8. There is a common misperception that the law prevents state and local governments from taxing online sales, but it does not (Lunder and Pettit 2013).

9. U.S. Senate, Subcommittee on Communications of the Committee on Commerce, Science, and Transportation, *S. 442, Internet Tax Freedom Act*, 105th Cong., 1st sess. (1997), p. 34.

10. Interview with interest group official, October 9, 2015.

11. The House version passed by voice vote, while the Senate version passed on a 96–2 vote.

12. The widespread reach of the SSTP and the gubernatorial letter should be interpreted as evidence of state officials' efforts to grapple with a new issue. It does not imply that more than forty states supported collecting sales taxes on online purchases.

supporters of an online sales tax in Wisconsin argued that their efforts would bring "more fairness to the state's tax code" by putting "Wisconsin small business on a level playing field with out-of-state Internet sellers." Meanwhile, Republicans in the state voiced their opposition by stating that it was "not the time for tax increases" (Lindquist 2009). Nearly all our interviewees emphasized the persistence and centrality of the fairness frame. An elected official who has worked on the issue for twelve years explained, "The argument for [collecting online sales tax] is fairness. . . . That is the argument I've been using the entire time."[13]

The preceding description of the e-commerce debate resonates with the theoretical underpinnings of the framing literature. Proponents emphasized a fairness frame to justify change, while opponents responded with a tax increase frame. This lack of convergence is exactly what framing scholars would expect (Riker 1996). However, framing falls short as an explanation of recent policy change, especially in Republican-led states. Republican governors have led the last three states to join the SSUTA, and other conservative leaders have argued that Congress should allow states to collect sales taxes on online purchases. The ubiquity and stability of the "fairness" versus "tax increase" debate cannot account for the growing openness of Republican leaders to altering the status quo. That is to say, the frames have not changed, but the outcomes have—at least somewhat. As the next subsection explains, this shift is better explained by analyzing how proponents used engagement to attempt to win conservative allies.

Elite Engagement and Policy Change

Engagement occurs when competitors debate the same policy dimension rather than focusing on different concerns. When engagement is used to persuade mass publics, the primary arena in which its impact has been assessed, the two sides can treat the same dimension differently. In her analysis of President Clinton's Health Security Act, Jerit (2008: 18) provides an example along the dimension of complexity. Opponents claimed the proposal was too complex, while proponents argued that it was straightforward and efficient. In this particular example, one still sees competitors "talking past" each other in a way that resonates with the framing literature.

When elites communicate with each other, engagement requires more than simply addressing the same issue dimension. Building on the previous example, legislators who believe a proposal is too complex will almost

---

13. Interview with elected official, August 25, 2015.

assuredly not change their mind because a partisan opponent tells them that it is actually straightforward and efficient, particularly in an era of partisan polarization. However, engagement can be persuasive if proponents engage their opponents and simultaneously connect their arguments to their opponents' broader goals. Returning a final time to the Health Security Act example, supporters could assert that its efficiency would trim government spending, linking their claim with a key Republican objective. This connection to broader principles might give advocates a better chance of persuading elite opponents who are already familiar with the basic contours of the debate.

The persuasive potential of the engagement strategy helps explain the recent openness of Republican officials to collecting sales taxes on online purchases. Supporters continue to rely on the "fairness" frame, but they have supplemented it with a rhetorical strategy that relies on engagement. Specifically, they increasingly focus on the issue of taxes, engaging with the argument that policy change is a tax increase. This rhetorical turn is not unprecedented; it relates to supporters' insistence that online sales taxes are not new taxes but rather taxes that are going uncollected. The key rhetorical innovation is linking this claim to the broader philosophical and policy goals of the contemporary Republican Party. Earlier efforts to engage on the taxation dimension were ineffectual because they involved competing claims and counterclaims rather than attempting to convince foes that policy change serves their interest.

How could proponents simultaneously link their arguments for e-commerce taxation to the dimension of taxes and argue that change was compatible with the broader Republican agenda? A state elected official answered this question by explaining how his fundamental argument depends on the partisan nature of his audience: "I would say to Democrats . . . here's more money to provide the services you'd like the state to provide more of. . . . [For] Republicans, for those who do not think there should be any increase in taxes, fine! You can use the additional money [brought in by e-commerce taxation] to reduce other taxes or even the overall sales tax rate if you want to."[14] This rhetorical strategy is a recent innovation that many proponents of online sales tax collection have embraced. It enables them to connect policy change to Republican goals by describing the collection of taxes on e-commerce as a tool for cutting taxes. An interest group official explained that this rhetorical strategy increased some Republican state legislators' openness to change

14. Interview with elected official, August 25, 2015.

because "[Republicans] don't want to raise taxes, but they're willing to fund the taxes that are due, especially if you're going to use them to reduce other taxes."[15]

Recent developments in several Republican-leaning states support these claims. In Texas, for example, Tea Party state legislators recently criticized Senator Ted Cruz (R-TX) for opposing national legislation permitting online sales taxation; they emphasized that the increased revenue the state received would be used to lower the margins tax levied on Texas businesses (Hailey 2013). Similarly, when the issue arose in Florida, a vice president of the state's Chamber of Commerce pointed to Ohio and Wisconsin as models to be emulated, and his rationale was revealing. The two states, he noted, "which happen to have conservative governors—are supporting [national e-commerce taxation legislation] with the anticipation that [they] will use the added sales taxes from the Internet transactions to lower income taxes" (Dunkelberger 2013).

Indeed, Ohio and Wisconsin illustrate how elite engagement can facilitate policy change. In Ohio, Republican governor John Kasich strongly opposed online sales taxation when he chaired the Budget Committee in the US House of Representatives in the mid- to late 1990s. His position as governor is quite different, however. In 2013 the governor signed an executive order instructing the state's tax commissioner to seek full membership in the SSUTA. Also, he has recently described e-commerce tax legislation as a "tax cutting mechanism," explaining, "If we're going to get more revenue, we should cut people's taxes with it" (Provance 2015).[16]

Developments in Wisconsin also hint at the potential efficacy of engagement. Like Ohio, Wisconsin is one of a growing number of conservative states that has pledged to use additional revenue from an online sales tax to lower other taxes. This promise aligns with Republican governor Scott Walker's strong stance against higher taxes (Umhoefer 2011), and the governor has taken two actions that emphasize the coherence between policy change and this broader objective. First, after the US Senate endorsed the Marketplace Fairness Act of 2013, the governor sent the Wisconsin congressional delegation a letter explaining his stance on the issue. Alluding to the goal of providing tax relief to middle-class families, Governor Walker explained, "I want to make clear, should federal

15. Interview with interest group official, October 9, 2015.
16. This justification supplemented, rather than supplanted, the fairness frame. In his 2013 executive order, Governor Kasich noted that the interstate compact "levels the playing field so that local 'brick-and-mortar' stores and remote sellers operate under the same rules, thus ensuring that all retailers can conduct their business in a fair, competitive environment" (John R. Kasich, Governor of Ohio, Executive Order 2013-09K, July 9, 2013).

Marketplace legislation become law, my intention would be for any resulting additional revenue [to] be used to provide individual income tax relief for Wisconsin's taxpayers."[17] Strikingly, the letter neither used the language of fairness nor praised the legislation for creating a level playing field for local retailers. Governor Walker's second noteworthy action occurred in 2014, when he signed into law a biennial state budget that automatically reduces the state income tax if Congress passes legislation permitting the collection of online sales taxes (Laffer 2014). In Ohio and Wisconsin, conservative governors both altered the way they discuss the issue and supported concrete legislative actions to facilitate e-commerce taxation. Their actions suggest that the engagement strategy helped alter state policy choices. This ability to spur policy change stands in sharp contrast to the more tenuous connection between framing effects and legislative decisions.

The preceding analysis suggests that some initially skeptical Republicans have become more open to applying sales taxes to online purchases, justifying this policy shift by linking it to their broader philosophical and policy goals. Conservative governors such as Scott Walker of Wisconsin and John Kasich of Ohio have claimed that the additional revenue generated by a change will enable them to reduce other taxes, a central goal of the contemporary Republican Party.[18] Supporters still use the fairness frame that has been ubiquitous since the late 1990s. Recently, however, they have supplemented this rhetorical strategy with elite-level engagement, addressing the concerns raised by opponents *and* connecting change to opponents' broader principles. The justifications advanced by Republican supporters suggest that the engagement approach has been somewhat successful.

As we discuss in the next section, the e-commerce example suggests that efforts to gain ACA support from Republicans by emphasizing the popular components of health care reform may be misguided. Instead of attempting to reframe the ACA, advocates may be better served by trying to engage Republicans on the same dimensions their opponents are emphasizing while also connecting their claims to broader Republican principles.

17. Governor Scott Walker, "Dear Congressman" letter, May 15, 2013. The entire letter can be viewed at www.standwithmainstreet.com/getobject.aspx?file=Letter%20from_Governor_Scott _Walker.

18. The growth of electronic commerce makes this argument more appealing than it was a decade ago, since it implies that the resulting tax cuts will be larger. Indeed, a recent analysis of the US Senate finds that both partisan affiliation and state revenue foregone were significant predictors of Senators' votes on the Marketplace Fairness Act of 2013 (Karch and Rosenthal 2016). In this sense, the engagement strategy is rendered more effective by the rising economic costs of maintaining a suboptimal tax policy.

Implications for the ACA

As supportive lawmakers, organized interests, and foundations try to overcome partisan resistance to the ACA, pursuing an engagement strategy might prove effective. Backers of health care reform often claim that the adoption of a specific component of the ACA will free Republican officials to pursue other objectives. The recent expansion of Medicaid in Arkansas, dubbed the "private option," is a case in point. The rhetorical debate surrounding the Medicaid expansion often pits supporters making the moral case for action against opponents who worry about the long-term financial implications of this commitment. The "Arkansas model" provides premium support for certain enrollees to purchase private insurance on the marketplace (Thompson et al. 2014). Its reliance on the private sector enhances its appeal to conservative officials who believe that its cost is more predictable, and who worry about expanding the reach of a governmental program. Officials in Montana, Kentucky, Louisiana, and elsewhere have pointed to the private option approach as a potential model to be emulated. It illustrates the potential power of engagement, addressing cost concerns and linking change to Republicans' other goals. Not only has the policy idea itself diffused; the political rhetoric surrounding this reform has spread as well, with conservative lawmakers describing it as something distinct from either the Medicaid expansion or the traditional Medicaid program (Grogan, McMinn Singer, and Jones 2017).

Importantly, the broader objectives invoked by an engagement strategy need not be limited to health care reform. Certain components of the ACA have been linked to tax cuts in ways that resonate with the electronic commerce example. Reformers in Texas, for instance, claim that the state's unwillingness to embrace the Medicaid expansion means it is foregoing significant revenue. This argument is not novel, but increasingly advocates link this revenue to property tax reform. One supporter recently explained, "There is some interest now by some Republican state senators because of the potential to reduce local property taxes" (Feibel 2015). By emphasizing the economic dimension and tying it to tax cuts, Texas reformers are using an elite-level engagement strategy. Time will tell if this approach proves successful.

In drawing lessons for the ACA, it is essential not to overstate the independent power of engagement. The strategy has diffused widely in the context of electronic commerce, but the recent pace of adoptions remains slow. Pursuing engagement is not sufficient for success. Sometimes it leads to policy change; sometimes it does not. The challenge is to identify the political and institutional conditions that make success more or less likely. Fortunately, the scholarly literature and the e-commerce example offer valuable guidance.

In *The Strategy of Rhetoric*, William Riker (1996) distinguishes between rhetoric and heresthetic. Rhetoric invokes argumentation and persuasion. Heresthetic describes "the art of setting up situations . . . in such a way that even those who do not wish to do so are compelled by the structure of the situation to support the heresthetician's purpose" (Riker 1996: 9). This distinction implies that, in addition to engaging opponents, supporters must be attentive to the "rules of the game." One episode in Texas is especially revealing. In September 2010 the state sent Amazon a bill for $269 million in uncollected sales taxes, citing the company's distribution center in Irving as evidence of its "physical presence" in the state. Amazon responded by announcing the closure of the distribution center (CanagaRetna 2012). The dispute lingered into the next legislative session, when the legislature endorsed and Governor Rick Perry vetoed a bill that sought to clarify what constituted physical presence. In response, supporters embedded the proposal in a "fiscal matters" bill during a special legislative session. The "fiscal matters" bill was "must-pass" legislation that was necessary for the budget to be certified by the state comptroller. Governor Perry had no choice but to sign it.[19]

This example helps demonstrate that the success of engagement may depend on the institutional setting within which decisions are made. Legislative rules and procedures are paramount. The trajectory of click through legislation in Minnesota provides another illustration, as a law was adopted through an omnibus budget bill in 2013 after a stand-alone proposal was unsuccessful in 2011. For ACA supporters, one potential lesson is that embedding policy changes within omnibus tax, budget, or health care bills provides two key advantages. First, omnibus bills have a greater likelihood of passage. Second, the discussions surrounding omnibus initiatives are an especially propitious setting for an elite-level engagement strategy. It is easier to link policies to broader principles such as cost containment and tax reduction when those issues are already under consideration, and that context might facilitate the sort of compromise that allows progress to occur. This dynamic can occur in non-budgetary and non-legislative settings, including bureaucratic amendments to a state's insurance code.

19. Interview with state representative, October 2, 2015.

The e-commerce example offers other useful lessons for ACA supporters. Just as states have joined the SSUTA, adopted click through legislation, enacted bills that are contingent on congressional action, and taken other actions to collect sales taxes on online sales, health care reform is "a comprehensive package of policy elements and a mix of regulatory and redistributive features" (Jacobs and Mettler 2011: 928–29). In both contexts, the salience of these alternatives varies. Some prominent features of the ACA, such as the Medicaid expansion and health insurance marketplaces, are freighted with enough political baggage that engagement may not always lead immediately to policy change. Developments in Arkansas, where low-income uninsured individuals enroll in exchange-sponsored health plans instead of Medicaid, nonetheless illustrate the strategy's potential. In contrast, the law's regulatory changes to the health insurance market and the delivery of health care services may prove especially amenable to engagement.

Looking ahead, significant uncertainty remains over state implementation of the ACA. There are open questions about whether and how states will expand Medicaid as well as ongoing governance decisions affecting the operation of health insurance marketplaces. Moreover, beginning in January 2017 states can apply for State Innovation Waivers through Section 1332 of the ACA. According to John E. McDonough (2014: 1109), this section "has the potential to be a significant and unpredictable game changer in future directions in federal and state health care policy." States that receive waivers can implement innovative strategies that retain the law's basic protections while providing residents with access to high-quality, affordable health insurance. The waivers can be used to pursue an unusually wide range of objectives, such as expanding the enrollment base to promote sustainability, streamlining operations, facilitating delivery system reform, enrolling consumers in optimal plans, and smoothing the "sharp edges" of the law (Howard and Benshoof 2015). As a result, they have been linked to everything from the establishment of a single-payer system in Vermont to the expansion of the Arkansas model (McDonough 2014). Thus, the waivers might facilitate the diffusion of a new round of health care policy innovations. The comprehensive nature of the waivers — and the fact that they can be merged with waivers associated with Medicare and Medicaid reform — makes engagement particularly appealing.

An engagement strategy will not be a panacea for the partisan polarization that characterizes responses to the ACA, and we do not expect it to lead to a rapid about-face in public attitudes. However, it offers a viable alternative to the framing strategy that has dominated discussions of the

ACA and is represented by the quotation from Secretary Burwell with which this article began. The framing process can occasionally lead to policy change over the long term (Baumgartner, De Boef, and Boydstun 2008), but most discussions of framing effects emphasize ephemeral changes in individual attitudes (Jacobs and Mettler 2011). Under certain conditions, many of which appear relevant to the diffusion of the ACA, an engagement strategy offers an approach that is more responsive to the elites who make the actual decisions that will determine the future course of health care reform in the United States.

Conclusion

In addition to its promise as a political strategy for ACA supporters, elite-level engagement deserves a more prominent place in academic studies of policy change and its causes. Existing research on framing effects illuminates the psychological bases of political attitudes, but there is ample reason to question whether subtle shifts in rhetoric are sufficient to cause well-informed elites to endorse policies that they had previously opposed. The recent trajectory of the e-commerce debate, in contrast, suggests that engagement can occasionally spur previously reluctant state officials to endorse change. Many questions remain about the institutional and political contexts in which engagement is most likely to succeed, and these questions offer numerous fruitful avenues for future research.

For example, the potential impact of an engagement-based rhetorical strategy on policy change offers two valuable lessons for policy diffusion scholars. Existing diffusion research tends to focus on various political, economic, and demographic correlates of adoption over which state leaders have little to no control. These background conditions (and many others) are undoubtedly influential, but it is equally important to recognize the dynamic nature of the policy process. The strategic and tactical choices that are made by institutionally critical actors such as governors and legislative leaders may help explain why a policy innovation either takes root in a seemingly inhospitable environment or fails to gain enactment under what seem to be favorable conditions. To be sure, rhetoric alone is rarely sufficient to explain policy change. The policy-making context might increase or decrease the power of a specific rhetorical strategy, as when the growing scope and scale of electronic commerce enhanced the size of the potential tax cuts that a change in policy would facilitate. However, diffusion scholars must be more attentive to the rhetorical and other strategic choices made by the individuals with the power to decide a policy's fate. Like policy innovations, the strategies themselves may diffuse through media coverage, advocacy organizations, or other means. Understanding whether and how advocates in late-adopting states learn about and employ rhetorical claims that proved successful in early adopters therefore has the potential to illuminate the impact of various diffusion mechanisms.

At its core, policy diffusion scholarship investigates whether the existence of a given program in one jurisdiction affects the likelihood that it will be adopted elsewhere. Most studies in this research tradition emphasize the adoption decision, but the second lesson of the preceding analysis is that the impact of external developments may be felt during the earlier stages of the policy process (Karch 2007). In the electronic commerce example, the rhetorical strategy of linking policy change to tax policy spread from one state to another as advocates viewed it as a way to try to convince unsupportive state officials to change their views. The geographic spread of this engagement approach suggests that the impact of diffusion can influence the nature of the political agenda and the portrayal of existing policy alternatives in ways that precede, but ultimately may affect, decisions concerning final passage. This insight has implications for both the future trajectory of the ACA and future research on the forces that facilitate or hinder the spread of innovative policies.

▪ ▪ ▪

Andrew Karch is Arleen C. Carlson professor of political science at the University of Minnesota. He is the author of *Democratic Laboratories: Policy Diffusion among the American States* and *Early Start: Preschool Politics in the United States.*

Aaron Rosenthal is a PhD candidate in political science at the University of Minnesota. His research interests include policy feedback, political participation, political inequality, and state politics.

References

Bartels, Larry M. 2008. *Unequal Democracy: The Political Economy of the New Gilded Age.* Princeton, NJ: Princeton University Press.

Baumgartner, Frank R., Suzanna L. De Boef, and Amber E. Boydstun. 2008. *The Decline of the Death Penalty and the Discovery of Innocence.* New York: Cambridge University Press.

Butler, Daniel M., Craig Volden, Adam M. Dynes, and Boris Shor. 2015. "Ideology, Learning, and Policy Diffusion: Experimental Evidence." *American Journal of Political Science*. doi: 10.1111/ajps.12213.

CanagaRetna, Sujit M. 2012. "Amazon and the States: New Momentum for States to Recoup Sales Taxes on E-Commerce." In *Book of the States*, edited by Audrey S. Wall, 409–15. Lexington, KY: Council of State Governments.

Carter, Ray. 2003. "Governor OK's Sales Tax, Park Fee Legislation." *Journal Record Legislative Report*, June 9.

Chong, Dennis, and James N. Druckman. 2007. "Framing Theory." *Annual Review of Political Science* 10: 103–26.

Chong, Dennis, and James N. Druckman. 2013. "Counterframing Effects." *Journal of Politics* 75, no. 1: 1–16.

Day, Martin V., Susan T. Fiske, Emily L. Downing, and Thomas E. Trail. 2014. "Shifting Liberal and Conservative Attitudes Using Moral Foundations Theory." *Personality and Social Psychology Bulletin* 40, no. 12: 1559–73.

Delli Carpini, Michael X., and Scott Keeter. 1997. *What Americans Know about Politics and Why It Matters*. New Haven, CT: Yale University Press.

DiJulio, Bianca, Jamie Firth, and Mollyann Brodie. 2015. *Kaiser Health Tracking Poll: September 2015*. Menlo Park, CA: Kaiser Family Foundation.

Dunkelberger, Lloyd. 2013. "Support Sought for Online Sales Tax." *Sarasota Herald Tribune*, July 20.

Entman, Robert M. 1993. "Framing: Toward Clarification of a Fractured Paradigm." *Journal of Communication* 43, no. 4: 51–58.

Feibel, Carrie. 2015. "How Texas is Learning to Like Obamacare." *Kaiser Health News*, November 3.

Feinberg, Matthew, and Robb Willer. 2015. "From Gulf to Bridge? When Do Moral Arguments Facilitate Political Influence?" *Personality and Social Psychology Bulletin* 41, no. 12: 1665–81.

Ferraiolo, Kathleen. 2013. "Is State Gambling Policy 'Morality Policy'? Framing Debates over State Lotteries." *Policy Studies Journal* 41, no. 2: 217–42.

Geewax, Marilyn. 2001. "Congress under the Gun on Internet Taxes." *Cox News Service*, August 29.

Gilens, Martin, and Benjamin I. Page. 2014. "Testing Theories of American Politics: Elites, Interest Groups, and Average Citizens." *Perspectives on Politics* 12, no. 3: 564–81.

Gollust, Sarah, and Julia Lynch. 2011. "Who Deserves Health Care? The Effects of Causal Attributions and Group Cues on Public Attitudes about Responsibility for Health Care Costs." *Journal of Health Politics, Policy and Law* 36, no. 6: 1061–95.

Gormley, William T., Jr. 2012. *Voices for Children: Rhetoric and Public Policy*. Washington, DC: Brookings Institution.

Green-Pedersen, Christoffer, and Peter B. Mortensen. 2015. "Avoidance and Engagement: Issue Competition in Multiparty Systems." *Political Studies* 63, no. 4: 747–64.

Grogan, Colleen, Phillip McMinn Singer, and David K. Jones. 2017. "Rhetoric and Reform in Waiver States." *Journal of Health Politics, Policy and Law* 42, no. 2: 247–84.

Hailey, Mike. 2013. "Republican Lawmakers See Tax Loophole Ban as Ticket to Business Levy Reduction in Texas." *Capital Inside*, October 4.

Howard, Heather, and Galen Benshoof. 2015. "State Innovation Waivers: Redrawing the Boundaries of the ACA." *Journal of Health Politics, Policy and Law* 40, no. 6: 1203–12.

Jacobs, Lawrence R., and Timothy Callaghan. 2013. "Why States Expand Medicaid: Party, Resources, and History." *Journal of Health Politics, Policy and Law* 38, no. 5: 1023–50.

Jacobs, Lawrence R., and Suzanne Mettler. 2011. "Why Public Opinion Changes: The Implications for Health and Health Policy." *Journal of Health Politics, Policy and Law* 36, no. 6: 917–33.

Jerit, Jennifer. 2008. "Issue Framing and Engagement: Rhetorical Strategy in Public Policy Debates." *Political Behavior* 30, no. 1: 1–24.

Jones, Bryan D. 1994. "A Change of Mind or a Change of Focus? A Theory of Choice Reversals in Politics." *Journal of Public Administration Research and Theory* 4, no. 2: 141–77.

Jones, David K., Katharine W. V. Bradley, and Jonathan Oberlander. 2014. "Pascal's Wager: Health Insurance Exchanges, Obamacare, and the Republican Dilemma." *Journal of Health Politics, Policy and Law* 39, no. 1: 97–137.

Karch, Andrew. 2007. *Democratic Laboratories: Policy Diffusion among the American States*. Ann Arbor: University of Michigan Press.

Karch, Andrew, and Aaron Rosenthal. 2016. "Vertical Diffusion and the Shifting Politics of Electronic Commerce." *State Politics and Policy Quarterly* 16, no. 1: 22–43.

Kinder, Donald R. 2007. "Curmudgeonly Advice." *Journal of Communication* 57, no. 1: 155–62.

Laffer, Arthur B. 2014. "E-fairness Still Needed to Spur Economic Growth." *Politico*, March 3.

Lax, Jeffrey R., and Justin H. Phillips. 2012. "The Democratic Deficit in the States." *American Journal of Political Science* 56, no. 1: 148–66.

Lindquist, Eric. 2009. "Democrats Defend Proposed Budget." *Leader-Telegram*, February 20.

Lunder, Erika K., and Carol A. Pettit. 2013. *"Amazon Laws" and Taxation of Internet Sales: Constitutional Analysis*. Washington, DC: Congressional Research Service.

Maguire, Steven. 2013. *State Taxation of Internet Transactions*. Washington, DC: Congressional Research Service.

McDonough, John E. 2014. "Wyden's Waiver: State Innovation on Steroids." *Journal of Health Politics, Policy and Law* 39, no. 5: 1099–1111.

Mucciaroni, Gary. 2011. "Are Debates about 'Morality Policy' Really about Morality? Framing Opposition to Gay and Lesbian Rights." *Policy Studies Journal* 39, no. 2: 187–216.

New York Times. 2005. "Internet Sales Tax." Editorial, July 5.

Nugent, John D. 2009. *Safeguarding Federalism: How States Protect Their Interests in National Policymaking*. Norman: University of Oklahoma Press.

O'Sullivan, Sheila, Lynly Lumibao, Russell Pustejovsky, Tiffany Hill, and Jesse Willhide. 2013. *State Government Tax Collections Summary Report: 2012*. Washington, DC: US Census Bureau.

Provance, Jim. 2015. "Amazon to Collect Sales Tax in Ohio." *Blade*, May 30.

Rasinski, Kenneth A. 1989. "The Effect of Question Wording on Public Support for Government Spending." *Public Opinion Quarterly* 53, no. 3: 388–94.

Rigby, Elizabeth, and Jake Haselswerdt. 2013. "Hybrid Federalism, Partisan Politics, and Early Implementation of State Health Insurance Exchanges." *Publius: The Journal of Federalism* 43, no. 3: 368–91.

Riker, William H. 1996. *The Strategy of Rhetoric: Campaigning for the American Constitution*. New Haven, CT: Yale University Press.

Scheppach, Raymond C., and Frank Shafroth. 2008. "Intergovernmental Finance in the New Global Economy: An Integrated Approach." In *Intergovernmental Management for the Twenty-First Century*, edited by Timothy J. Conlan and Paul L. Posner, 42–74. Washington, DC: Brookings Institution.

Sides, John. 2006. "The Origins of Campaign Agendas." *British Journal of Political Science* 36, no. 3: 407–36.

Sigelman, Lee, and Emmett H. Buell. 2004. "Avoidance or Engagement? Issue Convergence in US Presidential Campaigns, 1960–2000." *American Journal of Political Science* 48, no. 4: 650–61.

Stimson, James A., Michael B. MacKuen, and Robert S. Erikson. 1995. "Dynamic Representation." *American Political Science Review* 89, no. 3: 543–65.

Sun, Lena H. 2015. "Top Obamacare Official Says She Wept for Joy after Supreme Court Victory." *Washington Post*, June 27.

Thompson, Joseph W., J. Craig Wilson, Andrew Allison, and Mike Beebe. 2014. "Arkansas's Novel Approach to Expanding Health Care Coverage." *Journal of Health Politics, Policy and Law* 39, no. 6: 1277–88.

Umhoefer, Dave. 2011. "His Own Budget Proposes Some Increases, According to Nonpartisan Fiscal Bureau." *Politifact*, May 19.

Wolsko, Christopher, Hector Ariceaga, and Jesse Seiden. 2016. "Red, White, and Blue Enough to Be Green: Effects of Moral Framing on Climate Change Attitudes and Conservation Behaviors." *Journal of Experimental Social Psychology* 65: 7–19.

Yin, Robert K. 1989. *Case Study Research: Design and Methods*. Newbury Park, CA: Sage.

Commentary

Policy Diffusion in Polarized Times: The Case of the Affordable Care Act

Craig Volden
University of Virginia

Abstract With increasing ideological polarization both within states and across states, policy makers face new challenges in developing and refining policies. This essay explores these challenges in the context of the spread of health policies across the states under the Affordable Care Act, highlighting key arguments and findings from the authors in this Special Issue. I discuss how common mechanisms of policy diffusion, the attributes of policies themselves, and the conditional nature of policy diffusion all play somewhat different roles during polarized times. In addition to new challenges to policy makers, polarization offers new opportunities for experimentation and learning that may be valuable to scholars and practitioners alike.

Keywords policy diffusion, Affordable Care Act, ideological polarization

After decades of state experiments with varying policies of health insurance coverage, the Obama administration and Democratic Congress took a major step in 2010 toward nationwide universal coverage in the Affordable Care Act (ACA). In so doing, they changed the balance of state and national policy making in the area of health care, and brought to light the degree of ideological and partisan polarization that has arisen in American politics in recent years. Many Republican-controlled states refused to set up their own health care exchange websites and turned down highly subsidized grants for Medicaid expansion. When Republicans gained control of Congress, they voted repeatedly to repeal "Obamacare." And yet, as time has passed, and the ACA policies have spread across the states and taken greater effect, such polarization has presented both opportunities and

Journal of Health Politics, Policy and Law, Vol. 42, No. 2, April 2017
DOI 10.1215/03616878-3766762   © 2017 by Duke University Press

challenges for politicians and the public alike, as they work through the complexities of the new health care landscape.

Many view the ACA as a substantial centralization of health insurance policy in the United States. The degree to which policies are centralized or decentralized in federal systems is a crucial choice that impacts how well those policies address public needs. Policies that are determined at the state or local level tend to feature benefits such as horizontal competition, with policy makers seeking to innovate and hold down costs in order to attract and retain residents and businesses (Tiebout 1956). States and localities can experiment with various policy models, learn from one another, and spread successes to others (Walker 1969). Policies can be tailored to local circumstances and can be formulated by policy makers attuned to local knowledge. And the heterogeneous preferences of different populations can be reflected in diverse state and local policies (Volden 2005).

On the other hand, centralized policy making helps limit the spillovers that occur beyond local or state jurisdictions, attenuating harmful externalities. "Races to the bottom" that undercut the preferred policies and shred the social safety net can be halted before they start (Peterson and Rom 1990). And economies of scale can be realized, without all of the redundancies in policy making and implementation that decentralized policies bring about.

Peterson (1995) succinctly captured many of these benefits in his articulation of the argument that developmental policies are best left at the state and local level where they can be tailored to local needs, whereas redistributive policies are best handled nationally to avoid adverse state and local competition. Health care is a complicated policy area, fitting neatly in neither the developmental nor redistributive categories. Certainly, healthy citizens and a healthy workforce are critical to a robust economy. But providing such health care, especially during an era of high income inequality, involves some redistribution to those who cannot afford health insurance and health care services on their own.

In advancing the ACA, policy makers attempted to thread the needle between centralized and decentralized approaches, hoping to capture all of the benefits of each. Universal health insurance coverage could only be accommodated with some degree of redistribution, with subsidized premiums for low-income Americans. Thus, a national program was deemed essential to avoid the race-to-the-bottom incentives in state or local provision. Yet, the benefits of state experimentation might still be possible if there were some flexibility in how states developed the policy's specifics, and therefore the ACA encouraged state-run health exchanges and allowed for waivers to various parts of the policy to best meet local circumstances.

However, in this article, I argue that this attempt to capture all the best features of American federalism has been dramatically influenced by the highly polarized environment in which American politics is operating today. Observers of American politics cannot miss the partisan bickering and ideological polarization found in the US Congress. And such divisions are finding their way into numerous state legislatures (Shor and McCarty 2011). Not only are there strong ideological and partisan divides between "red states" and "blue states," but those divides are also evident in the policy-making processes *within* states. These polarized environments are broadly affecting how American federalism functions today (e.g., Conlan and Posner 2016), and polarization influences how the ACA has been and will continue to be implemented.

This special issue of the *Journal of Health Politics, Policy and Law* has brought together influential scholars to analyze and comment on one aspect of health policy making under the ACA. Specifically, the essays herein each speak to the diffusion of health policy choices across the states in the wake of the ACA. Within political science, scholars have come to define policy diffusion as occurring when one government's decision about whether to adopt a policy innovation is influenced by the choices made by other governments (Graham, Shipan, and Volden 2013: 675). With this definition in mind, each essay in this issue takes a different angle, ranging from the roles of framing and rhetoric in the spread of reforms to the importance of changing public opinion, from the important political and policy drivers of ACA enrollment to how advocates could use the diffusion process to their greatest advantage. As such, each contributes in different ways to our understanding about the future of health policy in the United States. In total, these contributions tell the story of policy makers across the ideological spectrum struggling with the implementation of a landmark policy reform.

Moreover, the timing of this special issue could not be better. With Section 1332 "State Innovation Waivers" becoming available to the states in 2017 (McDonough 2014; Howard and Benshoof 2015), innovation and policy diffusion under the ACA may soon be more robust than ever. More profoundly, if the new Trump administration and Repulican Congress follow through on their promise to repeal and replace Obamacare, a new era of state-level experimentation will begin. Rather than merely summarizing the authors' contributions, I instead encapsulate them in a broad discussion of what we know about the diffusion of policy choices across the American states, how that knowledge may help us understand the past, present, and future of the ACA, and how both the ACA and policy diffusion more generally have been significantly affected by the polarized times in which we live.

Across the past two decades, scholars of policy diffusion have moved significantly away from the narrow view of diffusion being the geographic clustering of policy choices to a much more robust and theoretically grounded understanding of the complexities of policy choice across governments. We have come to: (1) identify a small set of driving mechanisms of diffusion; (2) highlight how the attributes of policies themselves have influenced their diffusion; and (3) explore how policy diffusion has been conditional on politics within potential adopting states. In this essay, I will focus on each of these three lenses for viewing policy diffusion, assessing how ideological and partisan polarization shapes their applicability to our understanding of state adoption and diffusion of the Affordable Care Act.

The Mechanisms of Policy Diffusion

Although various authors have invented more than one hundred adjectives and metaphors to colorfully describe policy diffusion processes (Graham, Shipan, and Volden 2013: 690), scholars have recently coalesced around a small number of concrete mechanisms through which policies spread across governments (e.g., Simmons, Dobbin, and Garrett 2006; Shipan and Volden 2008; Maggetti and Gilardi 2016). Here, I focus on the four mechanisms of learning, imitation, competition, and coercion, each of which comes into play in the spread of ACA policy choices across the states.

Learning

When states experiment with solutions to policy problems, they present an opportunity for other governments to learn from their experiences. Policy successes will spread, while failures will be abandoned, with little cost to those who do not engage in the experiment (e.g., *New State Ice Co. v. Liebmann*, 285 U.S. 262, 311 [1932] [Brandeis, J., dissenting]; Volden 2006). Such learning has been identified in health policy areas ranging from children's health insurance programs to antismoking policy choices. Under the Affordable Care Act, states had a variety of choices to make— most notably whether to set up a health care exchange and whether to expand Medicaid. Within these broad choices were many smaller choices, each of which could be made in light of the decisions of other states and the successes or failures of those policies.

Polarization within and across the American states affects policy learning in a number of ways. Potentially limiting learning and policy diffusion is the possibility that some policy options are completely dismissed due to ideological biases. Regardless of a policy's success or failure, its perceived ideological location may be so divergent from what is deemed acceptable to state policy makers as to render the policy's effectiveness immaterial (Volden, Ting, and Carpenter 2008). However, recent evidence from survey experiments of local officials across the United States suggests that such ideological biases can be substantially reduced and potentially overcome (Butler et al. 2017). If the earlier policy has been adopted by co-partisans or has a high degree of success, policy makers are at least willing to find out more about the policy, if not adopt it in the end.

Polarization might also lead to a proliferation of policy models from which others can learn. Rather than merely gravitating to the first policy that seems to address a problem, ideologically diverse policy makers may seek out something quite different. In the extreme, two or more quite divergent models may be attempted across the states, potentially with important lessons to be learned across key evaluative criteria. Such starkly different models may be very beneficial in helping policy makers understand the impacts of policy choices and ideological viewpoints. Recent competing models to respond to gun violence provide a case in point. Liberal policy makers have been pushing for gun control while conservatives have advocated for expanding gun rights. Such dramatically different policies may make each side very uncomfortable with one another's choices, but they certainly provide the opportunity to learn about the effects of different policies.

When the federal government takes a major new role in a policy area, such learning and experimentation may be diminished. The implications of health insurance experiments from Oregon to Massachusetts may not yet have come into full view by the time of the adoption of the ACA. As much as advocates of universal coverage argued that the law had been too long in coming, proponents of a federalism approach instead suggested that there had yet to be sufficient state experimentation on which a national law could be based. Whether the ACA gives states sufficient flexibility to still experiment and learn from one another is an open question ripe for additional research and examination.

Imitation

Separate from learning, states may adopt policies found elsewhere through the diffusion mechanism commonly referred to as "imitation." Imitation involves the copying of a policy found elsewhere without regard to its effectiveness. Largely what is involved in imitation is a sort of herding activity, wherein states are hesitant to be first movers but also do not desire to be left behind and appear out of sync with others, especially if doing so casts a negative light on elected policy makers.

Polarization adds a wrinkle to the classic imitation model. No longer are policy makers solely looking to do what is popular or widely accepted. Now they are looking to do what is widely accepted within their (potentially isolated) ideological community. If most other Democratic governments are adopting state health exchanges and Medicaid expansions, it becomes very difficult and politically dangerous for other Democratic policy makers to seek a different course. Likewise, a potentially treacherous road lies ahead for Republican governors and legislators who wander in such a liberal direction.

The role of polarization and imitation pressures as part of the ACA are very much on display in the essays within this special issue. For example, Callaghan and Jacobs (2017) show a strong negative relationship between Republican state policy makers and the adoption of state exchanges and Medicaid expansions. Grogan, McMinn Singer, and Jones (2017) highlight the challenges faced by conservative policy makers who nevertheless wanted to adopt a Medicaid expansion. They could not do so in a cookie-cutter manner of imitation that would make them seem to endorse Democratic proposals, but instead had to find the modifications and rhetoric needed to differentiate themselves from such a liberal position.

Competition

When states compete with one another, they may take actions to try to attract business from other states or to offer lower taxes and more efficient services. Sometimes such competition produces poor results as the quality and generosity of services are significantly reduced along with tax cuts. In an ideologically polarized environment, such competition may be reduced somewhat. States may differentiate their policies from others more for ideological reasons than to attain nonpolitical competitive advantages. Diminished competition therefore reduces both the benefits arising from adding market discipline to government policy making and the race-to-the-bottom costs found in competitive federalism.

Competition across states in their health policy choices under the ACA may therefore be limited. While citizens moving across state lines may find greater access to Medicaid benefits in certain circumstances, the ACA largely serves to diminish state-by-state differences. Nevertheless, the combination of learning, imitation, and competition led to a robust environment in which states made a variety of important decisions about how to implement the ACA. Early adoptions set the stage for what could be learned by others, and for the broad understandings of what would be seen as prototypical liberal or conservative policies.

In this special issue, Boehmke, Rury, Desmarais, and Harden (2017) establish how crucial the order of such initial policy adoptions was. They show that the right mix of innovative initial states with neighbors engaging in learning, imitation, or competition can dramatically speed up the adoption of many policy innovations. With regard to Medicaid expansion typically opposed by Republicans, which states' conservative policy makers act first, what arguments they make, and how others react will go a long way in determining whether key elements of the ACA take broader hold across the country or leave the health care landscape deeply divided. Policy advocates interested in a broader impact on that landscape may wish to target their state-level efforts carefully in light of the authors' findings.

Coercion

Coercion is common in the spread of policies due to attempts of one government to force the hand of another, such as with trade restrictions across countries. In the US federal system, coercion mainly comes through top-down pressures from the federal government on the states in the form of regulations, preemptive policies, and intergovernmental grants.

The ideologically polarized environment both within Congress and in the states at the time of the passage of the ACA deeply influenced the coercive nature of the policy. Looking to attract bipartisan support and a sizable enough coalition in the Senate to overcome a possible filibuster, the percentage of federal funding for Medicaid expansion increased to very high levels. This made Medicaid expansion attractive to most Democratic governors and state legislatures. But it put Republican policy makers in the states in a difficult position. They could continue to promote small government policies and the private sector by limiting their Medicaid expansions. But, in so doing, they would be turning down a substantial amount in federal subsidies, while still likely supporting medical coverage for poorer families through other policies designed to help doctors and hospitals with unpaid bills.

More generally, when designing intergovernmental grant conditions, federal policy makers need to be mindful of the responses of the states (Volden 2007). During polarized times, the responses of one set of states may differ from those with different ideological positions. A grant sufficient enough to induce liberal policy makers to adopt a programmatic change may be insufficient to bring along conservatives. And yet, grant conditions targeting conservative lawmakers in the states may be inappropriately set for liberal officials. On top of such policy considerations are the political calculations, such that the majority party in Congress may be more concerned about state responses only by their own co-partisans, or may look to put politicians of the other party in a difficult political position, as with Republicans deciding how to react to incentives to expand Medicaid under the ACA.

The Role of Policy Attributes

Beyond the mechanisms that influence the spread of policies across states and localities, attributes of the policies themselves help determine which policies diffuse, and at what speeds. Makse and Volden (2011) apply the attributes typology of Rogers (2003) to policy diffusion. They establish that greater relative advantage, compatibility, observability, and trialability of policies enhances their diffusion across states, whereas policies' complexity reduces their spread. Moreover, they show that the mechanisms of diffusion are influenced by the policies' attributes.

"Relative advantage" captures the extent to which a new proposal is perceived to be an improvement over existing policy in a particular area. "Compatibility" characterizes the consistency between the new policy and prior laws, values, and experiences. "Observability" is the degree to which policy makers can see the choices of others and their effects. "Trialability" captures the possibility that a policy can be adopted and later abandoned at a low political or budgetary cost. And "complexity" characterizes whether a policy is difficult to adopt, understand, or implement.

Each of these policy attributes may be understood differently during ideologically polarized times than absent such divisions. For example, a policy seen to have a relative advantage by some policy makers may be perceived quite differently by others, who evaluate that policy according to different criteria. In this special issue, Karch and Rosenthal (2017) describe how Medicaid expansion is seen as less of an advantageous policy approach by Republicans than by Democrats. Until they started framing the policy as allowing lower taxes due to the increased federal subsidies, the expansion was perceived in a mainly negative light as an undue step away from the free market and toward big government.

Compatibility is also relevant in implementation of the ACA. Depending on their prior policy choices, some states could more easily select health care exchange models that matched their needs and values (e.g., Noh and Krane 2016). Such choices would in turn affect enrollment levels (Callaghan and Jacobs 2017). Grogan, McMinn Singer, and Jones (2017) highlight how Section 1115 waivers have allowed states to enhance the compatibility of Medicaid expansion to both past policy and the current political environment. More generally, as liberal and conservative policy choices diverge, many new policy proposals may be seen as incompatible with existing laws by one group or another. Increasing the flexibility of policy options may be crucial to the diffusion of such policy ideas.

Observability may be simultaneously enhanced and undermined given political polarization across the states. On the one hand, there may be many new experiments and models that states could observe and learn from. However, as discussed above, some policy makers may be hesitant to look to ideological opponents for such policy ideas. Such trade-offs in observability may apply not only to political elites but to the public as a whole. Pacheco and Maltby (2017) demonstrate how citizens in neighboring states take note of other governments' experiments and begin to demand change at home. They establish that the resulting shifts in public opinion in turn influence policy choices.

Trialability in the ACA may be enhanced by policy options, including state-by-state waivers such as those explored by Grogan, McMinn Singer, and Jones (2017). Yet, ideological polarization and the high-profile nature of state ACA policy choices make trying and then abandoning a policy politically perilous. Policy makers may be hesitant to abandon policies that seem to be failing in their states if doing so means they need to admit to their own failings in their earlier policy choices (e.g., Volden 2016).

Finally, there is little doubt that the Affordable Care Act is complex, both in itself and in how it affects state policy. Whether judged by the nearly two-thousand-page law itself or by the thousands of pages of regulations that followed during the implementation process, the details that needed to be spelled out were immense. As state policy makers waded into this area for their own purposes, they began to struggle with the complexities of matching the ACA's provisions to their own existing policies. From this point of view, difficult policy choices regarding implementation of the ACA and adapting the law's provisions (and modifications) to different states' circumstances will continue for many years to come. Adding to this complexity is the polarization across state policy makers, with their different perspectives influencing how each new development in the health care debates is perceived.

The Conditions for Policy Diffusion

Interacting with the mechanisms of policy diffusion and the attributes of the policies themselves are the natural differences across states that lead to conditional patterns in which policies spread and where they are adopted. For example, Shipan and Volden (2006) highlight how interest group strength and state legislative professionalism influenced whether states adopted various antismoking policies. In a similar manner, Callaghan and Jacobs (2017) note the role of administrative capacity for understanding the rollout of the ACA across the states and for subsequent enrollment levels.

Whether policies spread also depends on the role of public opinion (Pacheco 2012). Given the polarized political climate, not every governor leapt to embrace the ACA, accept grant funding, and develop a state health exchange. Rather, some governors only came to that position following other states' actions and the public opinion shifts that arose in their own states as a result, as Pacheco and Maltby (2017) establish.

Moreover, the spread of policies across the states is conditional on finding or developing a political climate in which such a change would be broadly accepted by politicians as well as the public. The framing of Medicaid expansions in terms of tax relief (Karch and Rosenthal 2017) and the rhetoric surrounding ACA waiver usage (Grogan, McMinn Singer, and Jones 2017) both offered conditions under which health care policies could spread from one state to the next. Especially when moving toward a policy change that may be in poor ideological alignment with state policy makers' predispositions, political choices are very much conditioned by policy perceptions.

Conclusion

Throughout this special issue, the authors have wrestled with state policy choices under the Affordable Care Act. They have explored the nature of policy diffusion within this landmark program. In so doing, classic themes of the mechanisms of policy diffusion and the attributes of policies have come into view once again. However, both the mechanisms of how policies spread and the role of policy attributes in that diffusion play out somewhat differently given how ideologically polarized US state governments have become. Policy makers may be loath to learn from or imitate those from the other party. Policies that are seen as relatively advantageous by one group may be viewed with suspicion by others.

As policy makers take further steps to implement or modify the ACA, they will need to navigate treacherous political waters. The authors writing here offer some sage advice and some words of caution along these lines. Rhetoric and framing have become crucial to building a coalition for policy change. The early actions of some states influence both public opinion in other states and their likelihood of adopting similar policies. And each of these choices has major implications for enrollment levels, medical care provision decisions, and ultimately the degree of success or failure that states experience under the ACA. Hopefully, this special issue will guide future scholarship and an understanding of such important issues for years to come.

▪ ▪ ▪

Craig Volden is the associate dean for academic affairs and a professor of public policy and politics, with appointments in the Frank Batten School of Leadership and Public Policy and the Woodrow Wilson Department of Politics at the University of Virginia. He studies legislative politics and the interaction among political institutions, including within American federalism. His most recent book, *Legislative Effectiveness in the United States Congress: The Lawmakers*, coauthored with Alan Wiseman, explores the effectiveness of individual members of Congress in overcoming policy gridlock. His most prominent work on issues of federalism focuses on why some policies diffuse across states and localities while others do not. He has published numerous articles in such journals as: *American Political Science Review*; *American Journal of Political Science*; *Journal of Politics*; and *Publius: The Journal of Federalism*. Prof. Volden is co-director of the Legislative Effectiveness Project (www.thelawmakers.org).

References

Boehmke, Frederick J., Abigail A. Rury, Bruce A. Desmarais, and Jeffrey J. Harden. 2017. "The Seeds of Policy Change: Leveraging Diffusion to Disseminate Policy Innovations." *Journal of Health Politics, Policy and Law* 42, no. 2.

Butler, Daniel M., Craig Volden, Adam M. Dynes, and Boris Shor. 2017. "Ideology, Learning, and Policy Diffusion: Experimental Evidence." *American Journal of Political Science* 60, no. 3.

Callaghan, Timothy, and Lawrence R. Jacobs. 2017. "The Future of Health Care Reform: What Is Driving Enrollment?" *Journal of Health Politics, Policy and Law* 42, no. 2.

Conlan, Timothy J., and Paul L. Posner. 2016. "American Federalism in an Era of Partisan Polarization: The Intergovernmental Paradox of Obama's 'New Nationalism.'" *Publius: The Journal of Federalism* 46, no. 3: 281–307.

Graham, Erin R., Charles R. Shipan, and Craig Volden. 2013. "The Diffusion of Policy Diffusion Research in Political Science." *British Journal of Political Science* 43, no. 3: 673–701.

Grogan, Colleen, Philip McMinn Singer, and David K. Jones. 2017. "Rhetoric and Reform in Waiver States." *Journal of Health Politics, Policy and Law* 42, no. 2.

Howard, Heather, and Galen Benshoof. 2015. "State Innovation Waivers: Redrawing the Boundaries of the ACA." *Journal of Health Politics, Policy and Law* 40, no. 6: 1203–12.

Karch, Andrew, and Aaron Rosenthal. 2017. "Framing, Engagement, and Policy Change: Lessons for the ACA." *Journal of Health Politics, Policy and Law* 42, no. 2.

Maggetti, Martino, and Fabrizio Gilardi. 2016. "Problems (and Solutions) in the Measurement of Policy Diffusion Mechanisms." *Journal of Public Policy* 36, no. 1: 87–107.

Makse, Todd, and Craig Volden. 2011. "The Role of Policy Attributes in the Diffusion of Innovations." *Journal of Politics* 73, no. 1: 108–24.

McDonough, John E. 2014. "Wyden's Waiver: State Innovation on Steroids." *Journal of Health Politics, Policy and Law* 39, no. 5: 1099–1111.

Noh, Shihyun, and Dale Krane. 2016. "Implementing the Affordable Care Act Health Insurance Exchanges: State Government Choices and Policy Outcomes." *Publius: The Journal of Federalism* 46, no. 3: 416–40.

Pacheco, Julianna. 2012. "The Social Contagion Model: Exploring the Role of Public Opinion on the Diffusion of Antismoking Legislation across the American States." *Journal of Politics* 74: 714–34.

Pacheco, Julianna, and Elizabeth Maltby. 2017. "The Role of Public Opinion—Does It Influence the Diffusion of ACA Decisions?" *Journal of Health Politics, Policy and Law* 42, no. 2.

Peterson, Paul E. 1995. *The Price of Federalism*. Washington, DC: Brookings Institution.

Peterson, Paul E., and Mark C. Rom. 1990. *Welfare Magnets: A New Case for a National Standard*. Washington, DC: Brookings Institution.

Rogers, Everett. 2003. *The Diffusion of Innovations*. 5th ed. New York: Free Press.

Shipan, Charles R., and Craig Volden. 2006. "Bottom-up Federalism: The Diffusion of Antismoking Policies from U.S. Cities to States." *American Journal of Political Science* 50, no. 4: 825–43.

Shipan, Charles R., and Craig Volden. 2008. "The Mechanisms of Policy Diffusion." *American Journal of Political Science* 52, no. 4: 840–57.

Shor, Boris, and Nolan McCarty. 2011. "The Ideological Mapping of American Legislatures." *American Political Science Review* 105, no. 3: 530–51.

Simmons, Beth A., Frank Dobbin, and Geoffrey Garrett. 2006. "Introduction: The International Diffusion of Liberalism." *International Organization* 60, no. 4: 781–810.

Tiebout, Charles M. 1956. "A Pure Theory of Local Expenditures." *Journal of Political Economy* 64, no. 5: 416–24.

Volden, Craig. 2005. "Intergovernmental Political Competition in American Federalism." *American Journal of Political Science* 49, no. 2: 327–42.

Volden, Craig. 2006. "States as Policy Laboratories: Emulating Success in the Children's Health Insurance Program." *American Journal of Political Science* 50, no. 2: 294–312.

Volden, Craig. 2007. "Intergovernmental Grants: A Formal Model of Interrelated National and Subnational Policy Decisions." *Publius: The Journal of Federalism* 37, no. 2: 209–43.

Volden, Craig. 2016. "Failures: Diffusion, Learning, and Policy Abandonment." *State Politics and Policy Quarterly* 16, no. 1: 44–77.

Volden, Craig, Michael M. Ting, and Daniel P. Carpenter. 2008. "A Formal Model of Learning and Policy Diffusion." *American Political Science Review* 102, no. 3: 319–32.

Walker, Jack L. 1969. "The Diffusion of Innovations among the American States." *American Political Science Review* 63, no. 3: 880–99.

Commentary
Policy Diffusion across Disparate Disciplines: Private- and Public-Sector Dynamics Affecting State-Level Adoption of the ACA

Rena M. Conti
University of Chicago

David K. Jones
Boston University

Abstract The ACA entails a number of provisions that are profoundly changing the way the states ensure access to medical care, including the expansion of Medicaid and the maintenance of health insurance exchanges. Here, we argue that while federal policy is the originating force of whether these provisions are adopted, individual state decisions are made within a larger ecosystem. This ecosystem has two main components: (1) complementary and competing state and federal policies; and (2) medical provision by a variety of suppliers. Specifically, the merits, costs, and uncertainties associated with adopting these provisions cannot be considered by the states in a vacuum—they may interact with a large set of simultaneously launched or existing local, state, and federal policies aimed at ensuring access to medical care. They may also interact with specific state and federal reimbursement policies and other requirements facing local hospitals and medical providers. We illustrate by example how these interactions may have important implications for the diffusion of ACA provisions. One implication of this perspective is that future empirical work on the rate, determinants, and impacts of ACA coverage expansions on individual and aggregate well-being must incorporate systematic study of this complex public–private sector ecosystem.

Keywords insurance, medical care, Affordable Care Act, 340B drug discount program, diffusion

Conti's effort on this article was generously funded by the Robert Wood Johnson Foundation and the Health Care Cost Institute in collaboration with the National State Health Policy Association and the John and Laura Arnold Foundation. Neither the funders nor the University of Chicago are responsible for the conduct of the study, model interpretations, or results.

Journal of Health Politics, Policy and Law, Vol. 42, No. 2, April 2017
DOI 10.1215/03616878-3766771   © 2017 by Duke University Press

Introduction

The 2010 Patient Protection and Affordable Care Act (ACA) entails a number of provisions that are profoundly changing who accesses medical care and how it is provided in the United States. Many of the law's provisions and subsequent regulations allow, indeed require, individual states to make decisions about whether and how to participate. This includes the expansion of Medicaid and the development and maintenance of health insurance exchanges. As other contributors to this special issue suggest, there is considerable interest among policy makers and health policy researchers regarding whether, which, and when states adopt these provisions, the determinants of these decisions, and their impact on individual and aggregate well-being.

In this commentary, we argue that the decision to adopt specific ACA coverage provisions by the states must be viewed within a larger ecosystem. This ecosystem has two main components: (1) complementary and competing state and federal policies; and (2) medical provision by a variety of private actors. As many other scholars have pointed out, including those in this special issue, state policy diffusion operates within a larger federal system and within state and interstate dynamics (Karch 2007, 2012; McCann, Shipan, and Volden 2015). However, not as many scholars have detailed how the diffusion of specific policies may interact with a large set of simultaneously launched or existing local, state, and federal policies; nor have the potential intended (and unintended) impacts of private actors been fully considered, namely, the panoply of medical care providers and health care organizations that operate within the health care system. Like all interest groups, health care providers have their own objectives and are subject to specific state and federal policies, such as reimbursement and other regulatory requirements. However, due to ACA enactment, hospitals and local medical providers face decisions about whether to participate in alternative payment arrangements, such as an Accountable Care Organization, and to what extent to care for additional Medicaid and/or exchange-insured patients. The diffusion of decisions made by these providers in the private sector has important implications for the diffusion of policy decisions made by leaders in the public sector. This is importantly separate from any direct lobbying they do in state capitals. Viewed from this vantage point, empirical study of the diffusion of ACA-based coverage expansion decisions must consider how federal policy creates a new private-sector environment at the state level, and how this then impacts state decision making regarding ACA policy.

Political scientists have examined the impact of private-sector decision making on state policy designs and decision making. Titmuss (1951), for example, long ago highlighted the important role of the private sector in the provision of welfare. More recently, Hacker (2002) highlights what he calls a *"Divided Welfare State"* where government provides direct public provision through programs such as Medicare and Social Security, and indirect private provision through taxation policies such as the Earned Income Tax Credit or tax exemptions for Employer-based Health Insurance. Hacker details how government both encourages private-sector involvement and is impacted by its involvement, and examines the unique politics that emerges under private provision. Morgen and Campbell (2011) also highlight another form of private-sector impact in their book, *The Delegated Welfare State*, by analyzing how government contracts with private actors similarly encourage involvement in policy, which in turn creates a new private-sector environment that impacts the political process of Medicare policy making. In particular, private-sector involvement in Medicare serves several purposes, including a way for policy makers to mask the role of government; it also gives government leaders an opportunity to win buy-in from potential allies who have helped a given reform succeed. By building on these insights and drawing on research from health economics, which focuses on how public policy impacts private actors, we suggest two main areas for further consideration in future research: (1) studies of policy diffusion should move beyond the focus on the diffusion of one policy to incorporate the reality that states must consider multiple policy decisions all at once—what we call "policy packages"; and (2) we need to consider how federal policy directly changes the private marketplace, which then interacts with and impacts state policy decisions. We discuss each of these points in the context of the ACA in the following sections.

The Diffusion of Policy Packages

One of the most underappreciated challenges of understanding the determinants of ACA state coverage policies is the fact that there were and are multiple specific ACA policy decisions simultaneously under consideration. For example, after the passage of the ACA, states had to make high-level decisions about whether to run their own exchange, and subsequently a myriad of programmatic decisions about what type of exchange to establish and how to do this. States also had to decide whether to expand Medicaid, and along with the Medicaid expansion decision they had to decide how to define an essential health benefits package and establish new rate review procedures. The ACA also triggered a number of decisions not explicitly spelled out in the law but implicit in the changing terrain, including whether to continue the temporary increase in Medicaid reimbursement rates for primary care physicians, and how to regulate changes in health care delivery and financing.

These policy decisions were not isolated from each other. While the political process of each decision might appear separate because regulatory policies with low public salience are made largely within state agencies and highly salient policies involve complicated legislative politics, the dynamics of one policy debate frequently spilled over to debates about other policies. Grogan (1994), for example, has shown how the dimensions of Medicaid policy interact where generous benefit policies have an impact on eligibility policy through budgetary trade-offs. Similarly, focusing on the diffusion patterns of each individual ACA policy may miss the complex interactions between policies—not just through the budget constraint but by creating a changed political dynamic. For example, interest groups in New Hampshire wanted the state to extend the Medicaid fee increase, but chose not to bring it up on the political agenda because they cared more about Medicaid expansion and did not want to confuse or dilute their message framing to legislators (Wilk, Evans, and Jones 2016). Idaho is another illustrative example of political interactions between ACA policies. The political capital and time spent on passing the exchange legislation was so significant that there was nothing left when the Medicaid expansion legislation was introduced in 2013 or since (Jones, forthcoming).

Further, just as the collection of ACA policies should be thought of as a policy package, we should consider how federal planning grants shift the baseline conditions in each state. Whether a state receives and adopts a planning grant will change the capacity facing each state to adopt future policies—not just bureaucratic capacity but private-sector preparedness, as many of the planning grants intended. The grants to establish health insurance exchanges are an important example. The federal government badly wanted states to run their own exchanges, and so offered a $1 million planning grant and open-ended, noncompetitive establishment grants. It also offered a small number of states approximately $30–45 million for an "early innovator grant." The goal was for a handful of states to take the lead on developing exchange technology and then to share lessons with the rest of the country. State leaders were involved in regular conference calls and meetings to learn from each other about what to put in these grants and how to move forward. At the same time, groups opposed to the ACA worked to undermine these grants. Florida and Louisiana led the resistance, with each governor deciding in early 2011 to return the planning grants they had just received. The governors of Oklahoma, Kansas, and Wisconsin soon returned their early innovator grants. In this way, state decisions regarding federal planning grants change the baseline conditions in each state for consideration of other ACA policies in subsequent years. All of these decisions are closely intertwined and have to be examined as such.

The Larger Ecosystem

State policy diffusion should also be viewed within a larger ecosystem of medical care organization and delivery. Health care providers are subject to specific state and federal incentive programs and regulatory policies, and the way they react to these policies shapes the private delivery system, which in turn impacts state policy decision making.

There are numerous examples in the health policy and economics literature suggesting the diffusion of certain types of medical care organization and delivery can be both an anticipated and unanticipated product of state or federal policy. Section 340B of the 1993 Public Health Service Act was intended to provide assistance to medical providers who serve poor, underinsured patients, and is a good example of how federal policy impacts the private market, which in turn impacts state policy. For purposes of illustration, we detail this example below and describe why it is important for state policy diffusion research.

The 340B program provides enrolled hospitals and other providers with deep discounts on the acquisition costs of outpatient drugs, whether those drugs are later administered by physicians or dispensed by pharmacies, to enable underfinanced medical providers to purchase otherwise expensive drugs for the outpatient treatment of their patients. By statute, the program does not require 340B entities to pass on the drug discounts to the patients they treat, or to the insurance plans that cover those patients. Neither does it require these entities to limit the patients who receive the discounted drugs to those who are poor and in need. Instead, 340B entities, alone or via their contract pharmacies, can dispense discounted drugs to all their patients (except, in some cases, those insured by Medicaid), and keep the profits they make when they bill insurers and patients for the drugs as if they had purchased them at full price.

Critics speculate that the opportunity to profit from this provision has created an impetus for 340B-qualified hospitals to push the envelope on the program's intent—by opening outpatient clinics or pursuing affiliations with outpatient clinics in affluent communities where most patients are well-insured. By so doing, hospitals increase their opportunity to profit from dispensing discounted drugs while being reimbursed at retail rates, but divert from the goal of the program, which is to provide services to the poor. Conti and Bach (2014) empirically evaluated this contention, using nationally representative data on program participants in 2012, matched to US Census Bureau data on local communities' socioeconomic characteristics. They found that 340B-qualified hospitals are expanding their base into communities that tend to be affluent and well-insured, consistent with the most profitable expansion strategy that counters the objectives of the program. Moreover, these activities drive up costs of providing care—and ultimately, commercial insurance premiums—since hospital outpatient contracts tend to be much more generous than physician office contracts and charge facility fees on top of service charges to payers and patients.

Similar to this example, there are a handful of ACA provisions that may have intended and unintended consequences for medical care organizations. For example, the ACA requires providers to collect and report quality metrics for their Medicare beneficiaries. The quality metrics attempt to encourage cooperation across different types of care, such as mental and physical health. The ACA also uses financial incentives to encourage providers to take care of patients in high-value, low-cost settings (e.g., outpatient over inpatient provision of care). Still further, the ACA encourages—through federal Medicare policy incentives—the use of alternative organizational structures for the practice of medicine, including but not limited to Accountable Care Organizations (ACOs) (Bekelman et al. 2013). The main idea behind this delivery model reform is that payers are able to reimburse defined, predictable payments for each patient for a set period of time, and providers have the freedom to practice medicine without being micromanaged by payers. Clearly, the intent of these policies is to change the US delivery system for the better. While the verdict is still out on whether the delivery system has substantively improved, we do know that the ACA has brought on enormous private-sector changes, including a number of new organizational forms—such as the adoption of ACOs—as hoped. Clearly, this changed private-sector landscape has important implications for state policy decision making regarding how to work with private insurers on the exchanges and in their Medicaid programs, such as how to set network requirements given changes in the supply of different providers and organizational types.

Conclusion

In sum, this commentary seeks to contribute to future research by highlighting two key areas for further consideration. First, the ACA is a major piece of legislation with multiple policies. Most studies of policy diffusion tend to focus on the diffusion of one or two policies as separate processes; the problem, especially in the case of the ACA, is that states need to consider multiple policy decisions all at once, and a decision in one domain almost certainly impacts the decision in another domain. We need to take account of the reality that states are adopting "policy packages." Therefore, future research should theorize and model the diffusion of policy packages. Second, future research should incorporate how ACA policies are targeted at private actors and the ultimate impact on state decision making. In particular, a large set of federal regulatory and incentive policies have changed private behavior, creating a new private delivery system environment, which in turn has an impact on state policy decision making.

▪ ▪ ▪

Rena M. Conti is an associate professor of health policy in the Department of Pediatrics, section of hematology/oncology, and the Department of Public Health Sciences at the University of Chicago, and is an elected member of the Conference on Research in Income and Wealth. She is an expert on the financing, regulation, and organization of medical care. Her work has been published in the leading health policy and health economics journals. She has provided expert testimony on prescription drug shortages in front of the US Congress Senate Finance Committee.

David K. Jones is an assistant professor in the Department of Health Law, Policy and Management at Boston University's School of Public Health. He is editor-in-chief of the *Public Health Post*. His research focuses on the politics of health policy. His forthcoming book with Oxford University Press examines how states made decisions about implementing the ACA's health insurance exchanges. He is working on a new book on health in the Mississippi Delta, retracing Robert Kennedy's steps in this region. He also studies Medicaid, CHIP, and health reform in France. His work has appeared in periodicals such as the *New York Times*, the *Washington Post*, the *Wall Street Journal*, and *Politico*. He was the winner of AcademyHealth's Outstanding Dissertation Award in 2015.

References

Ackerberg, Daniel A. 2003. "Advertising, Learning, and Consumer Choice in Experience Good Markets: An Empirical Examination." *International Economics Review* 44, no. 3: 1007–40.

Balla, Steven J. 2001. "Interstate Professional Associations and the Diffusion of Policy Innovations." *American Politics Research* 29, no. 3: 221–45.

Bekelman, Justin E., Miranda Kim, and Ezekiel J. Emanuel. 2013. "Toward Accountable Cancer Care." *Journal of the American Medical Association Internal Medicine* 173, no. 11: 958–59.

Berenson, Robert A., Paul B. Ginsburg, and Nicole Kemper. 2010. "Unchecked Provider Clout in California Foreshadows Challenges to Health Reform." *Health Affairs (Millwood)* 29, no. 4: 699–705.

Berry, Frances Stokes, and William D. Berry. 1990. "State Lottery Adoptions as Policy Innovations: An Event History Analysis." *American Political Science Review* 84, no. 2: 395–415.

Capps, Cory, David Dranove, and Richard C. Lindrooth. 2009. "Hospital Closure and Economic Efficiency." *Journal of Health Economics* 29, no. 1: 87–109.

Cenepa, Alessandra, and Paul Stoneman. 2001. "Financial Factors and the Inter-firm Diffusion of New Technology: A Real Options Model." EIFC Working Paper No. 2001-08, University of Warwick, Coventry, UK, December 2001.

Conti, Rena M., and Peter B. Bach. 2014. "The 340B Drug Discount Program: Hospitals Generate Profits by Expanding to Reach More Affluent Communities." *Health Affairs (Millwood)* 33, no. 10: 1786–92.

Cutler, David M., and Fiona Scott Morton. "Hospitals, Market Share, and Consolidation." *Journal of the American Medical Association* 310, no. 18: 1964–70.

Dafny, Leemore. 2009. "Estimation and Identification of Merger Effects: An Application to Hospital Mergers." *Journal of Law and Economics* 52: 523–50.

Gaynor, Martin. 2011. "Health Care Industry Consolidation." Statement before the Committee on Ways and Means Health Subcommittee, US House of Representatives. Washington, DC. September 9. Available at: waysandmeans.house.gov /UploadedFiles/Gaynor_Testimony_9-9-11_Final.pdf.

Gaynor, Martin, and Robert Town. 2012. "The Impact of Hospital Consolidation— Update." Princeton, NJ: Robert Wood Johnson Foundation. Policy Brief No. 9. Available from: www.rwjf.org/content/dam/farm/reports/issue_briefs/2012/rwjf 73261.

Gilardi, Fabrizio. 2016. "Four Ways We Can Improve Policy Diffusion Research." *State Politics and Policy Quarterly* 16, no. 1: 8–21.

Ginsburg, Paul B. 2010. "Wide Variation in Hospital and Physician Payment Rates Evidence of Provider Market Power." HSC Research Brief No. 16. November. Washington, DC: Center for Studying Health System Change.

Grogan, Colleen M. 1994. "The Political-Economic Factors Influencing State Medicaid Policy." *Political Research Quarterly* 47, no. 3: 589–622.

Hacker, Jacob. 2002. *The Divided Welfare State: The Battle over Public and Private Social Benefits in the United States.* Cambridge: Cambridge University Press.

Haider-Markel, Donald. 2001. "Policy Diffusion as a Geographical Expansion of the Scope of Political Conflict: Same-Sex Marriage Bans in the 1990s." *State Politics and Policy Quarterly* 1, no. 1: 5–26.

Jones, David K. Forthcoming. *Exchange Politics: Opposing Obamacare in the States.* Oxford: Oxford University Press.

Jones, David K., Katharine W. V. Bradley, and Jonathan Oberlander. 2014. "Pascal's Wager: Health Insurance Exchanges, Obamacare, and the Republican Dilemma." *Journal of Health Politics, Policy and Law* 39, no. 1: 97–137.

Joynt, Karen E., Paula Chatterjee, E. John Orav, and Ashish K. Jha. 2015. "Hospital Closures Had No Measurable Impact on Local Hospitalization Rates or Mortality Rates, 2003–11." *Health Affairs (Millwood)* 34, no. 5: 765–72. doi: 10.1377/hlthaff.2014.

Karch, Andrew. 2007. *Democratic Laboratories: Policy Diffusion among the American States*. Ann Arbor: University of Michigan Press.

Karch, Andrew. 2012. "Vertical Diffusion and the Policy-Making Process: The Politics of Embryonic Stem Cell Research." *Political Research Quarterly* 65, no. 1: 48–61.

Kocher, Robert, and Njikhil R. Sahni. 2011. "Hospitals' Race to Employ Physicians — The Logic behind a Money-Losing Proposition." *New England Journal of Medicine* 364, no. 19: 1790–93.

Lindrooth, Richard C., Anthony T. Lo Sasso, and Gloria J. Bazzoli. 2003. "The Effect of Urban Hospital Closure on Markets." *Journal of Health Economics* 22, no. 5: 691–712.

McCann, Pamela J. Clouser, Charles R. Shipan, and Craig Volden. 2015. "Top-Down Federalism: State Policy Responses to National Government Discussions." *Publius: The Journal of Federalism* 45, no. 4: 495–525.

Mintrom, Michael. 1997. "The State-Local Nexus in Policy Innovation Diffusion: The Case of School Choice." *Publius: The Journal of Federalism* 27, no. 3: 41–60.

Mooney, Christopher Z., and Mei-Hsien Lee. 1995. "Legislative Morality in the American States: The Case of Pre-Roe Abortion Regulation Reform." *American Journal of Political Science* 39, no. 3: 599–627.

Mooney, Christopher Z., and Mei-Hsien Lee. 1999. "The Temporal Diffusion of Morality Policy: The Case of Death Penalty Legislation in the American States." *Policy Studies Journal* 27, no. 4: 766–80.

Morgen, Kimberly J., and Andrea Louise Campbell. 2011. *The Delegated Welfare State: Medicare, Markets, and the Governance of Social Policy*. Oxford: Oxford University Press.

Newcomer, Lee N., Bruce Gould, Ray D. Page, Sheila A. Donelan, and Monica Perkins. 2014. "Changing Physician Incentives for Affordable, Quality Cancer Care: Results of an Episode Payment Model." *Journal of Oncology Practice* 10, no. 5: 322–26. doi: 10.1200/JOP.2014.001488.

Shipan, Charles R., and Craig Volden. 2008. "The Mechanisms of Policy Diffusion." *American Journal of Political Science* 52, no. 4: 840–57.

Titmuss, Richard Morris. 1951. *Essays on the Welfare State*. London: Allen & Unwin.

Welch, W. Pete, Alison Evans Cuellar, Sally C. Stearns, and Andrew B. Bindman. 2013. "Proportion of Physicians in Large Group Practices Continued to Grow in 2009–11." *Health Affairs (Millwood)* 32, no. 9: 1659–66. doi: 10.1377/hlthaff.2012.1256.

Wilk, Adam, Leigh Evans, and David K. Jones. 2016. "Extending the Fee Bump: Expanding Medicaid Access without Expanding Medicaid?" Paper presented at the annual meeting of the American Political Science Association, Philadelphia, September 1.

Behind the Jargon

Mere Mortals: Overselling the Young Invincibles

Deborah Levine
Providence College

Jessica Mulligan
Providence College

Abstract This article traces the emergence of the term "young invincible" in health policy literature, the health insurance industry, and popular media. Young invincible is the label given to adults under thirty-five who opt not to purchase health insurance because they perceive that they will not need it and would rather spend their money elsewhere. As uninsurance rates climbed, policy makers tried to figure out who the uninsured were and why they lacked coverage. Young adults rightly assumed importance in these conversations because they were disproportionately represented among the uninsured and their numbers were growing. However, the term "young invincible" had the contradictory effect of centering a white, male, high-income chooser as the subject of health policy discourses rather than the far more diverse mix of people who make up the uninsured. This character was imputed preferences and tastes based in economic theory and in long-standing cultural ideals: he was a risk taker, overly optimistic, and preferred cash now to security later. We argue that this heightened concern over young invincibles distorts understanding of the demographics of people who do not have health insurance. It also stokes intergenerational conflict, and frames structural constraints and high prices as a simple consumer "choice."

Keywords Affordable Care Act, young invincibles, adverse selection, history of health reform

The authors would like to thank the Providence College School of Professional Studies for providing funding. Deepest thanks are also due to editor David Frankford and reader Sara Rosenbaum for their thoughtful comments and suggestions on this material. Thanks also to Jon Gruber, Kyle Kusz, Catherine McLaughlin, Jack Ochs, and Scott Podolsky, who provided helpful suggestions in the early stages of research. Both authors contributed equally to this article.

Journal of Health Politics, Policy and Law, Vol. 42, No. 2, April 2017
DOI 10.1215/03616878-3766781   © 2017 by Duke University Press

In the fall of 2013, the news was full of stories about whether Obamacare would survive until spring. "Obamacare Is Really, Really Bad for You, Especially If You're Young," claimed Rituparna Basu on Forbes.com. In a line of argument that was commonplace on conservative media outlets, she argued that insurance rates were going up for the young, more than doubling for some. A few months later, Sarah Kliff at the *Washington Post* boldly took on "Five Myths about 'Young Invincibles.'" Kliff predicted that young adults would indeed sign up for coverage because it was affordable, they wanted it, and they needed it. Young adults, often termed "young invincibles"[1] in media stories, were seen as key to the health law's success. Battles were waged on cable television and social media over whether the law benefited these young adults, and pundits speculated as to whether or not they would enroll in coverage.

So how did this strange figure—the young invincible—come to play such an important role in the passage and implementation of the Affordable Care Act? Young invincible is the label given to adults under thirty-five who opt not to purchase health insurance because they perceive that they will not need it and would rather spend their money on something else. They were thought to be crucial to the law's success because young people are more likely to be uninsured, but they also generally use less medical care, which makes them desirable additions to balance out insurance risk pools. Voluntary health insurance markets have long been vulnerable to the problem of adverse selection, the notion that those who need coverage due to higher risk or existing illness will enroll while the young and healthy will opt out. The individual mandate provision of the ACA was designed to construct more favorable risk pools on the exchanges by requiring that nearly everyone obtain health insurance coverage or pay a fine. Ideally, younger and healthier individuals would sign up for the plans, which would offset the cost of covering the health care of older, sicker members of the risk pool. Young invincibles, then, in addition to gaining coverage in case they become ill, are believed to be the cure to the adverse selection that ails the exchange marketplaces.

In this article, we trace the emergence of the term "young invincible" in the health policy literature, the health insurance industry, and the popular media. We also examine some of the cultural assumptions that work to make the term so compelling yet, ultimately, misleading. We argue that this heightened concern over young invincibles distorts our understanding of

---

1. The term "young invincible" appears in popular media in various forms, sometimes capitalized, and often in quotation marks. In this piece we follow the usage of our sources wherever possible, and otherwise use quotation marks only in this first instance.

the demographics and behaviors of people who do not have health insurance. Young adults who are uninsured are more likely to be low income, minority, and immigrants whose status makes them ineligible for coverage (KFF 2012), rather than the affluent and white subjects so prominently featured in marketing campaigns and media stories. Furthermore, when surveyed, young people indicate that they do value health insurance, but cannot afford it (Collins and Nicholson 2010; Cunningham and Bond 2013). In addition to these demographic inconsistencies, the myth of the young invincible is overinvested in generational discourse, which converts this liminal stage of life enjoyed by some into a hard and fast, immutable population with a false presumption of shared interests and economic motivations between them. Finally, there is a gender politics in the use of this term that expresses a heightened concern over the fate of young men's lives but is not equally concerned with young women's fates. We found that almost all references to the young invincible — be they in scholarship or in advertising — were references to young men.

Making Up the Young Invincibles

If the term "young invincible" seems an almost too literary, romantic turn of phrase for an industry usually lacking in poetry, that's because the phrase has at least some of its roots in nineteenth-century literature. It was also put to use by behavioral scientists in the early twentieth century and applied in clinical literature on risky behavior at century's end. It wasn't until the 1990s that the term was discussed by health policy scholars, though it was used colloquially in the insurance industry earlier. As these various actors together "made up" the young invincible, his key attributes emerged: a risk taker, optimistic, usually male, and affluent enough to afford coverage, but unwilling to buy it. By the end of the twentieth century, the young invincible came to play an outsized role in health policy and health reform.

Born in a century known for flowery English prose, the notion of the young invincible was used in nineteenth-century European and American literature to evoke the unique power of the young to ignore danger. The young invincible was a white man engaging in romanticized, masculine, risky pursuits such as battle, rebellion, and colonial settlement, and agricultural tasks that included breaking in particularly wild horses (Tynan 1894). In the US context, during the American Civil War (1860–65), there were real-life regiments known as "the young invincibles" that captured the public's imagination and were written about in novels and magazines. One such novel, *Patriotism at Home, or The Young Invincibles* (1865), tells the story of two white teenage boys from the North who establish a children's unit in the Union Army. The boys in this sentimental tale are simultaneously celebrated as brave and lamented as doomed.

Young white men, unaware of or disregarding the dangers around them, racing headlong into harm's way for the sake of adventure, thrill, and patriotic glory—it doesn't sound like a group looking to buy a sensible, comprehensive, and probably costly health insurance plan, does it? In a society where coming to grips with human frailty and capacity for suffering remains an infrequent and unusual focus of public discourse, the idealized vision of independent, daring young men runs counter to planning for the inevitable.

Another set of historical roots for the young invincible come from the fields of psychology and behavioral medicine. Drawing on influential psychologist G. Stanley Hall's groundbreaking early twentieth-century ideas about adolescence as a period of "storm and stress" and a uniquely transformative period of life, particularly for males, subsequent practitioners considered the period as dangerous but of central importance to the formation of self (Hall 1904; Arnett 2006). Hall's work and the work of his students cement into American culture the idea of adolescence as a volatile period in a young man's life, characterized by risk-taking behaviors with a distressing lack of regard for danger (Bederman 1995). This conception of adolescence informs later claims by insurance theorists that young invincibles callously forego insurance and instead risk experiencing an accident or major illness with no insurance to break their fall.

In the 1970s and 1980s, clinicians focused on ways to help adolescents navigate this "storm and stress," countering what they perceived to be this group's notions of invincibility (Werner and Smith 1982). In the early years of the HIV/AIDS epidemic, many sexual health experts published on the unique challenges of reaching young people who think themselves invincible to death or disease, as Phillip Wishon did when he wrote, "The young, when they die, they die despairing—lamenting the future they've been denied, shattering in convulsive fashion the heartfelt myth of the young, that they are invincible" (Wishon 1988: 213). Oncologists, too, have long discussed the psychosocial impact of cancer diagnoses on young patients (Schrijvers and Meijnders 2007), and some have noted that young patients, particularly after treatment ends, need to be monitored for excessive risk-taking behavior because "teens and young adults see themselves as immortal and have a compulsive need to prove that they are invincible" (Epelman 2013, 328). As these examples show, excessive risk taking by young people had become common sense in a wide variety of fields. It is not surprising, then, that this idea of the young risk taker also found fertile ground in the insurance industry, whose primary concern is to understand and profit from risk.

The term appears to have been used first colloquially in the industry to refer to the young men who are often absent in traditional insurance markets. By the early 1990s, the terms "young invincible" and "young invincible theory" were in some use in the academic literature. It does not play an important role in the early 1990s Clinton health reform plans, but the idea makes occasional appearances in literature about health insurance choice and population purchasing behaviors. In 1993, in one of the earliest examples we identified, Catherine McLaughlin argued that pricing—and not a cultural or generational aversion to coverage—was to blame for the problem of lack of coverage among young workers in small businesses. In a survey of small employers, McLaughlin's team found that, "Consistent with the young-invincible theory, . . . young (under twenty-five) unmarried workers are more likely to work for firms that do not offer insurance," and these workers do not seek coverage through other means, because they cannot afford it (McLaughlin 1993: 159). By foregrounding that coverage was not affordable for the low-wage workers in her survey, she expressly calls into question that young people choose to "go bare," opting out even when offered coverage, because of a feeling of invincibility (McLaughlin 1999). Here and elsewhere, the term is recognized as a colloquial, rather than technical, insurance industry term, and indeed it does not have an entry in the 1996 *Glossary of Insurance Terms* put out by Merritt Publishing or in any of the other guides we consulted.

As we have seen, central to the idea of the young invincible is the notion that young adults "choose" not to be covered. Some context here is necessary. As uninsurance rates climb in the 1990s and become of even greater concern in the new millennium, health policy makers tried to figure out who the uninsured were and why they lacked coverage. Young adults rightly assumed importance in these conversations because they were disproportionately represented among the uninsured and their numbers were growing. Some analysts explained these high uninsurance rates by giving demographic and structural reasons such as labor market factors and the price of coverage. But another influential group, made up mainly of economists, focused on young adults' behavioral choices and their decision to forego coverage.

A host of foundations and government agencies such as the Commonwealth Fund, the Kaiser Commission on Medicaid and the Uninsured, and the National Institutes of Medicine compiled descriptive reports detailing the demographic breakdown of the uninsured. Take, for example, the Commonwealth Fund's annual publication *Rite of Passage* (published 2003–10). Using evidence from census data and other large-scale surveys, the *Rite of Passage* reports presented what was known about the demographics of young uninsured adults and explained the structural constraints that kept them from gaining coverage.[2] This publication, and others like it, stressed that young adults were disproportionately represented among the uninsured, particularly low-income young adults who were less likely to be full-time college students and, hence, less likely to be able to remain on their parents' coverage. The nineteenth birthday was understood as a "crucial milestone" (Quinn, Schoen, and Buatti 2000: 2), a life transition that led to being uninsured because of aging out of parents' coverage or Medicaid, starting new jobs that are low paying and lack benefits, and job insecurity. To increase insurance coverage rates for young adults, policy changes were proposed such as expanding Medicaid eligibility to age 23, allowing young adults to stay on their parents' plans until age 23, and requiring college students to obtain coverage (Collins et al. 2004). These reports generally do not use the term young invincibles nor are young adults presented as actively choosing to be uninsured. Instead, they argue that young people take employer-based coverage when offered at about the same rate as other age groups, and that they also think insurance is important at about the same rate as other age groups: "The risks of being without health insurance are not so easily dismissed by young adults as conventional wisdom would have it," which calls into question a behavioral preference to go without coverage (Collins et al. 2004: 5). Overall, these reports focus on structural conditions and life cycle changes that lead to uninsurance while behavioral factors are minimized. The key to getting young adults covered is to change the system, not their behavior.

Another increasingly vocal camp, mostly economists, argued that uninsured people could afford insurance, but chose not to purchase it (Glied and Stabile 2000; Bundorf and Pauly 2006; Levy and DeLeire 2008; Baker and Siegelman 2010; Baicker, Congdon, and Mullainathan 2012). Acknowledging and trying to remedy the demographic focus of the foundation studies, economists instead emphasized behavioral choices and preferences, including that young invincibles were overly optimistic, underestimated their own risk, and live in the present rather than planning for future calamities. These preferences were deduced largely from economic theory and experimental studies. Whether it was that the uninsured

---

2. In 2000 the Commonwealth Fund published "On Their Own: Young Adults Living without Health Insurance," which appears to be the predecessor of the *Rite of Passage* reports considering similarities in argument, data sources, and even wording.

preferred jobs offering higher wages to those offering insurance (Glied and Stabile 2000), paid more for other necessities and vices and therefore did not prioritize insurance (Levy and DeLeire 2008), or simply needed a nudge in the form of a prize to buy in (Baker and Siegelman 2010), many economists focused on uninsurance as a voluntary choice. In a review piece summarizing the contributions of behavioral economics to understanding insurance uptake, Baicker and colleagues (2012) acknowledge that prices and information matter, but they are not the whole story. Multiple behavioral patterns, they argue, lead to low insurance take up, including: choice overload and complexity; misunderstanding of costs and benefits, which is exacerbated by complicated pricing; underestimating the risk of a major medical event; a tendency to procrastinate; and being put off by the difficulty of the purchasing process (Baicker, Congdon, and Mullainathan 2012: 114–18). Young invincibles are characterized as being overly optimistic, which leads them to underestimate their likelihood of needing coverage (117).

Some economists focused their studies exclusively on men. For example, Glied and Stabile (2000) asked if falling coverage rates for men had to do with changes in the labor market (less manufacturing, more part-time and temporary work) or were more related to the price of coverage. They concluded that "young men's low income, combined with their good health status, generally has led them to prefer cash to health insurance at this stage in their lives" (296). In another piece focused on young men, Baker and Siegelman (2010) propose solving this problem by introducing a new kind of insurance plan for men aged 19–29 who make more than 200 percent of poverty. The article argues that, since young invincibles won't otherwise buy health insurance, they should be "nudged" through the use of a product that pays them a rebate if they don't use the services. These authors also cite an "optimism bias" that leads young invincibles to under evaluate the need for insurance because they think they will be healthy and not need to use it, and their proposal harnesses the optimism bias to entice these men to bet on their own health. In these articles, men are emphasized and women are largely absent, appearing only in their role as mothers. Rather bizarrely, women make only a brief appearance in the Baker and Siegelman article with the exhortation that the young invincible (clearly gendered as he) will want to purchase insurance in order to make his mother happy (101–2).[3]

3. Selling and designing health insurance plans for young white men has an interesting history, see Kusz, Levine and Mulligan (forthcoming), "From Preferred Male Risk to "Brosurance:" Health Insurance Advertising Images in the United States." The article traces how insurance marketing has historically been to male head of households and how that has changed in the ACA era as mothers have come to assume an outsized role in getting their adult sons covered.

Women are insured at slightly higher rates than men and are more likely to have access to public programs such as Medicaid when they are pregnant and as parents, but it is also important to recall that the median (pre-ACA) Medicaid eligibility for parents was 61 percent of the federal poverty level (FPL) in 2013 (Paradise 2015; KFF 2016). Therefore, many poor and near poor women who were parents were also uninsured. Furthermore, women are also delaying childbearing, more likely to work in service jobs with no benefits, and less likely to be married than previously. In ignoring these factors, these economists make the conversation about the uninsured primarily a conversation about men and men's behavioral patterns. This implicitly leaves women, a sizable group of the uninsured population, behind. Additionally, not all women are mothers, and to assume otherwise is to fail to grasp the reality of the problems faced by uninsured young people in the United States.

Debates about insurance take up and the uninsured were largely academic and policy conversations, but occasionally pieces appeared in the media that brought the problem to wider attention. Media reports often combined the structural and behavioralist perspectives into a new commonsense explanation about why young adults were less likely to be covered. In 2007, *New York Magazine* ran an influential article that chronicled the misadventures of sick and injured young adults in New York City, ironically titled, "The Young Invincibles." The article both implies that young adults sometimes choose not to get insured because they overestimate their own health, and shows the structural factors that make getting covered so impossible:

> For the young who don't luck into a job that offers coverage, a certain outlook becomes inevitable: Premiums are a fortune, you can barely pay your rent, you rarely need a doctor, you decide to gamble. It's a state of mind so common, in fact, that the insurance industry has a name for it: . . . the "young invincibles," those who, betting they can get through their twenties relatively unscathed, "choose" to go without insurance. They are the fastest-growing segment of America's uninsured population. (Amsden 2007)

The article carefully details the structural constraints that make obtaining insurance coverage out of reach for so many young New Yorkers: low-paying part-time or temporary jobs; struggling to get established in their chosen fields; high rents and other outlays; and the lack of affordable insurance options. The supposedly invincible youth Amsden interviews also experience the dangers of not having a regular doctor or source of care, and employ quite a few strategies in order to avoid and minimize risk such as no jaywalking, no snowboarding, a kiwi a day, and regular yoga.

A few years into the new millennium, the young invincible had gone from being a romantic carryover from the nineteenth century to a powerful character in health policy debates. A white, male, high-income chooser was centered in health policy discourses rather than the far more diverse mix of people who make up the uninsured. This new character was imputed preferences and tastes based in economic theory: he was a risk taker, overly optimistic, likely to procrastinate, and preferred cash now to security later. When policy gets crafted based on wooing young invincibles, contradictory effects unfold, including generational infighting and insurance advertisements featuring keg stands.

Writing the Young Invincibles into Health Policy: MassHealth and the ACA

Policy makers concerned with expanding access to coverage were paying attention to the academic debates and popular lore about the young invincibles. When the Commonwealth of Massachusetts embarked on a major overhaul of the health care system with an aim of expanding coverage to as many as possible, stakeholders made sure that policies and marketing would reach uninsured young adults. This reform, which became the model for the Affordable Care Act, required residents to obtain coverage, expanded Medicaid eligibility, and provided income-based subsidies to make coverage more affordable. In the Massachusetts reforms, the young invincible population came to be viewed as a problem—and an opportunity. Jon Kingsdale, executive director of the Commonwealth Health Insurance Connector Authority, explained it thusly:

> The uninsured in Massachusetts are disproportionately young, male, single, and healthy. Those who can afford but choose not to purchase insurance do not subsidize the sick. Moreover, when they need emergency or hospital services, the costs of their bad debt are borne by premium payers. The mandate *converts the so-called young invincible from a financial drain to a net contributor* . . . these "invincibles" now subsidize premiums for the older population. (Kingsdale 2009: w590, italics added)

Under the Massachusetts law's reform of the health care system, when young invincibles buy into health coverage, they have insurance in case they become sick or injured. And if they do not get sick, the premium

Figure 1 2008 Advertisement for MassHealth. Note language: "Good thing *he's* got health insurance" (italics added).

Source: www.npr.org/sections/money/2014/04/24/306542078/how-one-state-convinced-its -young-invincibles-to-get-health-insurance.

money these "young, male, single, and healthy" men pay into the risk pool offsets the cost of paying for higher-utilizing residents of the state. To entice these men into the health care market, MassHealth enlisted "one of the foremost brands in New England, the Boston Red Sox baseball team," to advertise the plan to young men (Kingsdale 2009: w591). The campaign, called "Connect-to-Health," offered special opportunities to MassHealth participants at Fenway Park and at events with the Red Sox around the state. This and other advertising efforts (see fig. 1) were part of an explicit strategy of continuing to campaign for the law even after passage in order to ensure successful implementation, a strategy that would also be taken up by the ACA.

The data gathered after the passage of the Massachusetts reform law bolstered the premise that the young invincibles' full participation was key to the reform's economic and popular fate. Sharon Long of the Urban Institute credited the "creation of new young adult products for 19- up to 26-year-olds who do not have access to employer-sponsored insurance," as one of the key ways that MassHealth expanded coverage around the state. Long has also stated in multiple interviews and research reports that con-tinued outreach to this population was key to the success of the reform law (Long 2008: 3; Vedantam 2008). Long, Kingsdale, and others involved in promoting and evaluating the 2006 MassHealth reforms placed the young invincibles at the center of their model for expanding coverage and controlling system costs while still preserving the overall system of private insurance.

As the Patient Protection and Affordable Care Act was drafted, passed, and implemented by many of the same economists and policy makers who were behind MassHealth, the figure of the "young invincible" continued to play an important, and outsized, role. By this point, it had become a truism that, left to their own devices, young invincibles would choose to forego coverage. Policy makers and analysts saw the young invincible as the antidote to failed risk pools, or "death spirals." This prompted fierce marketing efforts on both sides of the debate that centered young white "bros" in a battle over covered lives and votes. In the political debates about the ACA, slippage was common between the insurance term and the coveted "millennial" advertising demographic, who will one day age out of the young invincible category (Howe and Strauss 2009). The result was heightened intergenerational tensions that pitted young against old.

Multiple allowances were made to get young adults—not only a desirable consumer demographic but also a key Obama constituency— covered under the Affordable Care Act (Goldman 2013). For example, the law allowed young adults to stay on their parents' coverage until age 26. The Medicaid expansion also helped young people since more than half of young adults aged 19–29 had incomes below the 133 percent FPL Medicaid cutoff in 2008. Together, these reforms addressed that key transitional moment, turning 19, when young adults graduate from high school and age out of pre-expansion Medicaid programs (Collins and Nicholson 2010). Finally, insurance being sold on the exchanges was meant to appeal to young people. They alone were eligible to buy catastrophic coverage, a low-premium, high-deductible form of insurance that would offer some financial protection in the event of a major medical episode, but would otherwise cover little for routine medical care. Age rating ensured that young people paid less than their older counterparts shopping on the exchange for the same insurance plan. The law allows for 1:3 age bands, meaning that premiums for older beneficiaries can be up to three times higher than for younger beneficiaries.

Since the law eliminated many of the practices that insurance companies used to combat adverse selection such as exclusions for preexisting conditions, excision, and gender rating, insurance companies wanted some assurances that the new Obamacare risk pools wouldn't be dominated by older, sicker, and female beneficiaries. If only medically needy populations sought coverage, this would drive up premiums and could ultimately endanger the viability of the marketplaces in what has been termed an insurance "death spiral" (Brill 2015: 280). Whether or not an insurance death spiral will occur on the exchanges is still hotly debated. The ACA contains multiple provisions designed to spread risk on the exchanges and make coverage attractive to consumers, such as age rating, risk corridors, and risk adjustment and reinsurance, as well as government subsidies and regulations that limit how much of one's income can be spent on coverage (Blumenthal 2014; Goodell 2014). The "death spiral" is itself a piece of economistic health policy jargon that imbues the task of regulating insurance markets with a sense of drama and urgency usually not associated with the actuarial sciences. The presence of failed risk pools in some sectors of health insurance does not fully explain why policy makers unquestioningly accept the practice of constructing insurance risk pools around the young. Medicare, for example, does not include very many young people in its ranks. The same is true for many employer-based health insurance plans in the United States, where older workers have always disproportionately enjoyed coverage (Collins, White, and Kriss 2007; Davis et al. 2009). As we have seen, the concern with young invincibles is not just about insurance risk pools, it is also about a larger cultural propensity to value young, affluent males.

The individual mandate provision of the ACA, which requires most Americans to purchase insurance or else pay a fine, is a major tool to combat adverse selection. Not surprisingly, the individual mandate became a partisan battleground during the implementation phase of the law and age-based arguments figured prominently in the "Repeal Obamacare" arsenal. In multiple arenas, from the Supreme Court to the far reaches of partisan Internet commentary, the individual mandate was framed by detractors as a paternalist imposition on young people's consumer choices. In the Supreme Court's deliberations, for example, constitutional challengers to the Affordable Care Act were encouraged when justices compared the mandate to purchase health insurance to a hypothetical government mandate to purchase broccoli (Mariner, Glantz, and Annas 2012; Rosen and Schmidt 2013). The "broccoli horrible," as it came to be known through the writings of Justices Scalia and Ginsburg, framed the debate over requiring taxpayers to purchase health insurance in part as a conflict between an overbearing parent and a young child being forced to eat his vegetables.

The ACA was also designed to make insurance affordable and appealing to young adults, who were the targets of marketing and outreach campaigns from the White House and organizations run by former Obama staffers such as Enroll America (Brill 2015: 298). "Funny or Die," a comedy website created by comedians including Will Ferrell, produced a number of pro-Obamacare spoofs, and Enroll America used data analytics to target young adults for outreach and enrollment. In 2009 the group that called itself Young Invincibles tried to reach out to people in this age group and encourage them to get coverage, even as they took a more sophisticated tack than most, acknowledging the problems with framing uninsured young adults as simply a problem of young people making poor choices. Cofounder Aaron Smith, for example, testified before Congress in 2010 that,

> The term "young invincible" is based on the false premise that young adults simply do not want to buy insurance coverage because they think they do not need it. The reality is much more complicated. Numerous factors act as barriers to coverage for young adults, from low incomes to the scarcity of entry-level jobs with benefits. In fact, evidence shows that young adults want and need health insurance and will buy it readily when given the opportunity." (US House of Representatives 2010: 22–23)

Still, many exchanges ran provocative advertisements targeted at the young invincibles that embraced the notion that young adults are out-of-control risk takers who would rather buy anything but health insurance. In Illinois, the Luck Health Plan campaign targeted young people and tried to convince them that they are not invincible and should therefore enroll in actual health insurance rather than relying on luck. In Colorado, a pro-ACA advocacy group pursued a campaign aimed at "Bros," in one instance picturing white men with a keg of beer (see fig. 2 below) and entreating them to get insurance: "Brosurance. Keg stands are crazy. Not having health insurance is crazier. Don't tap into your beer money to cover those medical bills. We got it covered. Now you can too. Thanks Obamacare!" Nationally, the AARP engaged in much of this same rhetoric in a campaign that encouraged their members to reach out to young people via clever e-cards imploring them to make their elders happy and purchase health insurance.

All of this attention paid to young people did not go unnoticed by the law's opposition, who reasoned that if young invincibles were central to making the ACA exchanges solvent, then dissuading them from buying coverage could lead to the collapse of the law altogether. Attempts to woo young invincibles by the Obama administration and its surrogates were lampooned by some media outlets and met with fierce opposition by

Figure 2 "Kegstand." Image from Colorado Exchange 2013 "Got Insurance?" Campaign.

Source: www.doyougotinsurance.com/index.php?id=6.

conservative groups.[4] The Koch brothers sponsored Generation Opportunity, which described itself as "a non-profit millennial advocacy organization," and promotes the idea that Obamacare is especially bad for young people. GenOpp aims to "put a stop to Washington's generational

---

4. Conservative media outlets cast Obamacare as a bad deal for bros. See, for example: Avik Roy's "The War on Bros: Exchange Subsidies Won't Protect Young People from Obamacare's Higher Insurance Premiums," in *Forbes*, 06/07/13, www.forbes.com/sites/theapothecary/2013 /06/07/the-war-on-bros-exchange-subsidies-wont-protect-young-people-from-obamacares-higher -insurance-premiums/; Rituparna Basu's "Obamacare Is Really, Really Bad for You, Especially If You're Young," from *Forbes.com*, www.forbes.com/sites/realspin/2013/08/21/obamacare-is -really-really-bad-for-you-especially-if-youre-young/; "Obamacare Kicks Young Men While They're Down," *American Interest*, www.the-american-interest.com/2013/05/14/obamacare-kicks -young-men-while-theyre-down/; and Tami Luhby's "Who Will Pay More under Obamacare? Young Men," from *CNN Money*, money.cnn.com/2013/05/14/news/economy/obamacare-premiums/. For some criticism of this trend, see: Garance Franke-Ruta's "Why Is Maternity Care Such an Issue for Obamacare Opponents?" in *The Atlantic*, www.theatlantic.com/politics/archive/2013/11/why-is -maternity-care-such-an-issue-for-obamacare-opponents/281396/.

Other notable examples of media coverage featuring young invincibles include: Sarah Kliff, "The Bros Just Might Sign Up for Obamacare Yet," Washington Post, 08/30/13, www .washingtonpost.com/news/wonkblog/wp/2013/08/30/the-bros-might-just-sign-up-for-obamacare -yet/; and Josh Vorhees, "Did Enough Young Invincibles Sign Up for Obamacare?" Slate.com, 04/18/14, www.slate.com/blogs/weigel/2014/04/18/obamacare_young_enrollment_percentage_of _young_invincibles_aca_enrollees.html.

Figure 3 Still from September 19, 2013, Press Release Associated with Generation Opportunity Spot, "The Glove."

Source: generationopportunity.org/press-release/young-people-should-opt-out-of-obamacare/.

theft schemes that rob us of future prosperity" (Generation Opportunity 2014). This message is promoted further through funding anti-Obamacare programming on college campuses and hosting tailgate parties promoting their "opt out" message (Stolberg and McIntire 2013; see also generationopportunity.org). Perhaps most famously, as seen in figure 3 above, Generation Opportunity ran advertising spots with a puppet-headed figure, who came to be known on social media as "creepy Uncle Sam," probing the orifices of young white women and men, taking a recurring theme over decades of anti-reform rhetoric—that reform would put "a government bureaucrat between you and your doctor"—to an absurd and disturbing extreme. Generation Opportunity put tremendous financial resources into discouraging millennials from enrolling in the Obamacare exchanges.

Despite these efforts, the first year saw 31 percent of enrollment on exchanges coming from young adults aged 18–34 (Blumenthal and Collins 2014: 278), though this did fall short of the 40 percent of the uninsured made up of young people (Levitt, Claxton, and Damico 2013). What this means, however, was hotly contested. Some argued that the impact on premiums would be minimal (Levitt, Claxton, and Damico 2013), while others blamed premium increases and insurers such as

United and Aetna opting to withdraw from the exchanges on the scarcer than anticipated young invincibles (Herman 2016).

Overselling the Young Invincibles

"Young invincibles" is a term which has become influential and important in health reform, a centerpiece of both the marketing message of the ACA *and* the economic balance on which the law is supposedly based, yet it rests on shaky ground. When it comes to coverage debates, focusing so closely on the young invincible, is inherently problematic.

First, it places too much focus on a subset of young adults who have high rates of insurance coverage. This diverts attention from those who are truly in need of affordable insurance in greater numbers: black and Hispanic young adults, poor and near poor adults, and immigrants in ineligible statuses. Young invincibles featured in advertisements, and press and academic coverage are predominantly presumed to be white, high income, and male. This is not merely a problem of representation in marketing materials, although that is troubling, but it also perpetuates the idea that our current health system is fine so long as young white men are covered. Ultimately, shining the light brightly on young invincibles makes it difficult to see clearly who is still uninsured and why. Income and pricing are more essential to understanding insurance than generational stereotypes, as organizer Smith himself understood when he testified before Congress in 2010, citing census data and concluding that, "young adults with higher income levels are far more likely to have insurance. The uninsured rate is just 14 percent for young adults living over 400 percent of the FPL, but rises to 46 percent for young adults making less than 200 percent of FPL. With about 37 percent of young adults living below 200 percent of the FPL, it is no surprise that young adults have the highest uninsurance rate of any age group" (US House of Representatives 2010: 19).

Second, this inordinate attention to the notion of the young invincible creates a false permanence to the category of "young." One upshot of this distortion is that it can amplify resentment between segments of the population, as seen in the debates over whether young adults would enroll in the ACA. Sure, there might be 23-year-old healthy men now who resent paying for health insurance they don't feel they "use," but, if all goes well, one day those 23-year-old men will be older. Some of the healthy will be sicker. Some of the unattached men will one day have partners and/or children whom they might like to see benefitting from insurance coverage. As in the nineteenth-century novels, the young and invincible do not remain so for long. By pumping up generational discord, we are ignoring how the broader community benefits when everyone is covered.

Third, from the earliest references to the idea, even the most prominent experts have questioned whether or not the idea of the young invincible opting out of health insurance coverage, not because of price prohibitiveness, but because of a belief that they will not need medical care, is an accurate reflection of behavior in the real world. Behavioral economists, demographic researchers, and activists since the early 1990s have questioned the legitimacy of the "so-called young invincible theory" or the "myth of the young invincible." Yet, the idea has persisted through the Massachusetts health reforms and is an important part of the Affordable Care Act, permitting our national conversations over insurance coverage to continue to center around private insurance and demographic consumer purchasing patterns, avoiding politically difficult but necessary discussions about price controls or single-payer models.

▪ ▪ ▪

Deborah Levine is an assistant professor of health policy and management at Providence College. Trained as a historian of science, her research focuses on the history of medicine and disease in the United States. She is currently at work on a book about diet, nutrition, and obesity in the United States. She has authored several journal articles on the histories of health policy, medical education, and patient experiences of disease.

Jessica Mulligan is an associate professor of health policy and management at Providence College, where she teaches courses in public health, health policy, and medical anthropology. Her current research explores insurance, financial security, and health reform from the perspective of the newly insured and those who continue to lack coverage. She is co-editor of *Covered? Risk, Inequality, and Experiences of Health Reform in the United States* (New York: NYU Press, forthcoming). She is also the author of *Unmanageable Care: An Ethnography of Health Care Privatization in Puerto Rico* (New York: NYU Press, 2014), and multiple journal articles.

References

American Interest. 2013. "Obamacare Kicks Young Men While They're Down," *American Interest*, www.the-american-interest.com/2013/05/14/obamacare-kicks -young-men-while-theyre-down/.

Amsden, David. 2007. "The Young Invincibles." *New York Magazine*, October 22.

Anderson, IH. 1866. *Patriotism at Home or The Young Invincibles*. Boston: William V. Spencer.

Arnett, Jeffrey. J. 2006. "G. Stanley Hall's 'Adolescence: Brilliance and Nonsense.'" *History of Psychology* 9, no. 3: 186–97.

Baicker, Katherine, William J. Congdon, and Sendhil Mullainathan. 2012. "Health Insurance Coverage and Take-Up: Lessons from Behavioral Economics." *Milbank Quarterly* 90, no. 1: 107–34.

Baker, Tom, and Peter Siegelman. 2010. "Tontines for the Invincibles: Enticing Low Risks into the Health-Insurance Pool with an Idea from Insurance History and Behavioral Economics." *Wisconsin Law Review* 1: 79–120.

Basu, Rituparna. 2013. "Obamacare Is Really, Really Bad for You, Especially If You're Young." *Forbes.com*, www.forbes.com/sites/realspin/2013/08/21/obama care-is-really-really-bad-for-you-especially-if-youre-young/.

Bederman, G. 1995. *Manliness and Civilization: A Cultural History of Gender and Race in the United States, 1880–1917*. Chicago: University of Chicago Press.

Blumenthal, David. 2014. "The Three Rs of Insurance." Commonwealth Fund, www.commonwealthfund.org/publications/blog/2014/mar/the-three-rs-of-health -insurance.

Blumenthal, David, and Sara R. Collins. 2014. "Health Care Coverage under the Affordable Care Act—A Progress Report." *New England Journal of Medicine*, (July 2): 1–7. doi: 10.1056/NEJMhpr1405667.

Brill, Steven. 2015. *America's Bitter Pill: Money, Politics, Backroom Deals, and the Fight to Fix Our Broken Healthcare System*. New York: Random House.

Bundorf, M. Kate, and Mark V. Pauly. 2006. "Is Health Insurance Affordable for the Uninsured?" *Journal of Health Economics* 25, no. 4: 650–73.

Collins, Sara R., and Jennifer L. Nicholson. 2010. "Rite of Passage: Young Adults and the Affordable Care Act of 2010." Commonwealth Fund. www.commonwealth fund.org/~/media/Files/Publications/Issue%20Brief/2010/May/1404_Collins_rite _of_passage_2010_v3.pdf.

Collins, Sara R., Cathy Schoen, Katie Tenney, Michelle M. Doty, and Alice Ho. 2004. "Rite of Passage? Why Young Adults Become Uninsured and How New Policies Can Help." Commonwealth Fund.

Collins, Sara R., Chapin White, and Jennifer L. Kriss. 2007. "Whither Employer-Based Health Insurance?: The Current and Future Role of US Companies in the Provision and Financing of Health Insurance." Commonwealth Fund.

Commonwealth Fund. 2008. "Evaluating Massachusetts Health Reform—The Commonwealth Fund." www.commonwealthfund.org/publications/spotlights /2008/evaluating-massachusetts-health-reform.

Cunningham, Peter J., and Amelia M. Bond. 2013. "If the Price is Right, Most Uninsured—Even Young Invincibles—Likely to Consider New Health Insurance Marketplaces." Research Brief. Center for Studying Health System Change, www.rwjf.org/content/dam/farm/reports/issue_briefs/2013/rwjf407851.

Davis, Karen, Stuart Guterman, Michelle M. Doty, and Kristof M. Stremikis. 2009. "Meeting Enrollees' Needs: How Do Medicare and Employer Coverage Stack Up?" *Health Affairs* 28, no. 4: w521–w532.

Epelman, Claudia L. 2013. "The Adolescent and Young Adult with Cancer: State of the Art—Psychosocial Aspects." *Current Oncology Reports* 15, no. 4: 325–31.

Franke-Ruta, Garance. 2013. "Why Is Maternity Care Such an Issue for Obamacare Opponents?" *The Atlantic*, www.theatlantic.com/politics/archive/2013/11/why-is -maternity-care-such-an-issue-for-obamacare-opponents/281396/.

Generation Opportunity. 2014. Mission. generationopportunity.org/about/mission/.

Glied, Sherry, and Mark Stabile. 2000. "Explaining the Decline in Health Insurance Coverage Among Young Men." *Inquiry* 37: 295–303.

Glossary of Insurance Terms. Santa Monica, California: Merritt Company, 1996.

Goldman, T. R. 2013. "Health Policy Brief: Young Adults and the Affordable Care Act." *Health Affairs*, December 16, 2013. healthaffairs.org/blog/2013/12/16 /recent-health-policy-brief-young-adults-and-the-affordable-care-act.

Goodell, Sarah. 2014. "Health Policy Brief: Risk Corridors." *Health Affairs*, June 26, 2014, healthaffairs.org/healthpolicybriefs/brief_pdfs/healthpolicybrief_118.pdf.

Hall, G. Stanley. 1904. *Adolescence: Its Psychology and Its Relations to Physiology, Anthropology, Sociology, Sex, Crime, Religion, and Education*, vol. 2. New York: Appleton.

Herman, Bob. 2016. "What, Me Buy Insurance? How Slow Uptake by 'Young Invincibles' is Driving the ACA's Exchange Rates Higher." *Modern Healthcare*, www.modernhealthcare.com.

Howe, Neil and William Strauss. 2009. *Millennials Rising: The Next Great Generation*. New York: Vintage.

KFF (Kaiser Family Foundation). 2012. "The Uninsured: A Primer. The Kaiser Commission on Medicaid and the Uninsured." Menlo Park: CA.

KFF (Kaiser Family Foundation). 2016. "Women's Health Insurance Coverage," kff.org/womens-health-policy/fact-sheet/womens-health-insurance-coverage-fact -sheet/.

Kingsdale, Jon. 2009. "Implementing Health Care Reform in Massachusetts: Strategic Lessons Learned." *Health Affairs* 28, no. 4: w588–w594.

Kliff, Sarah. 2013a. "The Bros Just Might Sign Up for Obamacare Yet," *Washington Post*, August 30, www.washingtonpost.com/news/wonkblog/wp/2013/08/30/the -bros-might-just-sign-up-for-obamacare-yet/.

Kliff, Sarah. 2013b. "Five Myths about 'Young Invincibles.'" *Washington Post*, November 26.

Kusz, Kyle, Deborah Levine, and Jessica Mulligan. Forthcoming. "From Preferred Male Risk to 'Brosurance': Health Insurance Advertising Images in the United States."

Levitt, Larry, Gary Claxton, and Anthony Damico. 2013. "The Numbers behind 'Young Invincibles' and the Affordable Care Act." Kaiser Family Foundation, kff.org/health-reform/perspective/the-numbers-behind-young-invincibles-and-the -affordable-care-act/.

Levy, Helen, and Thomas DeLeire. 2008. "What Do People Buy When They Don't Buy Health Insurance and What Does That Say about Why They Are Uninsured?" *Inquiry* 45, no. 4: 365–79.

Long, Sharon K. 2008. "Who Gained the Most under Health Reform in Massachusetts?: Massachusetts Health Reform Survey Policy Brief." Washington DC: Urban Institute.

Long, Sharon. K., and Stockley, K. 2010. "Sustaining Health Reform in a Recession: An Update on Massachusetts as of Fall 2009." *Health Affairs* 29, no. 6: 1234–41.

Long, Sharon. K., Stockley, K., and Yemane, A. 2009. "Another Look at the Impacts of Health Reform in Massachusetts: Evidence Using New Data and a Stronger Model." *American Economic Review* 99, no. 2: 508–11.

Long, Sharon. K., Zuckerman, S., and Graves, J. A. 2006. "Are Adults Benefiting from State Coverage Expansions?" *Health Affairs* 25, no. 2: w1–w14.

Luhby, Tami. 2013. "Who Will Pay More under Obamacare? Young Men." *CNN Money*, money.cnn.com/2013/05/14/news/economy/obamacare-premiums/.

Mariner, Wendy K., Leonard H. Glantz, and George J. Annas. 2012. "Reframing Federalism—the Affordable Care Act (and Broccoli) in the Supreme Court." *New England Journal of Medicine* 367, no. 12: 1154–58.

McLaughlin, Catherine G. 1993. "The Dilemma of Affordability: Health Insurance for Small Businesses." In *American Health Policy: Critical Issues for Reform*, edited by Robert Helms, 152–66. Washington, DC: AEI.

McLaughlin, Catherine G. 1999. "Health Care Consumers: Choices and Constraints." *Medical Care Research and Review* 56, supplement 1: S24–S59.

Paradise, Julia. 2015. "Medicaid Moving Forward." Kaiser Commission on Medicaid and the Uninsured, kff.org/health-reform/issue-brief/medicaid-moving-forward/.

Quinn, Kevin, Cathy Schoen, and Louisa Buatti. 2000. "On Their Own: Young Adults Living without Health Insurance." Commonwealth Fund, May 2000.

Rosen, Mark D., and Christopher W. Schmidt. 2013. "Why Broccoli? Limiting Principles and Popular Constitutionalism in the Health Care Case." *UCLA Law Review*, 61, 66.

Roy, Avik. 2013. "The War on Bros: Exchange Subsidies Won't Protect Young People from Obamacare's Higher Insurance Premiums" *Forbes*, www.forbes.com/sites/theapothecary/2013/06/07/the-war-on-bros-exchange-subsidies-wont-protect-young-people-from-obamacares-higher-insurance-premiums/.

Schrijvers, D., and Meijnders, P. 2007. "Palliative Care in Adolescents." *Cancer Treatment Reviews* 33, no. 7: 616–21.

Stolberg, Sheryl Gay, and Mike McIntire. 2013. "A Federal Budget Crisis Months in the Planning." *New York Times*, October 5.

Tynan, Patrick. 1894. *The Irish National Invincibles and Their Times*. London: Chatham and Company.

US House of Representatives. 2010. *Are Mini-med Policies Really Health Insurance?: Hearing Before the Committee on Commerce, Science, and Transportation*, United States Senate, 111th Cong., 1st sess., December 1. Washington, DC. House of Representatives.

Vedantam, Shankar. 2008. "Study Praises Mass. Health-Care Program." *Washington Post*, June 4.

Vorhees, Josh. 2014. "Did Enough Young Invincibles Sign Up for Obamacare?" *Slate.com*, www.slate.com/blogs/weigel/2014/04/18/obamacare_young_enrollment _percentage_of_young_invincibles_aca_enrollees.html.

Warwick, Ian., and Aggleton, Peter. 1990. *Adolescents, Young People and AIDS Research*, edited by P. Aggleton, and P. Davies, 89–102. London: Falmer.

Werner, Emmy E. and Smith, Ruth. 1982. *Vulnerable but Not Invincible: A Study of Resilient Children*. New York: McGraw Hill.

Wishon, Phillip. M. 1988. "Children and Youth with AIDS." *Early Child Development and Care* 39, no. 1: 123–37.

Books

Review

Judith N. Lasker. *Hoping to Help: The Promises and Pitfalls of Global Health Volunteering.* Ithaca, NY: Cornell University Press, 2016. 262 pp. $89.95 cloth, $19.95 paper.

Judith Lasker's new work, *Hoping to Help*, is an eminently accessible book that anyone involved in international medical volunteering should read. Lasker writes about an important trend: short-term volunteering in international health, specifically by citizens of rich countries who spend brief periods working on health projects in poor countries at their own expense. By short-term, the author means less than six months, although one to two weeks is the average length of trips. She asks logical, commonsense questions about this trend and answers them concisely but without eliminating complexity and ambiguity. Readers wanting to know more about how Lasker came to these conclusions can consult the appendix describing research methods. Before signing off, Lasker offers help for potential volunteers and host communities by developing a framework for evaluating the possible benefits and harms of such programs. *Hoping to Help* is a model of clear communication. Judith Lasker's writing is pristine, free of jargon, and uncluttered by excessive citations.

Hoping to Help asks and answers the questions we want to know: Why do the organizations sponsoring short-term medical volunteering do it?

Journal of Health Politics, Policy and Law, Vol. 42, No. 2, April 2017

What motivates the volunteers themselves? And, do the projects benefit the receiving communities? These questions are justified by the tremendous growth of this kind of volunteering (often, not coincidentally, among universities and their students), and are posed in a spare framework of opinion and scholarship. Lasker contrasts the growth of international medical volunteer programs and the assumption that they must be doing good with a summary of critiques of this "white savior industrial complex" (13). The critiques are drawn from a few well-chosen popular and scholarly works. This bare-bones framing works because the empirical issue is so comprehensible. The result is a book that is accessible to a broad audience. The downside of this theoretical minimalism, however, is that Lasker forfeits the opportunity to relate her study to social science research on the motivation and impact of international volunteers or on the involvement of religious missions in overseas medical projects. An appendix with further theoretical discussion might prove more satisfying for academics.

Religious organizations are the largest subset among the groups sending medical volunteers abroad. Their motivations often mix the desire to lend medical assistance with the imperative to share the good news of salvation. These groups, along with nongovernmental organizations (NGOs) of every stripe, offer short-term medical volunteer trips that have become very popular among students. Lasker asks about the impact of these types of trips both within the target community and for the volunteers themselves. The mixed outcomes she reports are sure to resonate with many students. On one end of the spectrum are trips designed for medically unskilled volunteers such as students and church groups; on the other are highly trained professionals such as surgeons who make one-shot visits to offer discrete interventions such as cleft palate repair. Unsurprisingly, the latter trips earn better marks, especially if they offer technology transfer, training of local practitioners, and follow-up patient care, but they are often too short and irregular to fulfill these needs.

All in all, Lasker is not opposed to medical volunteer trips that benefit the givers as well as the hosts. She accepts the complexity of human motivation and recognizes that such trips can lead to volunteers becoming better global citizens. But she thoroughly delineates the unintended negatives for the host communities. Particularly alarming for this reader were the many instances of medical students delivering care to patients they would not be allowed to touch in their home countries. Lasker also sensitizes the reader to the many ways in which the very presence of foreign volunteers and their need for help in adjusting to local conditions fritter away the valuable time of scarce domestic medical personnel.

Judith Lasker's conclusion that better results, from the point of view of the host community, would come from longer placements by skilled volunteers begs for examination. Many readers will immediately think of Doctors Without Borders (*Médecins Sans Frontières* or MSF), the international organization that sends physicians and other medical professionals into conflict zones on six- to twelve-month assignments to provide care and train local professionals. Lasker rejects the comparison by saying that MSF is a different type of organization because it pays its staff and responds to a different category of situations: humanitarian emergencies (220). True on both counts, yet the salary paid to physicians (starting at about US$1,900 gross per month according to its website), and the difficult and often dangerous conditions in which its staff work, mean that they almost certainly see themselves as volunteers. And while MSF does run projects in zones of armed conflict, disasters, and epidemics, it also provides services in locations where people are simply too marginalized to access care.

It is probably not fair to suggest that Lasker should have included MSF in her detailed study of short-term volunteering. But rather than rejecting the idea altogether, I submit that such a comparison would be a logical next step. If length of stay and volunteer skill level are critical independent variables, then why not vary them and see how the hypotheses play out? Another direction for further research would be to explore the history of faith-based medical "missions" and compare it to the very short-term trips of the present day. These sorts of explorations should bring us closer to figuring out what type of medical volunteering, if any, justifies the impact on host communities.

Hoping to Help benefits from clear writing and the use of summaries and boxes to break up long chunks of text. Judith Lasker's writing style should serve as a model for other social scientists. Still, this unidimensional delivery of information would be more interesting if non-textual devices were mixed in. There is not a single graphic or photo in the entire book. Relatively simple additions could include visual representations of the project's questions or hypotheses, a global map of the volunteer cites discussed, and a table categorizing survey respondents.

These are small points in an overall excellent book, one I intend to assign to an upper-level undergraduate global health class.

—Mary A. Clark, Tulane University

DOI 10.1215/03616878-3766790

■ ■ ■

Mary A. Clark is an associate professor of political science and associate dean in the School of Liberal Arts at Tulane University. She is the author of *Gradual Economic Reform in Latin America: The Costa Rican Experience*, and many articles on development and health policy. She is currently working on a book on noncommunicable diseases and governance regimes in Latin America and the Caribbean.

Books

Review

Anthony Ryan Hatch. *Blood Sugar: Racial Pharmacology and Food Justice in Black America.* Minneapolis: University of Minnesota Press, 2016. 184 pp. $87.50 cloth, $25.00 paper.

The concept of metabolic syndrome has emerged across disciplines in the biomedical and health sciences as a loosely defined set of statistical risk factors that purport to predict heart disease, diabetes, and other poor health outcomes (Hatch 2016). While there remains little consensus over how to define metabolic syndrome, to what extent the syndrome is a predictive factor of heart and digestive-related diseases, and what factors cause metabolic syndrome, there have been recent attempts to create standardized definitions. Most recently, the National Cholesterol Education Program (NCEP) defined metabolic syndrome using measurements of blood pressure, fasting blood sugar, LDL and HDL cholesterol, and abdominal circumference. Anthony Ryan Hatch's *Blood Sugar: Racial Pharmacology and Food Justice in Black America* explores the consequences of creating standardized definitions of metabolic syndrome by questioning how research on this syndrome shapes knowledge of racial health disparities, and to what extent it benefits people on ground level who are rarely diagnosed with this syndrome.

Journal of Health Politics, Policy and Law, Vol. 42, No. 2, April 2017

Blood Sugar is an important contribution to the field of science and technology studies. While science and technology studies scholars often draw on Foucault's theory of biopower, they less often draw on critical race theory. Hatch's utilization of critical race theory provides an important intervention because it provides details to histories of New World systems of racial oppression and classification that the theory of biopower does not expound on in as much depth. Now, in order to challenge and prevent the re-essentialization of race, critical analyses must have an astute understanding of how the concept of race permeates through highly specialized discourses in the biomedical and nutrition sciences. Hatch employs biomedicalization theory to help with this process.

Through analysis of his own personal narrative of his experience with diabetes, specialized discourses of risk and race in the biomedical sciences over the last two centuries, and a history of the role that sugar has played in New World slavery and industrial agricultural capitalism, Hatch develops his main argument: metabolic syndrome perpetuates a Foucauldian form of biopower and is a new form of scientific racism. In this review, I discuss how Hatch effectively defends this argument by employing the theories of critical race theory, biopower, and biomedicalization.

Despite critical race theorists cogently debunking the myths of scientific racism, biomedical research has continued to define race as something that can be identified within genetic and metabolic processes. Defining race as biological elides the complex sociopolitical history of sugar and how it relates to African American health. In following the tradition of critical race theory, *Blood Sugar* departs from overly simplistic analyses of race and racism in making clear that racism should not be theorized as measures on individual attitudes or prejudices. The book is less concerned with the question of whether or not individual scientists intentionally infuse research design with racializing discourse than it is with the study of disjunctures, that is, how knowledge systems bring forth and at other times close off racializing concepts of metabolic syndrome.

Hatch (2016: 100) explains that, "Over the course of its colonial and industrial history, sugar production has increased more rapidly than any other agricultural commodity." Soon after Christopher Columbus introduced sugar cane to the New World in 1493, it would burgeon into a cash crop of chattel slavery. Sugar fields labored by enslaved Africans profited countries such as the United States, Portugal, Spain, Italy, Belgium, the Netherlands, England, and France. Though many accounts of the introduction of sugar into African American diets do include a history of slavery, these accounts seldom consider the continued growth of sugar into the twenty-first century that has been made possible through labor exploitation, racial and ethnic-based food marketing which disproportionately targets African American communities, and the increase in the amount of food products with added sugars. These structural accounts cannot necessarily prove that sugar causes metabolic syndrome. Proving such a claim would be methodologically challenging due to competing definitions of what metabolic syndrome is, and ethically problematic because it would require individuals to be exposed to foods we know are harmful. Nonetheless, Hatch convincingly argues that the social, political, economic, and agricultural systems that center on sugar production have deep entanglements with the continuation of racial and socioeconomic status (SES) health disparities into the twenty-first century.

To understand the larger political purposes of metabolic syndrome, Hatch analyzes how lifestyle discourses of health applied to research to describe African Americans' metabolic health outcomes hold together a form of biopower and biocapitalism. Hatch's work draws on Foucault's theory of *biopower*, which can be defined as the processes by which states exercise a control over life through discourses and technologies of governance and surveillance. Hatch also draws on biomedicalization theory's concept of biocapitalism, which describes how bodies become sites of exploitation and profit for biomedical and government collaborations. Diabetes management programs, made possible through research on human metabolism and technical developments that measure metabolic processes, can be considered one such technology of surveillance and exploitation. To wit, while individuals are encouraged to manage their diabetes through carbohydrate counting and insulin pumps, multinational food corporations expand their markets and bypass strict surveillance.

Practices of surveillance and control of individuals are also made possible through the development of "killer applications." For example, in chapter 4, Hatch describes killer applications as a type of one size fits all approach to drug development. Metabolic syndrome is commonly defined as a set of risk factors that predict heart disease and that should be targeted as a secondary mode of prevention. Nonetheless, within the world of pharmaceutical capitalism, which calls for an ever-increasing expansion of the drug market, killer applications are brought to market which purport to treat the risks associated with metabolic syndrome, such as LDL cholesterol, as diseases in and of themselves. Equally troubling, by drawing on clinical trials that utilize decontextualized concepts of race, the development of killer applications often re-essentializes race as something that lies within metabolic processes. With constant disagreement over what biomarkers and risk factors actually constitute metabolic syndrome, the efficacy of killer applications for metabolic syndrome remains questionable. Furthermore, the practice of unreflexively using the concept of race in drug development remains highly problematic.

What discourses and practices made possible the usage of the concept of race in killer applications that purport to treat metabolic syndrome? Throughout the book, Hatch describes key moments in the history of research on metabolic syndrome and how different modes of research stitched together a racial framework that would later be used to develop killer applications. These moments, most notably physician Jean Vague's studies of male and female obesity, demonstrate how physicians in Western medicine shifted away from examining only individual patients' presentations of symptoms. Instead, they began looking at population-level statistics and drawing on essentialist notions of race and ethnicity by comparing these statistics with individual-level examinations in order to identify risk. Consequently, population-level trends were construed as evidence to support the idea that there are distinct racial populations. Hatch employs biomedicalization theory's studies of the concept of risk in order to understand how these processes took place. Biomedicalization theory describes how social problems—in this case, health disparities—are recast as problems that can be solved through biomedical and technoscientific expertise (Clarke et al. 2010: 2, 53). Within the process of biomedicalization, racial and ethnic minorities become at-risk populations "that require institutionalized forms of metabolic examination, surveillance, and regulation" (Hatch 2016: 61).

By bringing together the theories of critical race theory, biopower, and biomedicalization, *Blood Sugar* does great work in making biomedical jargon more accessible to those in the humanities, social sciences, and health and social policy concerned with the role that biomedicine plays in challenging or upholding essentialist concepts of race. *Blood Sugar* can and should be taught to undergraduate and graduate students in disciplines and fields as diverse as sociology, history, science and technology studies, heath policy, environmental studies, and ethnic studies. Ultimately, Hatch's works calls for the continuation of interdisciplinary analyses of why we are seeing a "resuscitation" of race across the domains of law, medicine, criminal justice, and food production (Roberts 2011). *Blood Sugar* also falls in the recent tradition of seeking to bridge the gap between medical and environmental sociology (Brown, Morello-Frosch, and Zavestoski 2011). While Hatch provides rich data and analysis for multiple disciplines, the discussion of the problem of connecting risk factors to supposedly distinct racial populations can be furthered if read alongside scholarship that works to unpack the political assumptions and consequences made by constructing obesity as one of those supposed risk factors (Kirkland 2008; Kirkland 2011).

Hatch does not end the book by providing specific policy recommendations, but rather a guide to how we can critically question the future of metabolic health and research on metabolic syndrome. By providing this guide, Hatch's important work helps prevent another *disjuncture* that may close off the much needed critical appraisal of the politics of the development and application of biomedicine.

—Peter Kent-Stoll, Vanderbilt University

DOI 10.1215/03616878-3766799

▪ ▪ ▪

Peter Kent-Stoll is an M.A. candidate at the Center for Medicine, Health, and Society at Vanderbilt University. Before coming to Vanderbilt, he received his B.A. in public health policy from the University of California, Irvine. He has research interests in science & technology studies, social movements, gender & sexuality, and race & ethnicity. He studies the ways in which discourses of cancer advocacy and other forms of disease activism in the United States are impacted by and impact racial and gender inequality.

References

Brown, Phil, Rachel Morello-Frosch, and Stephen Zavestoski, eds. 2011. *Contested Illnesses: Citizens, Science, and Health Social Movements*. Berkeley and Los Angeles: University of California Press.

Clarke, Adele E., Laura Mamo, Jennifer Ruth Fosket, Jennifer R. Fishman, and Janet K. Shim, eds. 2010. *Biomedicalization: Technoscience, Health, and Illness in the U.S.* Durham: Duke University Press.

Kirkland, Anna. 2008. *Fat Rights: Dilemmas of Difference and Personhood*. New York: New York University Press.

Kirkland, Anna. 2011. "The Environmental Account of Obesity: A Case for Feminist Skepticism." *Signs*, 36, no. 2: 463–85.

Roberts, Dorothy. 2011. *Fatal Invention: How Science, Politics, and Big Business Re-create Race in the Twenty-First Century*. New York: New Press.

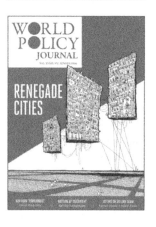

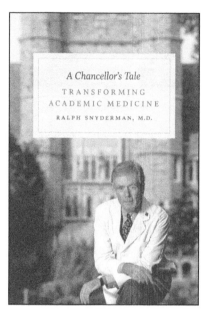

Printed and bound by CPI Group (UK) Ltd, Croydon, CR0 4YY

13/04/2025

14656483-0002